Batboys and the World of Baseball

Studies in Popular Culture
M. Thomas Inge, *General Editor*

Batboys and the World of Baseball

NEIL D. ISAACS

UNIVERSITY PRESS OF MISSISSIPPI
Jackson

Copyright © 1995 by the University Press of Mississippi
All rights reserved
Manufactured in the United States of America

98 97 96 95   4 3 2 1

The paper in this book meets the guidelines for permanence and durability of the Committee on Production Guidelines for Book Longevity of the Council on Library Resources.

Library of Congress Cataloging-in-Publication Data

Isaacs, Neil David, 1931–
    Batboys and the world of baseball / Neil D. Isaacs.
        p.   cm. — (Studies in popular culture)
    Includes bibliographical references (p.   ) and index.
    ISBN 0-87805-771-4 (alk. paper). — ISBN 0-87805-772-2 (pbk. : alk. paper)
        1. Bat boys—United States—Biography. 2. Baseball—United States—History. I. Title. II. Series: Studies in popular culture (Jackson, Miss.)
    GV865.A1I73   1995
    796.357′092′2—dc20
    [B]   94-42700
                                                                   CIP

British Library Cataloging-in-Publication data available

*To Josh and Emmi
with love and
parental pride*

CONTENTS

PREFACE

The story of this study's origins is worth repeating. It was like a scene from *The Graduate*, only instead of a pool party it was a Tuesday night poker game. My friend Burt Dietch, whom I've known since Mrs. McQueeney's fourth grade class at Roger Sherman School in New Haven, knowing that I was finishing up my book on Grace Paley and undecided about what the next project would be, said, "I have one word for you: BATBOY."

That word was father to much thought, grandfather to research, progenitor of the project. I discovered that no one had tapped the enormous resource of baseball lore and legend in the memory banks of former batboys, that fears about the difficulty of accessing sources were groundless, and that the subculture of clubhouse and dugout has its own rites and myths and charm.

Everyone I talked to about the project seemed to know someone who had been a batboy, and every one of them I tracked down knew two or three others. I did my usual backgrounding in the Library of Congress, wrote a hundred letters, made a thousand phone calls, prowled stadiums long hours before game time, drove a few tough interview subjects to Atlantic City after a Phillies game, and in Detroit, against the advice of security people, walked out Michigan Avenue to the corner of Wabash where someone thought Eddie Forester, who had batboyed for Ty Cobb, still lived.

Why hadn't anyone thought of it before, I was asked over and over again, and what can we do to help? With few exceptions, the former batboys of every era were receptive. As the appendix makes clear, some chose to write me, some to tape-record their own reminiscences, some to be interviewed by phone, and some to welcome personal visits. Many followed up with additional installments. Of the exceptions, there were a couple of Californians who feared I would trash them by digging up scandalous material, a few bright younger ones who wanted to write their own books, a venerable historian whose failing health precluded interviews, and a Chicago television newsman who responds to neither phone nor fax.

I have had a legion of helpers along the way, for which these expressions of thanks are but modest tokens. Burt Dietch not only whispered the original suggestion in my ear, but also wrote letters, made contacts, and conducted a couple of preliminary interviews, along with Phil and Marilyn Isaacs. Uncle Phil Taylor, the Orioles' Bob Brown, and Mel Proctor provided many good leads. Tom Dolan, Jim Walczy, and Clyde Taylor gave both pragmatic and psychological support, and without the help of my wife, Ellen Isaacs, who took me to a ball game on our first date, nothing that matters ever gets done around here.

Once and perhaps future editors, whose encouragement kept me going—especially when expressed in the form of what my brother calls "rave rejections"—include Eric Swenson, Ed Burlingame, Al Silverman, Ken Cherry, Mel Helitzer, Larry Malley, and Dick Wentworth. Peter Stine published a version of the prologue, "The Importance of Being Batboy," in the "Sports in America" issue of *Witness* (1992), which is now being reprinted by Wayne State University Press.

I doubt that I can remember everybody whose leads, advice, or remarks were valuable, but several come to mind: Harold Rosenthal, Bill Gildea, Frank Mazzone, Jon Miller, Jack Buck, Stacey Berger, Dave Sislen, Seymour Steiglitz, Don Stevens, Bob and Mercy Coogan, Bill Bechill, Bill Tosheff, Tom Boswell, Ken Denlinger, Gerald Strine, Larry King, Shirley Povich, Phil Hochberg, Marvin Lowe, Jack Higgs, Michael Olmert, Rich Drozd, Charley Rutherford, John Caughey, Larry Mintz, Tom Inge, and Rich Abel. A number of baseball front office or PR people gave more than routine attention: Bill Beck, Jay Hinrichs, Bill Squires, Jim Ferguson, and Larry Shenk.

Equipment and clubhouse managers were the mainstream of support in identifying sources, lining up interviews, generously cooperating, and enthusiastically supporting the project. Special thanks, among them, to Butch Yatkeman, Frank Ciensczyk, Dennis Liborio, Frank Coppenbarger, Jim Ksicinski, Jim Schmakel, Jeff Ross, John Silverman, Joe Macko, Buddy Bates, Leonard Garcia, Mike Murphy, Brian Prilaman, Jim Wiesner, Cy Buynak, Willie Thompson, and, last but not least, Yosh Kawano. A few sources extended themselves above and beyond their own interviews: Jim Ryan, Steve Winship, and Bob Recker.

Players, coaches, and other personnel at all levels of the game who were generous with their time and thought include Eddie Logan, Jimmy Reese, Ken Reitz, Pete Rose, Jr., Art (Caveman) Kusnyer, Ernie Tyler, Sr., Rob Ogle, Jim O'Neill, Bob Bauman, Bill Zeigler, George Brett, and Dan Schatzeder. Special appreciation and regards go to Brooks Robinson. (No wonder they say that some players have candy bars or restaurants named for them, but Brooks Robinson has sons named after him.)

I owe my greatest debt to the men listed in the appendix, who, whether or not their voices are heard in the following pages, are really coauthors of this book. For edited versions of many of their stories, told entirely in their own words, see my book *Innocence and Wonder: Baseball through the Eyes of Batboys* (Masters Press, 1994). I am especially indebted to Tom Bast for his efforts in publishing that work, and to Mark Montieth, its editor, I am prepared to present a writer's MVP award. Equally deserving in the league of university presses is the wise and resourceful Seetha A-Srinivasan. Finally, for the extraordinary generosity of his constructive guidance throughout, offered with the kind of unconditional regard characteristic of a good therapist rather than a critic, I am deeply grateful to Jerry Klinkowitz.

Batboys and the World of Baseball

PROLOGUE **The Importance of Being Batboy**

Chad Blossfield figures he had shined about twelve thousand pairs of shoes in his four years working for the Milwaukee Braves. The polish came from containers as big as cookie tins, and it was the most tedious part of the batboy's job. And then in the fourth game of the 1957 World Series it suddenly became the most important part of all.

Leading two games to one, the Yankees had come from behind on Elston Howard's three-run ninth-inning homer off Warren Spahn to send the game into extra innings and then had taken the lead in the tenth on Hank Bauer's triple. Fred Haney sent up Nippy Jones, a rarely used utility man playing his last season, with instructions to get on any way he could in the Braves' tenth.

Jones skipped over a low curve and promptly headed for first base as if he'd been hit by the pitch. Augie Donatelli called him back, ruling that the ball had missed him. Meanwhile Chad Blossfield retrieved the ball from the backstop. "Gimme that ball, Bloss," said Jones. The next day newspapers around the country printed a picture

The batboy at the turning point of the 1957 World Series: Chad Blossfield retrieved the ball at the screen and umpire Augie Donatelli changed his call, awarding Nippy Jones first base when the shoe polish on the ball proved the batter had been hit by the pitch. Chad (far left) had shined Jones's shoes before the game, and he still has that ball. In the Milwaukee uniforms are third base coach Connie Ryan (# 8), on-deck batter Red Schoendienst (# 25), and Jones (# 4). The Yankees catcher is Yogi Berra. (courtesy of Charlie Blossfield)

of Yogi Berra, Nippy Jones, Augie Donatelli, and Chad Blossfield examining the ball and seeing clearly the mark of the polish that Chad had applied hours before.

Jones was awarded first base, Johnny Logan's double tied the game, and Eddie Mathews's home run won it, providing Spahn with the win that, together with Lew Burdette's three masterworks, won the Series for the Braves in seven games. "That turned it all around— the shine on Nippy's shoe and the home run by my personal hero; it was decisive, like the third day at Gettysburg," says Blossfield. "You know, as an FBI man, I once caught one of the ten most wanted fugitives, but the biggest thrill of my life was that home run by Mathews." And he still has the ball marked by the polish of that twenty-four thousandth shoe he'd shined.

Baseball fans take batboys for granted. But the position is of fairly recent vintage, a contemporary of the lively ball and the relief pitcher, though more venerable than such semi-fixtures as designated hitters and artificial turf. The batboy originates in the coming together of four separate elements or functions: the mascot, the support staff that accompanies commercialization of sports, the equipment that develops with professionalization, and the habit of boys to hang around ballparks and ballplayers.

At the turn of the century, these elements might be found here and there (though players usually cared for their own equipment) but not in combination. John McGraw is said to have kept a humpback mascot with the Giants from 1903 on, and W. P. Kinsella presents (1986) a fantasy of 1908 baseball in which Frank Chance's Cubs have a "hunchbacked midget" who tends the bats while the Iowa Baseball Confederacy All-Stars adopt an "albino" youngster to do the same. But until World War I it was common practice for players, managers, and clubhouse men to choose boys on their way into the ballpark and give them free admission in return for running errands and helping out with equipment.

When clubhouse management stabilized, however, some boys became regulars who performed routinized tasks in the clubhouse and on the field. By the end of the twenties, they were uniformed, too, and though some were still called mascots they were mostly underpaid, underage drudges who willingly served their heroes.

It is a unique characteristic of baseball that the drudges wear the uniform of the club. The very idea of a football waterboy in helmet and pads is absurd. Only in baseball, too, do the aging or even aged managers and coaches also suit up. The uniform, then, becomes emblematic of the special-club character of the game. Once firmly established in tradition, the investiture of the batboy is a momentous turning point—for the individual and the institution alike.

Batboys are supposed to be inconspicuous, nameless, part of the equipment on the field, the furniture in the clubhouse. "Most of us [baseball writers] don't think of them as people," Thomas Boswell said when research for this study was just getting started, and he acknowledged that batboys could be a great untapped source to be heard from. A Cincinnati Reds PR man, answering a request for names, said, "They're more or less anonymous. They come and go and no one knows where." Overstating the difficulty of identifying

In Griffith Stadium in 1937, batboy George Catloth's uniform is still not quite official. Behind him in jacket is rookie Senators speedster George Case, whom Catloth helped train for a match race with Olympics champion Jesse Owens. (courtesy of George Catloth)

and contacting subjects, he was also expressing an attitude (not shared by many other baseball insiders) of disregard for batboys.

In fact, batboys often achieve their moment in the limelight, their fifteen minutes of Warholian fame, either by being in the right place at the right time or by doing the very things they are supposed to be doing. On rare occasions they achieve a measure of celebrity by performing beyond the call of duty.

The care of the bats, the most obvious and routine function for the boys, may itself lead them to a place in the sun. Gus Tham, for example, was the Giants batboy in the mid-sixties and had a close-up view of the infamous confrontation between Juan Marichal and John Roseboro. The press called Gus "heroic" because he was the one to take the bat from Marichal's hands. Gus says that he knew something was going to happen that day, and that when it did there was no time for thought; he acted on an adrenaline rush and was a little surprised when Gene Moreno of the grounds crew, who always looked after the boys, grabbed him and pulled him out of the melee. On another occasion, instinctively running to pick up a bat in Los Angeles, he collided with Dodgers catcher Jeff Torborg. A subhead in the paper next day read, "Batboy Only Injury in Giant Loss."

Neil Cashen's injury came in the Baltimore clubhouse in 1973. A kid had somehow gotten in and snatched a couple of bats when Neil spotted him and instinctively took off to rescue the equipment. The fleeing young thief shut a glass door behind him, and Neil's arm slammed through (the bats were dropped at the sound). Earl Williams and Elrod Hendricks got him to the hospital for stitches, but the picture for the Baltimore *Sun* taken next day in the clubhouse showed Boog Powell with the bandaged-up batboy. Maybe Neil had rescued Boog's big bats.

Roger Hailey (oldest son of author Arthur) also was pictured in the paper for rescuing bats. One night with the California Angels, who were still playing their home games in Dodger Stadium, a sudden downpour deluged the field and flooded the dugout. Roger was photographed "swimming" to retrieve the equipment.

Photos and equipment can make a batboy ambivalent. Bob Recker was kneeling in the on-deck circle with Dick Stewart when Bill Mazeroski's home run won the 1960 World Series for the Pirates. Bob ran to the plate to greet Maz—he had a sure instinct for being part of a photo opportunity—but then he "looked around and saw thousands of people coming down to the field right at me. I grabbed every piece of equipment I could and ran for the clubhouse as fast as I could. It was scary. Everybody was looking for a souvenir, but I think I saved most of the bats."

If there is a dispute on the field about pine tar or cork, the batboy is sure to be involved, but not by choice. The Cardinals batboy for the visiting team, who wishes to remain nameless now, was caught in the middle when Whitey Herzog challenged Howard Johnson's bat, and both clubs and the umpires all demanded that the kid surrender the bat to them. He still shudders at the many replays on national TV showing his dilemma.

Steve Winship was in the same position in Kansas City, when the visiting team, the umpire, and catcher Darrell Porter all wanted Steve to turn over a suspected bat to them. What made it particularly embarrassing was Steve's special relationship with the player. Porter had met his wife Deanna in Steve's father's Royals Stadium suite, and for months Steve had been their go-between, carrying courtship messages back and forth.

The most famous of pine tar incidents brought Billy Martin nose to nose with George Brett at the plate in 1983. And there in the middle, along with the umpire and catcher Rick Cerone, is Merritt Riley in the picture that the wire services picked up. Amid Merritt's collection of bats in his Levittown, New York, home, a framed copy of that picture, signed by all the principals, takes pride of place. Merritt is cool about it now, but at the time he took a lot of heat from the Kansas City dugout, where John Wathan especially got on him for not grabbing the bat quicker.

It is the eye of the camera, whether video or still, that usually frames a batboy for his shot at immortality. Paul Gonoud, who happened to be there to see Merritt Riley's moment of fame, had his own cameo appearance during a televised game against the Brewers at Yankee Stadium. Paul was running a batting glove from the clubhouse out to a batter when his mother and aunt, watching at home, were surprised by Phil Rizzuto's commentary: "It looks like the Yankees are bringing in a pinch runner . . . hey, no, it's the batboy. But look at that kid move, he's fast, and big, too. Holy cow, the Yanks ought to sign him."

Jim Sassetti had several radio and newspaper interviews during his five years batboying for the White Sox. But he is glad that he was not identified by name in the incident that got him the widest audience—on an NBC Saturday Game of the Week. With two men on in the eighth inning at Comiskey Park, a wild pitch headed straight for him where he sat in a folding chair at the base of the screen, his position for his duties that day as home plate ballboy. Jim nimbly dodged out of the way, carrying the chair with him. Unfortunately the ball in play bounced into the bag of balls at his station, occasioning a stoppage of play as players and umpires searched for the proper ball and the appropriate rule.

Kevin Cashen's triumphant television moment on Mel Allen's "This Week in Baseball" came from a seventh-inning-stretch prank by Rick Dempsey on the road with the Orioles in Seattle. The San Diego Chicken was performing that night, and Dempsey caught hold of him, picked him up, and stuffed him into the big basket on wheels that Kevin used for the bats. It was Kevin, then, who got to wheel the Chicken out to the bullpen, giving the Seattle fans (with their team on its way to ninety-eight losses) something to cheer about.

Sometimes, even without a photo op, a batboy may distinguish himself for the fans. For Payton Morris, working the foul line for the Atlanta Braves in 1989, the moment came in a Sunday game against the Mets that had gone through several rain delays, with fans drifting out of the stadium all afternoon. A foul line drive came so suddenly at Payton through the late-inning mist that he was only half out of his chair when he made a glove-hand grab of the ball, getting a big hand from the small crowd that remained.

Steve Winship, in a similar position for the Royals, often tried to make the outstanding play. His nickname Stretch may derive from the day he took four quick steps toward a foul liner off the bat of Jim Rice, speared it in a headlong dive, and slid on his stomach holding the ball up in the webbing of his glove. Not only did the fans roar their approval, but the press box, by consensus, awarded him the "play of the game."

When Tony Atlas made his best play in an Angels uniform in 1978, the problem was that the foul ball hit by Lyman Bostock was called fair by the first base umpire. Tony fielded it cleanly, feeling thirty-eight thousand eyes on him, and then, not knowing what to do, threw to second—a perfect one-hop throw. Rhubarb! Dale Ford sends the runner back to first. Angels protest. Atlas gets lectured, can't shrug it off. Grounds crewman Brian Nofziger says, "The best thing about it was he came up throwing." No, says Tony, "the best thing was the one-time fantasy of coming into the clubhouse after the game and finding reporters waiting around *my* locker for interviews. For days after that the players hounded me, chased me around with a ball, making crowd noises."

For Johnny Boggs in that special moment he was oblivious of camera and crowd. He had been a batboy for Ted Williams's Senators in 1969, but eight years later got to suit up for the World Series as one of Tommy Lasorda's "celebrity batboys." As it happened, his old teammate Rick LaCivita was producing the game for CBS Television, so J.B. was getting some coverage anyway. But when Dusty Baker was hit by a pitch and was being attended to by the trainer at the plate, there was Boggs standing at his leisure alongside Thurman Munson, gazing out into the monumental center field of Yankee Stadium, "living out an exhilarating fantasy."

If pictures are the proof of a batboy's significance, three historical items may be placed in evidence. One is the photograph of John McBride standing between Babe Ruth and Lou Gehrig in Comiskey Park just after Ruth had completed his home run trot in the third inning of the first All-Star Game in 1933. Another is the 1969 Topps bubble gum bobble of Aurelio Rodriguez: Rodriguez wasn't there for the card picture, so batboy Leonard Garcia in his Angels uniform posed in his place—and passed.

The third is arguably the best-loved baseball picture of all. Frank McNulty is president of *Parade* magazine, but it was the *Saturday Evening Post* that made him famous. Frank was the Boston Braves batboy in 1948 when Norman Rockwell posed him in a Cubs uniform, took about twenty-five individual shots of him in the dugout with the instruction to "look sad," paid him five dollars, and later sent him a signed copy of the cover (September 4, 1948) featuring Jolly Cholly Grimm and other Cubbies looking classically, immortally sad.

What makes a batboy feel important—other than that sense of belonging to the club, the game, the baseball world? To Ron Pieraldi, who batboyed for the championship Oakland A's in 1973, it was a ritual he shared with Vida Blue during his twenty-game-winning season. At the start of the game, instead of having new ball and rosin bag placed on the mound for the pitcher, as is usually done, Ron would walk to the mound and hand them to Vida. Even better for Ron was riding in his own car, with his name on it, in the World Series parade. Similarly for Paul Greco and Mike Rufino, it was

Aurelio Rodriguez's stats are on the back of the Topps card, but the picture on the front is that of Angels batboy Leonard Garcia. (courtesy of Mark Montieth)

leading the parade for the 1986 champions, the two batboys carrying the Mets banner down Broadway.

Batboys often talk about the luck that put them in the middle of things. Jim Ryan remembers Opening Day 1958, when he was taking his friend Bill Turner's place as batboy for the Senators. President Eisenhower threw out the first ceremonial ball to Whitey Herzog. When he threw the second, 6'7" pitcher Frank Sullivan reached for it but deflected it right into Ryan's hands. Jim followed Whitey to the presidential box, delayed by Jimmy Piersall who handed him another ball for Ike's signature, and then was greeted warmly by the president, who said, "You're the first batboy I have ever met."

Mark Sassetti and his brother Jim were made to feel important when asked to contribute suggestions for the design of the clubhouse in the new Comiskey Park. (The swimming pool for rehabilitation purposes may partly be their legacy to future White Sox personnel.) But both had been close to Harold Baines and his family and were upset when he was traded. Mark remembers that it

Mike Rufino (l.) and Paul Greco were the 1986 Mets batboys who carried the banner down Broadway at the head of the World Series parade. (courtesy of Paul Greco)

"brought a tear to my eye" to see Baines suit up in a Rangers uniform in the visiting clubhouse. And that's where Mark learned that the White Sox were going to retire Baines's number before the Sunday game.

When the player arrived at the ballpark, the batboy said, "H.B., congratulations." "For what?" "They're gonna retire your number today." "You're crazy, you're kiddin' me, they're not gonna do that." "You better start writing your speech," Mark said, wondering at his luck at being the bearer of such news.

It was Mickey Morabito's luck to be in the middle of an embarrassing situation on the field at Yankee Stadium. His position that night as ballboy was near the dugout right next to the phone connecting the press box to the field. In between innings, Bob Fishel, Yankees PR man, called down on behalf of the official scorer, asking Mickey to consult third base umpire Jake O'Donnell about a play the previous inning. But plate umpire Frank Umont, intercepted Mickey in his gruff, crew cut way, saying, "Where the hell you

President Eisenhower signs a ball for Cookie Lavagetto on opening day in 1958, while Whitey Herzog respectfully waits his turn and Jim Ryan, who can hardly believe his good fortune, is about to become the first batboy Ike ever met. (courtesy of Jim Ryan)

going?" "The press box wants me to check with Jake about scoring on that play at third," he said. "Goddammit," said the ump, promptly walking to the phone and screaming into it, "You guys are watching the game up there. Do your job up there, and don't be asking us for help." Morabito, now the A's traveling secretary, calls himself an "umpire fan."

Roy (Red) McKercher has many examples of his luck, and several memories of ways the batboy can be important. It was a coin toss, for example, that made him the first batboy for the San Francisco Giants instead of working the visiting clubhouse at Seals Stadium. And that's how he got to know manager Bill Rigney so well.

"He was the classiest guy in the world. Showering after games he'd ask my opinions, almost like talking to himself, and I just always agreed with him. Then one day he says, 'Red, what should I do with McCovey and Cepeda?' 'I dunno,' I said. 'Well, I think I'm gonna put McCovey at first—he's a natural first baseman—and play Cepeda in the outfield,' and his voice got louder and he said, 'Now, I want to know what you think and I don't want any bullshit answer this time.' I said, 'That's the greatest move in the world.' The next day after that move, Rig was fired, and he came over to me in the clubhouse and said, 'Red, it's not your fault.'"

That first year, 1959, McKercher was flown to New York to appear on "What's My Line?" Arlene Francis guessed what, and quickly, too. But back in San Francisco, Red got a stack of mail from that appearance. Willie Mays saw it in his locker and asked, "Why'd you put my mail in your locker?" Told what it was, Willie deadpanned, "One TV show and you get more mail than I do."

When a bench-clearing brawl erupted during one game, Red found himself on the field squaring off with the Cubs batboy. But the voice of umpire Al Barlick stayed his hand: "You hit him, you're gone." Not long after that came the incident that won McKercher the Batboy of the Year honor given by *Coronet* magazine. Resisting a holdup in a hamburger joint, Red had been badly beaten. What he remembers most vividly is that the basket of fruit delivered to the hospital from the Giants had an extra note from Johnny Antonelli that said, "IOU one apple."

The importance of being a batboy is something dreamlike to Tim Buzbee, now a Long Beach firefighter. "I can remember the first time, as an Angels batboy, running the game ball and rosin bag out to the mound to start the game, just me, in front of a sellout crowd, under the lights, and I was awed by it. It was ominous."

To Stretch Winship, it is more whimsical than portentous. It is the touching memories of his relationship with Dick Howser, about how they used to wave towels at each other, the manager from the dugout, the ballboy from his chair down the left field line, to signal "errors" of managerial judgment or the misplay of a foul ball. On one occasion, time was called by the third base umpire, who pointed to the dugout where Howser was waving—perhaps the only time major league play was stopped because of a ballboy's error.

Wes Patterson, another Royals batboy, points with pride to the significance of his own towel signal: "It's weird to think that a guy who makes six bucks an hour is the man who controls the start of the game. Everyone thinks it's the umpire saying 'play ball,' or the pitcher throwing the first pitch. Nope, it's me, the batboy. I stand outside the dugout, and when the pitcher says he's ready, I twirl the towel, and they start their little theme song, and we take the field. It's really a weird feeling to be in control, Opening Day in front of forty-two thousand screaming fans, and you've got the towel, getting ready to make them all erupt. It makes you feel like you're body-slinging Hulk Hogan in Madison Square Garden, heading for the title. Well, I guess it's not that exciting, but it's a neat feeling. I do that, they take the field, and the rest is cake."

Batboys perform largely in anonymity. (Their uniforms, alone among those worn in baseball, typically bear the legend "BAT BOY" rather than a name and rarely have a number.) Perhaps that accounts for the kind of neglect discovered in an otherwise comprehensive oral history like Peter Golenbock's *Bums*, in which seventy separate voices are heard from field, dugout, clubhouse, front office, press box, and grandstand, but not the voice of even one batboy.

The anonymity persists as a literary convention. In Bernard Malamud's *The Natural*, when Roy's "Wonderboy" splits, the batboy's part in the subsequent action is incidental to the point of nonexistence. In Barry Levinson's altered (corrupted) movie version, the batboy's role is significant but still anonymous, which probably contributes to the ironic effect when that scene is parodied in Ron Shelton's *Bull Durham*. Jerry Klinkowitz's *Short Season*, in which twenty-eight stories make us so familiar with minor-league personnel that we even know the bus driver by name and idiosyncrasy, the batboy is still anonymous, and the only role he plays, in the characteristically wry story "Nicknames" (79–84), is as close-up reporter of an invented piece of instant legend. And in Louis Phillips's short story "The Day the Walrus Hit .400," the line "I'd be lucky to end up as a bat-boy in Siberia" (71) underscores the image of batboy as the lowest icon among baseball's totems.

Yet the presence of batboys on the field, in the dugout, and in the clubhouse is a constant of the subculture, a persistent reminder of baseball's special quality as a separate world resistant to change. Most of us can only fantasize about the world that is seen close-up through the eyes of batboys. But a comprehensive picture, drawn from interviews with 170 of them who batboyed in nine different decades of baseball, delineates a role relatively unchanged, *mutatis mutandis*, since World War I. They experience dreams and memories, characters and incidents, whimsy and awe, duties and perqs, towels and cake—all as if for the first time but all like obligatory elements in a formulaic scenario.

The importance of being batboy is to take part, integrally if anonymously, as celebrant in the rituals that surround the game and fix it in a cultural continuity that seems almost sacred. Suiting up is an investiture in tradition. As Mike Murphy, once a Giants batboy and now equipment manager, says, "I wish there were a million clubs, to give a million kids the chance to be a batboy, to let 'em see what it's like working with ballplayers." Or listen to Gus Tham, who has been a batboy, a schoolteacher, an air freight truckdriver, and is now a rehabilitation counselor: "If every kid in America could do it, America would be a better place."

Wherever I have quoted former batboys without acknowledging a source, the quotation is drawn from firsthand contacts. These contacts have taken place in a variety of ways, as documented specifically in the appendix: live interviews or conversations, telephone interviews or conversations, taped monologues of reminiscences (in part responding to an open-ended questionnaire), and follow-up correspondence. Much of the material, edited to form coherent sets of remembrances, appears in *Innocence and Wonder*.

There are several benefits to be derived from looking at baseball and its world or subculture through batboys' eyes. Their reported memories provide unique details that cannot fail to enrich our appreciation of both the game and the separate world of its clubhouse. But they will modify that appreciation as well; more than an accretion of detail, this hitherto unexamined vantage provides a freshness that neither the popular nor the media-generated conceptions and perceptions of baseball in general have experienced. Common threads that help bind these reports are essential distinctions between insiders and outsiders. Batboys thrive on the insights of those distinctions, and like much twentieth-century fiction (and mythology) a central theme in their narration is illusion versus reality.

The interviews themselves may be labeled "participant observation," which at best produces a wealth of details—curious and familiar but always evocative—that bring a subculture to life. But these participants are not, after all, ethnographers, observing with a preconceived goal of illuminating their world and experience for outsiders.[1] Moreover, their observations are the stuff of oral history, filtered through sometimes very old memories and structured in part by the conventions and values of that world. This study is an attempt both to synthesize the memories and observations and to analyze them from and in a larger context. It presents, then, the subculture of baseball, described from within but viewed from the mainstream culture outside, a culture that has itself contributed greatly to a mythologizing of the subculture.

CHAPTER 1 The Subculture of the Ballpark

In August of 1993, I took two friends who had never been there to Oriole Park at Camden Yards. My seats are upper reserved on the third base side between home and third; they afford a wonderful view of the field and its setting, with the warehouse walls as a backdrop for the scoreboard straight ahead and, a half turn to the left, a view of Baltimore past the terraced bullpens and the picnic and bleacher areas. We entered through the tunnel next to the first aid station, and as we emerged into the summer afternoon Susan and John, in unison, uttered a loud gasp. The sparkling jewel of the diamond in its setting had taken their breath away.

I have heard and seen and read about that reaction a thousand times, whether from fans or from disinterested or alien observers. It is an instinctive though perhaps also a learned response to the beauty of a baseball field in its contexts of season and park and game and pastime and all the meanings and values we associate with it. Several batboys included a similar experience in accounting for their early fascination with the game. Years before he began to work at Memorial Stadium for the Cleveland Indians, Jeff Sipos remembers "the thrill of coming to the ballpark, getting to the top of the ramp, and looking down to see this bright green field with a diamond cut into it."

Similarly, Steve Friend recalls growing up in Montreal when "going to Olympic Stadium was like an adventure to me. When you're young, seeing Olympic Stadium is a thrill, and even though you're growing through the years the stadium seems to grow along with you. They were still constructing the tower which we hoped would hold the roof, but that came much later. People in Montreal often complained about the billion-dollar stadium that still didn't have a roof, but I can still remember the feeling of awe, sitting in the stands, just to be looking at the field. It was pretty spectacular, and I never imagined in those pre-batboy days that one day I'd be running out on the field."

Conventional wisdom has it that baseball is a significant reflection of American culture or is at least a commemoration of our pastoral heritage (which exists only in nostalgic dreams, but is no less treasured for that). But it seems to me that baseball is a subculture unto itself, that it derives its power, its appeal, its magical-mystery properties from the very fact of its isolation from the culture at large. I am using the term *subculture* in the sense that the prefix *sub* means "adjacent to" but "separate from" with the additional sense of "hidden from."

In recent decades the term *subculture* has taken on special meaning in the field of culture study. It has been used specifically to refer to individual groups within the youth culture at large, such as "punk," "rude boy," and "Rasta," but also to such deviant groups as street gangs, professional criminals, and the "teahouse trade." In this context, the prefix carries the connotations of "subterranean" and even "subversive."

We are relying, in the first place, on a definition of culture derived from anthropology. In Raymond Williams's "social" definition, culture is a "description of a particular way of life which expresses certain meanings and values not only in art and learning, but also in institutions and ordinary behaviour. The analysis of culture, from such a definition, is the clarification of the meanings and values implicit and explicit in a particular way of life, a particular culture" (41).

Describing a tendency of subcultural studies to rely exclusively on participant observation, Dick Hebdige says, "In such accounts, the subculture tends to be presented as an independent organism functioning outside the larger social, political and economic contexts" and the accounts are therefore "often incomplete" (76). Attempts to place subculture in context relative to mainstream culture produce observations such as Phil Cohen's: "Its latent function is to express and resolve, albeit magically, the contradictions which remain hidden or unresolved in the parent culture" (Hebdige 77). Even while contextualizing, however, a study like Walter Miller's analysis of gangs tends to argue that the values of the deviant group are distortions or heightenings of those of the parent culture.

In a folkloristic context, Tristram Coffin classifies baseball with "folk occupations" like cowpunching and seafaring, but not full-fledged. It is "a semi-folk occupation" because its lore is ". . . confined to the occupational portion of a man's life" (21), for while ballplayers "share the homogeneity and lore of their occupation during much of the day, even on a road-trip for a couple of weeks at a time, they do not carry this homogeneity or lore into their home-lives" (23). When the whole club becomes the focus, however, we can see its ways, lore, and values being internalized and carried into every aspect of life outside the clubhouse; at least that is the argument for my preference for *subculture* over *semi-folk occupation*.

To call baseball a subculture is to extend and modify and to a certain extent invert the definitions derived from anthropology and culture study. "Subterranean" does not apply, though those ways of the baseball world that are hidden from public view may be called "sub rosa." Yet the sense of "submergence" is present in the clubhouse, not so much to oppose or revolt against the values of the culture at large, but to *maintain* the presumed classical, older values of a culture undergoing transvaluations of values. The subculture justifies its submergence as a matter of preservation, conservation, and "subsistence" or survival. It acts as a kind of "sublimation" of the anger occasioned by the loss of treasured values and may even think of itself as heroic or "sublime."

It is not, I would argue, the specific nature of those values that makes baseball special, but the essential fact of its separation. That special quality has been legislatively proclaimed and judicially upheld in baseball's antitrust exemption.[2] It has also been reinforced by the game's establishment in a variety of self-aggrandizing ways.

The most egregious was the campaign of A. G. Spalding to establish once and for all that baseball was an American game invented by an American hero, Abner Doubleday. The Special Base Ball Commission, which Spalding single-handedly lobbied into existence and which consisted entirely of his handpicked members, not surprisingly issued its report in support of Spalding's own pet theory, thus establishing by edict in 1907 an official myth that all patriotic baseball fans, including President Theodore Roosevelt, could approve. The game was thus exempted not only from the law of the land but also from the pursuit of truth and from the rigors of historical evidence.

Spalding did more than any other individual to establish the especially *national* character of baseball (see Levine). In the succeeding century, however, while the specialness has persisted, the *publicly* jingoistic nature of the game has subsided—or gone underground. It is instructive to see Spalding's own brief comments (12–15) on the Commission's efforts, so dismissively accepting as to question the seriousness of the endeavor. It is also instructive to see how such professional historians as Voigt and Seymour disdain the Spalding-Doubleday myth. Baseball no longer institutionally recognizes the myth as history, yet honors it *as* myth with the site of its Hall of Fame at Cooperstown.

I would also argue that the separation is what makes baseball an attractive subject for writers of every stripe. Listening to the stories of batboys, one hears not only bits and pieces of the mystique that attaches to the sacred world of the game but also strains of the mythology through which the media have developed, institutionalized, embroidered, and reinvented that mystique. Trying to articulate his feelings about the game, for example, batboy Mike Mullane refers to a passage from Roger Kahn, whose creative nonfiction *Boys of Summer* has become part of a universal frame of baseball reference but whose *Seventh Game* is a forgettable novel. Mullane, however, cites *Good Enough to Dream*, a memoir of Kahn's season as an executive with the Utica Blue Sox (interwoven with other nostalgic baseball reminiscences), calling baseball "the door to the world of men." While Mullane may have had in mind Kahn's observation that there is "a certain bridge that separated the ball players from the civilians" (155), the twofold point remains—a quality of separateness and a literary articulation of that quality.

One other sense of the word *subculture* may have some appro-

priateness here, at the least in a punning way. That is its micro-
biological sense, which refers to a process of development in a new
or separate *medium*, an apt allusion since the media contribute
mightily to our perceptions of baseball as a subculture. Coffin ar-
gues that *legend* "is the only major form of folklore in the heritage
of ballplayers. However, there will be a wealth of minor, folk-literary
forms: a lot of jokes; many superstitions and beliefs; a host of customs; a few proverbs, proverbial sayings, and truisms; and a cant—
all working to maintain the homogeneity and ideals of a life separated 'by the foul lines' from the main culture" (31). Later, however,
he acknowledges "an elusive dream" of a "great national novel"
taking shape from the game (159). He mentions Malamud, but Jerome Charyn's *The Seventh Babe* is, I think, a more rewarding example of how *all* of Coffin's "forms" are integrated in a baseball
novel that transcends the weighty distractions of Malamud's mythic
rituals and icons. Charyn even employs the legend of the hunchback
batboy, "their own private brute, the middle-aged boy with unde-
veloped legs who delivered bats and rosin bags to them" (38), and
who plays Sam Gamgee to the Babe's Frodo.

Batboys' stories share a common thread with other treatments of
baseball, such as the coverage of beat reporters, the chronicles of
cultural historians, the anecdotal memories of fans, the autobiogra-
phies of star players, and the imaginative constructions of fiction
and film: all assume a relationship to the game that goes beyond
appreciation to a personal involvement and presumptive understanding, an intimacy of feeling that is translated into all sorts of
distortions and fantasized unrealities. (No doubt I am participating
in this process even as I describe it.)

I confess I cannot remember my first visit to a major league ballpark. Either it was my grandfather taking me to Yankee Stadium to
see "the great DiMaggio," a phrase that already had epithetic currency in the Isaacs household more than a decade before Hemingway
gave it its literary permanence in *The Old Man and the Sea*; or it
was my father taking me to the Polo Grounds to see the Giants. But I
know that it was the 1939 season—and not just because I also saw
the World's Fair on one of those trips from New Haven to New York.
It is firmly fixed in my memory that I saw DiMag get three hits
toward his first batting title, but my memory of that National
League game is clearer still.

It was Claude Passeau of the Cubs, on his way to the league lead in strikeouts, versus Carl Hubbell. Mel Ott hit a very short home run, and the Giants led 2–1 in the ninth, when the win was preserved by a double play I can see as vividly in my mind's eye today as I witnessed it in openmouthed awe fifty-five years ago. Man on first, one out, and Billy Herman the batter, with the defense playing him to pull. He hits a grounder just to the left of the mound. Hubbell fields it and turns to throw to second where Whitey Whitehead is *standing* on the bag. There's no chance for two because Whitey will have to pivot and throw from a set position, but here comes Billy Jurges racing across from deep shortstop to take the throw on the fly and with full momentum nailing Herman at first with the ball in Zeke Bonura's stretched-out glove. It has to be '39, with Passeau just come over to the Cubs from the Phillies while Jurges and Dick Bartell had exchanged shortstop uniforms as part of a six-player trade.

Grandpa Isaacs was a lifelong Yankees fan who, had he lived to see it, would have ignored the departure of the Giants and Dodgers from the other boroughs, kidded his sons about the loss of "their" teams, and scoffed at the very notion of a Mets team playing near the site of the Trilon and Perisphere at Flushing Meadows. He brought me to Yankee Stadium and to a grudging appreciation of the matchless grace of DiMaggio. My father, on the other hand, was a Giants fan (till 1958), and he spent another two decades of mounting bitterness over the move west, which he blamed neither on Walter O'Malley's greedy leadership nor Horace Stoneham's me-too avarice but on a general decline in the values of the society at large. (Uncle Bert was a Dodgers fan, in part because of a long friendship with coach Jake Pitler, but he mellowly adopted the Mets until embracing the Braves when they had settled in Atlanta and he in Charlotte.) I like to think that my own first allegiance, to the Detroit Tigers, was due to an idolization of Charlie Gehringer along with some ethnic bias toward the team of Hank Greenberg, but there was probably an element of sheer perversity as well.

In any case, what I remember are moments of splendidly meaningful movement. I was compelled to accept what I saw in DiMaggio—the image of the ideal ballplayer with his apparently effortless brilliance in center field. And to this day that is where I look for greatness. (The appreciation of pitching, the proverbial ninety percent of the game, is a more sophisticated and cerebral dimension of baseball attentiveness, the focus of most intellectual—and gambling—analysis. Despite the early model of Christy Mathewson for a generation of fictional baseball heroes, however, it is the position players that arouse the strongest feelings in fans and the boldest characterizations in fiction.) I probably underrate Barry Bonds because he plays in left (as I did Aaron and Clemente in right), tend to glorify Griffey and McRae the younger, and, when Jeffrey Hammonds arrived in an Orioles uniform in 1993 hoped for his eventual installation (anointing?) in center instead of the overmatched Mike Devereaux or the splendid *left* fielder Brady Anderson. I remember being dazzled by Terry Moore of the Cardinals, guiltily impressed by Duke Snider, and bewildered by the exploits and inconsistencies (the saga perhaps as much as the record) of Mickey Mantle. I saw him as a rookie strike out five straight times in a doubleheader at Fenway Park until merciful Casey Stengel removed him from the abusive Red Sox fans chanting "phe-nom, phe-nom." But I could also soon see an unmatched combination of speed, precision, and power. Still, it was the Mick *in potentia* (what he might have accomplished if healthy) and the charismatic character to be adored and reviled off field, that is, the popular-hero-of-modern-legend, that comes through most clearly in memories of Mantle.

With the coming of Willie Mays I experienced a whole new set of criteria for greatness. It was as if the quiet admiration for DiMaggio and the hero worship of the Babe had been combined and transcended in a nonpareil embodiment of both the skills and the joys of the game. You could see those qualities every time Mays made a play or swung the bat or ran the bases, and when you saw the statistical record there was a kind of shock that the numbers actually confirmed the larger-than-life perceptions in the worshipping mind's eye. I was gratified to learn from those I interviewed that the awe in which Mays was held by clubhouse personnel was universal and perhaps matched only by the feeling for Ted Williams.

I don't remember many uniform numbers, although it was numbers that attracted me to baseball in the first place—the stats. Computing averages and standings, reading a box score, and knowing how to score a game were some of the skills I acquired early on as merit badges when I was still a tenderfoot baseball fan. Then there were the bubble gum cards with their technicolor images that overrode the stats, but there were also endless hours my brother and I spent playing a dice baseball game for which we kept elaborate updated records. The numbers elevated the personalities of players, real and imagined, into mythic figures. They were realer than real, separate and special. Listening to play-by-play accounts on radio,

Roy McKercher, the first Giants batboy in San Francisco, was befriended by Willie Mays, whose generosity in the clubhouse matched his greatness on the field. (photo by Gene Tupper, Palo Alto *Times*, courtesy of Roy McKercher)

whether live or "recreations" from the wire, I had the freedom to envision a grand panorama peopled by my own projected images.

When I actually saw a game, the players became impersonal, abstract expressers of routinized movements, not only the drills of infield practice and the rituals of batting practice but even the actual playing of the games. Watching the play I saw the performance of rituals and lost sight of the participants as ennobled performers. This is not to say that I didn't love the play, whether routine or surprising, banal or astounding. But missing the embodiments of mythic qualities as charismatic figures (the images I attached to the names on my stat sheets, the pictures on my cards) I found myself scanning dugouts and bullpens in search of glimpses. Of what? Gestures, I suppose, or the dim outlines of faces, something—anything, really—with movements or features to which I could attach a larger-than-life quality.

Ted Williams sometimes got mixed reviews from fans and press but was universally revered in clubhouses. In Washington he took batboy brothers Scot (l.) and Tom MacDougal under his wings. (courtesy of Tom MacDougal)

The chatty nature of baseball reportage in those days encouraged that kind of popular mythologizing. Photos and caricatures and occasional interviews and what passed for public relations all supported the rather simplistic public assumptions and images of the game. It is one of the great ironies in our cultural history that the Black Sox scandal of 1919 changed public attitudes so little. And it is testimony to the gritty persistence of those attitudes that a majority of fans would vote Pete Rose into the Hall of Fame today (as they would have voted Joe Jackson in earlier, perhaps as a charter member).

The dominance of baseball as a national pastime had as its corollary the dominance of baseball as a sporting proposition. Among all the sports, it was baseball, by far, that attracted the most widespread betting, and for the largest stakes. (Horse racing stands outside this discussion, though I might point out historical relationships between baseball owners and horse owners, between baseball players and horse players.) Baseball had everyone's interest, and baseball meant action. You could find odds quoted on games and series in the mainstream press, not just tabloid and sporting papers, and game reportage often detailed specific wagers by famous high rollers. Looking back at the time of the Black Sox fix, Brendan Boyd's gambler narrator in *Blue Ruin* says, "Baseball and gambling mixed seamlessly. We were good company, and good copy; we brought thousands of otherwise reluctant spectators through the turnstiles" (124).[3]

Three factors changed all that. One was a belated righteousness (or pious hypocrisy, depending on one's angle of vision or attitude) that held good sport to be threatened or contaminated by gambling (as if stakes hadn't always been an essential part of competition), and that institutionalized opposition to legalized gambling (perhaps because illegal gambling had a nourishing symbiotic relationship with the game, as long as the game cynically disdained to acknowledge it). The other two factors were the coming of television and the development of the point spread.

The rhythms of baseball are not as neatly structured for television as those of football. But without the more attractive betting proposition of football with a point spread to "equalize" the action ("balance the book"), the National Football League could not so quickly have replaced baseball as the national pastime, and the Super Bowl could not have displaced the World Series as the premier event, a festive celebration on the public calendar now far more significant than Independence Day.

But if betting on baseball was a kind of ancillary but natural appendage to the game, point spread and "office pools" action are essential corollary activities with pro football and approaching that equivalence in basketball despite the scandals of fixes and point shaving that spot the last forty-five years of collegiate play.[4] The notion that sport is "clean" is as naive an American myth as George Washington's cherry tree, but in the case of baseball, with its "self-serving idealism," it is also "the self-deception that believes the lie."[5]

Complaints frequently appear about how television has changed the game of baseball, directly by dictating the schedule and lengthening the pauses for commercial purposes, indirectly by driving the financial factors to unforeseen heights and thus altering the values of pressure, performance, loyalty, incentive, physical conditioning, duration of careers, relations with management, and so forth. But television has also changed the ways in which the game is *perceived*, thought about, and *re-created*. It is a medium with a consuming nature, serving overstimulated and ever-unsatisfied appetites. It is both voyeuristic and cannibalistic. As a staple of television fare, baseball is *used* by fans to see the game and its players as never before—and to devour them.

What were rarely glimpsed personal features and gestures, dimly perceived nuances of motion and technique, are now seen in close-up, "slomo," and insistent instant replay. Before television, the game could generate a fantasy world of baseball fiction, translating its magic (however illusory it may have been) into the stuff of novelistic dreaming. Baseball fiction created a baseball of the mind, a baseball of the word, all sorts of parallel baseball universes that constituted their own subcultures *outside* the base lines.

The first phase of that re-creation produced novels for a juvenile audience that were no less moralistic or simplistically idealistic than Richardson designed *Pamela* to be when the English novel was in its infancy. The world of Gilbert Patten's Frank Merriwell, of the six ghost-written novels of Christy Mathewson himself, and of Edward Stratemeyer's (Lester Chadwick's) Baseball Joe persists,[6] even though it has been substantially eclipsed in several of the mature parallel worlds that evolved from that infancy. Among others, there are the fantasy world of H. Allen Smith's *Rhubarb*, George Abbott and Stanley Donen's *Damn Yankees*, and Clarence Brown's *Angels in the Outfield*; the world in which baseball and literature cohere, as in Kinsella, Philip Roth, and Mark Harris, all looking back to or askance upon Ring Lardner; the historical-novel world[7] of William Brashler, Brendan Boyd, Eric Rolfe Greenberg (Christy Mathewson as historical *character*), and preeminently Don DeLillo; and the world in which baseball partakes of larger mythic or ritual patterning, as in Charyn, Malamud, Lamar Herrin, and Robert Coover.

Other categories will suggest themselves to other readers, while my categorizing will seem arbitrary for other readings of the works named here as exemplary. But if a prevailingly nostalgic tone seems to cut across the borders of these separate provinces, that is only to point out their parallelism, reinforcing the process I have suggested even while challenging specific applications. It may be that "nostalgia" itself should constitute its own separate world; how else to categorize Irwin Shaw's *Voices of a Summer Day*, in which a sandlot game and several baseball memories provide the occasion and the structure of the whole novel? "The sounds were the same through the years," Shaw says through Ben Federov's consciousness, "the American sounds of summer, the tap of bat against ball, the cries of the infielders, the wooden plump of the ball into catchers' mitts, the umpires calling 'Strike three and you're out.' The generations circled the bases, the dust rose for forty years as runners slid in from third, dead boys hit doubles, famous men made errors at shortstop . . . . The distant mortal innings of boyhood and youth" (*Voices* 12). And how at all to categorize Dick Dillard's remarkable *First Man on the Sun*, in which the very processes of artistic re-creation and myth-making from the empirical and statistical details of the game are explored? A chapter called "The Game Itself" has this second paragraph:

> The game itself, the pattern of pitches and hits, the ball bouncing and twisting across the infield grass, a bat that cracks along the grain, the ball boy ducking behind the light pole as a foul tip stings the screen, the sun steady overhead holding the players to the field in the narrow circles of their shadows, the third-base coach's signs, the patterns of electric numbers across the scoreboard—the game itself, holding to what [Borges's] Herbert Quain called "the essential features of all games: symmetry, arbitrary rules, tedium." [73] We admire the symmetry on the field and on the scoreboard, and we admit the arbitrariness of the rules and the tedium, claiming all the while that, like the symmetry, they are informed with significance, that the game is game, is play, but that game and play are alive with the values by which we inform our lives, our life, from day to day. (199–200)

And then the chapter ends with a box score (!) of the game itself, an actual late-season Carolina League game between Salem and Winston-Salem.

Television has not destroyed the novelistic impulse to create a baseball of the mind, even though it has become the instrument of demythologizing. But that very process—voyeuristic and cannibalistic—paradoxically constitutes a re-mythologizing as well. From the perspective of what we can see so clearly now, know so intimately, and explicate so sophisticatedly, we tend to refashion an appreciation of baseball. Both the love and the separateness, to borrow Eudora Welty's phrase for an application she never dreamt (though Robert Penn Warren hints at its possibility in his analysis thereof), are insisted upon by baseball's establishment and its conventions. And for those of us outside, looking in or on or down through the most powerful of lenses, it is the separateness that nourishes the love.

It is not the purpose of this study to shatter a myth, nor to explore a sacred world in order to tear it down from within. The ninescore men interviewed would hardly countenance, never mind participate in, such a process. But it will necessarily serve as a corrective to some of the more passionate paeans and "overblown rhetoric."[8] It will present, from the vantage of "participant observers," a valuable but necessarily flawed depiction of what might be called the reality behind the mythology, but perhaps more accurately the reality *of* the mythology.

The following six chapters are loosely grouped around central *topoi* that may be seen as mechanisms for establishing and maintaining the gaps between the larger culture outside and the privileged subculture within. First come the places, those sacred precincts that delineate the boundaries. These are followed by the rites of initiation and passage through which clubhouse attendants ("clubbies," a generic term that includes batboys, ballboys, former batboys and ballboys who stay on as assistants, and young helpers aspiring to uniforms and on-field duties) become club members, then the calendar of pilgrimage that charts the habitual cycles of movement in which a game that knows no time moves according to its own timetable. A central pantheon of types is then derived from the views of the resident deities or heroes. Chapter 6 takes us through a game day for a batboy, showing how prescribed duties take on the coloration of ritual and eventually produce (or reinforce) an ethos held to be specific and special for the subculture. Chapter 7 attempts to portray the emotional commitment, the passionate devotion, engendered by the cycles, conventions, and practices described. The epilogue, finally, is a demonstration of how conventions and values, when embraced and internalized, may filter and structure the observation, memory, and judgment of participant-reporters.

In a sense, this study discovers a new species belonging to the genus "Baseball of the Mind." There are the several forms in fiction and film (as noted above), but also several forms in generations of media coverage, as well as several forms in the varieties of biography and autobiography, history and exposé. Perhaps more important, there are many forms of a baseball of the mind generated by public and personal experience, an architecture of fantasy and memory and convention built on the foundation of the game as perceived. These are the castles in air (or cyberspace, we must now add) erected from radio broadcasts, or trading cards, or scorecards and box scores, or rotisserie leagues, or dice baseball games, or family traditions, or childhood visits to ballparks with their fragmentary glimpses of players and bullpens and dugouts.

Donald Hall's famous essay brings the family-tradition aspect of the game to bright imagistic light. Irwin Shaw presents it in a fictional context:

> Federov had taken Michael to his first big-league game when Michael was six. The Giants were playing the Reds at the Polo Grounds. The Yankees were a more interesting team to watch, but it was at the Polo Grounds that Benjamin, aged six, had watched *his* first baseball game, at his father's side. An uprooted people, Federov had thought half-mockingly, we must make our family traditions with the material at hand. There was no ancestral keep to bring the male heir to; no hallowed family ceremonies into which to initiate a son . . . . So, bereft of other tribal paraphernalia, he took his son to the Polo Grounds, because when *he* was six *his* father had taken him to the Polo Grounds. (*Voices* 152–3)

In Coover, when Henry Waugh disappears *into* the world of his baseball game, the family-tradition aspect of the rituals is itself taken into a new dimension.

It may be that for every baseball fan, as well as for every baseball writer, there is a separate, idiosyncratic baseball of the mind. But I would argue that almost all of these are subspecies at best or most likely hybrids of the forms listed. For seven paragraphs, earlier in this chapter, I sketched some of the elements of my own variety of subspecies; I would also argue that most of them would fall under general rubrics depending on which forms provided the greater influences. The batboys themselves have usually experienced some of those very influences, which impinge on (or coincide with) batboys' perceptions and memories in many ways that may be suggested below.

I would also argue—and this study will be the vehicle of the argument—that there is a certain persistence and consistency that constitutes a Baseball of the Batboy's Mind. It is that characteristic, cohesive distinctiveness that reinforces the concept of baseball as a subculture. The gaps between the perceptions of baseball *imagined* from outside the clubhouse and the knowledge of it *experienced* from inside may help draw a clear line between appearances and realities, thereby acting as demythologizing, demystifying agents. But in the final analysis, in bringing the soaring flights of imagina-

The batboy's ground-level view of the action: Dennis Cashen in front of the visitors dugout at Memorial Stadium in Baltimore, with Carlton Fisk on deck (photo by Gene Boyars, Baltimore *News-American*, courtesy of Dennis Cashen)

tion down to the ground level of the batboy's perspective, a re-mythologizing takes place, a mystifying of the mundane, which may be as good a phrase as any to suggest the powerful hold that the subculture of baseball has on American culture writ large. Is this a great game, or what?

CHAPTER 2 Sacred Precincts

"If you build it, he will come," says the voice out of the Iowa corn-field in Kinsella's *Shoeless Joe* (3 et passim), and the reader, along with the narrator Ray, assumes that "it" is a ballpark, while "he" becomes increasingly ambiguous. In any case, what comes first is the shrine, the temple, the house of worship, with the green gem of the field and the cynosure of the diamond presented to the view of the visiting celebrants.

A recent book by Philip J. Lowry, *Green Cathedrals*, has as its subtitle, *The Ultimate Celebration of All 271 Major League and Negro League Ballparks Past and Present*. Celebration it certainly is, but hardly ultimate, since it was followed the same season by Lawrence Ritter's *Lost Ballparks: A Celebration of Baseball's Legendary Fields*. It is not my purpose to trace the literature of ballparks but to observe the sacramental and elegiac tone of such literature.[9]

Lowry's dedication ends, "May the cheers of fans, the crack of the bat, and the aroma of hot dogs never disappear from these sacred and cherished shrines of baseball." And Ritter begins his celebration by saying, "In a nation that has had a century-long love affair with baseball, it is not surprising that ballparks play a special role in the lives of Americans." Citing a *New York Times* feature on fans' ashes being scattered over Comiskey Park, Wrigley Field, and County Stadium in Milwaukee, he says, "People have been born in them, gotten married in them, ritually taken their children to them, died in them, and even had their final remains scattered over them" (1).

Ritter goes on to say, "For many older baseball fans, the first major league ballpark they ever entered occupies a hallowed niche in the corridors of memory, one of those few treasured childhood recollections that remain forever vivid" (1). Lowry's opening passage amplifies, perhaps even elevates, those sentiments. At times he sounds exalting, exhortative, or Zen-like:

> I spent a very long time searching for the right title for this book. The more I have studied ballparks, the more they have begun to resemble mosques, or synagogues, or churches, or similar such places of reverent worship. There is a scene of beauty at 21st and Lehigh in Philadelphia. Where once there was the Shibe Cathedral, also called Connie Mack Stadium, there is now the Deliverance Evangelistic Church. There is a message in this.
>
> My wife and I believe that each person travels his or her own unique religious path on their quest for that spiritual truth that will speak best to their own individual soul. I feel the same way about ballparks: that to fulfill their purpose in our National Pastime, they must be allowed to have their own personalities and characteristics, or, in other words, to be unique and asymmetrical.
>
> What I hope the title *Green Cathedrals* conveys is a quiet spiritual reverence for ballparks. For millions of baseball fans, a ballpark holds treasured memories and serves as a sanctuary for the spirit. *Green Cathedrals* celebrates the mystical appeal of the hundreds of ballparks, past and present, where the soul of the game of baseball resides. (1)

Set aside the utterly depressing context of the present scene at Twenty-first and Lehigh in urban-blighted Philadelphia, a point made in comprehensive detail by Bruce Kuklich in *To Every Thing a Season: Shibe Park and Urban Philadelphia*. And where Kuklich's neutral tone firmly resists the elegiac, nostalgic, or ironic implications of his subject, consider Lowry's language here: *reverence, ritual, hallowed niche, shrine, sanctuary, spiritual*, and *mystical*. This is not the language of ordinarily nostalgic childhood memory. It is the language of devotion to and faith in iconographic images that are superimposed on memories of ballparks and the blessed event of attending games therein.

These images have been maintained over time by a kind of magic, and the language of prestidigitation is not absent from these celebrants' usage. Ritter says, as lament gives way to consolation in the true function of elegy, "Most of yesterday's ballparks are gone, bulldozed into oblivion. They will never return, but there are indications that they are appreciated more today than has been the case for a long time. They had their faults, no doubt, but they had magic as well, magic that will live for years in the memories of those who were lucky enough to have passed through their turnstiles" (7).

Such extravagance can only be supported by the great value placed on the game itself. Here is Lowry: "The subtleties of the game of baseball are incredibly beautiful and balanced. A close play at the plate, a brilliantly executed double play, a diving catch over the outfield fence, an inside-the-park home run—these are every bit as wonderful as Michelangelo's *Pietà* or one of Beethoven's symphonies" (1).[10] Ritter is somewhat less breathless with adoration but equally awed: "For twenty-two ballparks that no longer exist— ballparks that are lost forever but that once bore clamorous witness to many wondrous and thrilling events—the following pages may convey to you some hint of the spell they once cast" (7).

Implicit (and eventually explicit) in both Lowry's and Ritter's views is the superiority of those old ballparks that brought the fans closer to the fields of play, to the action of the games, and to the players in action on the field. The memories from such ballparks may be more vividly rendered because the original sense impressions might themselves have been more vivid and immediate. But I suspect that at least some of the iconographic power of those structures derived from their function in housing, in a newly urbanized society, the sanctified plots of ground of a pastoral past.

James Harper, in his essay "Baseball: America's First National Pastime," has provided a precise analysis of the game's Janus-faced quality:

> Much of baseball's hold over the American sporting mind resulted from its ability to exemplify two seemingly contradictory sets of values. In one sense baseball was rural, calling fans back to simpler pastoral America or to the unhurried pleasures of youth. The green field

evoked images of the America of William Jennings Bryan or even that of Thomas Jefferson. In the 1920s the census for the first time registered that the majority of Americans no longer lived on the farm. Baseball offered a means of reacting to this change by looking backward. This nostalgic appeal was strengthened by those players who still hailed from rural America and by the game's tradition, its refusal to change its rules or dimensions.

On the other hand the growth of professional baseball had been clearly linked to the urbanization of America. Even before the turn of the century, Mark Twain had characterized the game as "the very symbol, the outward and visible expression of the drive and push and rush and struggle of the raging, tearing, booming nineteenth century." Baseball had grown with the spread of trolleys and urbanization. From 1920 to 1950 it benefitted from these continuing patterns of growth as well as by technological innovations such as the automobile, radio, and illumination. Thus, the sport was curiously the beneficiary of two seemingly contradictory trends and sets of values. (Baker and Carroll 56–57)

And it was the ballparks themselves that housed and perpetuated the ambivalence, carved the apparent contradictions as it were in stone and brick and concrete and steel.

Wes Ferrell's story of his 1927 arrival in Cleveland, at nineteen, to play for the Indians dramatizes several of these points:

I get off the streetcar, and I'm looking for a ball park. Now the only ball parks I'd ever seen were back home and in East Douglas [North Carolina], and what those were were playing fields with little wooden fences around them. So I'm looking around, and I don't see a ball park. Some kids were playing in the street, and I asked them where League Park was. They pointed and said, "That's it." Well, I turned around and looked up, and there's this great stone structure. Biggest thing I ever saw in my life. They called this a ball park? I couldn't believe it. Then I heard a little noise in the back of my mind: *major leagues*. The sound of those two words was like instant education.

At this point Ferrell is more a pilgrim to the shrine than a participant in the rites. His continuing response is that of a devotee describing an epiphany:

So I took a tighter hold on my suitcase and walked through the gate of that thing, staring up and around at everything like I was walking through a palace. I went past all those great stone pillars and got up onto a concrete runway and looked way down and there at the end was a beautiful green ball field and guys playing ball on it. There was a game going on. And all of a sudden the notion of baseball got as big as all get-out in my mind. Seeing it being played down there in that setting was just beautiful. It was inspiring. (Honig 1975: 18)

An ironic echo of Ferrell's story was heard by a batboy fifty-five years later. Richie Hebner became ill prior to his debut in the American League on Opening Day 1982 after being traded to the Tigers. The batboy drove him back to his hotel and was told that "when he was trying to find the ballpark he thought the stadium was a factory."

Fans, players, batboys, even writers, all acknowledge the potency of both ballpark and playing field among the totemic images of their devotion to the game. But the distance from the far reaches of the grandstand to the field-level vista is also a frequently heard refrain among hymns of praise. I find its clearest expression in Christopher Lehmann-Haupt's chronicle of a single baseball season. Baseball, he says, was a "collection of images" he carried around in his mind, generated by broadcasts and newspapers and nurtured in his imagination. His first live game, the Red Sox at Yankee Stadium in 1948, was experienced remotely, from "way off in the distance," and enacted by tiny figures in white and gray. Contrast this with the "elation," over forty years later, when, possessed of passes newly bestowed by Mickey Morabito (once a Yankees batboy, now Oakland A's traveling secretary), he emerges into "a day of brilliant Florida sunshine" at Fort Lauderdale Stadium, and looks out at "a perfect baseball field, as green and symmetrical as any I had every seen, set down in a perfect little joy of a park, complete with grandstands and advertising billboards" (19, 37). What has been bridged, clearly, is neither the geographical gulf between climates or topographies or particular ballparks nor the chronological pass of decades, but a perspectival gap between the entitlement of a general admission ticket and the priceless privilege of a passport to field and clubhouse.

Over and over in the recollections of former batboys, I heard similar reports of incremental heightening of devotion, from early excitement and awe as youthful audience in the stands to the subsequent thrill of being acolytes among the idols and icons on the field and in the clubhouse. Mike Doyle, the only batboy to my knowledge who became a diocesan priest (before becoming a sectarian TV producer), remembers the profound feeling, during his first experience as a ballboy for the Milwaukee Braves, of passing through the tunnel from the clubhouse to the field as "an emergence into a bigger-than-life closeness to the game." He was in the eighth grade and was one of twelve winners of an essay contest. All twelve were introduced like a starting lineup before a game against the Cubs, and it was Ernie Banks who put his arm around him to calm a nervous kid.

In a sense the ballpark takes on the trappings of a temple of worship because being there is the closest most fans ever get to the sacred world of the game. Colman McCarthy has called Yankee Stadium "the Sistine Chapel of sports" and remembers when "being a batboy for the Yankees was the only glory I wanted," only to discover the "grander dream, of having a boy of my own take the stadium mound"—one of the central icons in the chapel—in a collegiate all-star game. In *Fans!* Michael Roberts says, "Whatever mystique attaches to ballplayers and their deeds, belongs by extension to their tools and garments and the very bricks and girders of the places in which they play" (64). Batboys, then, experience a hands-on heightening of the awe that fans share from afar. If any contempt is bred by this familiarity it is likely to be a feeling of superiority toward those still outside among the hoi polloi rather than for the objects of their attention and adulation.

No one knows better than the batboy the separation, the distance, the clear demarcation between the fan in the stands and the denizen of the baseball subculture itself. That is in part because he is often called upon to serve at the interface between those worlds. It is the batboy who is sent to the stands for some players with a taste for concessionaire refreshment (though it is against the rules of most clubs). It is the batboy who is sent to find the occasionally wayward player who wanders into the alien territory of the fans (a habit of Mickey Rivers, for one). And it is the batboy who delivers notes, phone numbers, room keys, and other tokens of assignation between players and their more ardent fans.

The go-between role leads to occasional embarrassment. Pat McBride was bothered less by the passing of notes than the requirement to make small talk with the women. Rich Eberle had an opportunity to exercise mature judgment when Ron Santo asked him to deliver a message to the reigning Miss Texas in the Wrigley Field crowd; he kept the Cubs captain out of trouble by not making the delivery because he found the beauty sitting next to Don Kessinger's wife. Tom MacDougal says that he routinely discarded those notes, but might have gotten into trouble himself one day during a rain delay in Griffith Stadium, when he put the familiar message from Mickey Mantle ("See you after the game—#7") into the wrong blonde's hands. In the Dodgers visiting clubhouse, however, messages to players had to be routed by batboys through their boss, Jim Muhey. When the Cardinals were in town, Orlando Cepeda got the most billets doux, but perhaps only because Muhey didn't like Curt Flood and would fail to deliver.

Sometimes the go-between role is transformed into that of a surrogate. Batboys are occasionally asked to chauffeur players' wives and girlfriends, and a lucky few even get to escort the baseball "widows" to concerts when the team is on the road. The experience of Sid Bordman, describing his "new duty" in the Kansas City clubhouse in 1942, provides the clearest example: "One of our starting pitchers, Rinaldo (Rugger) Ardizoia, had me run up to the stands and give his wife a kiss before every game he started. And she was a beauty, too!"

Some of those intimate conversations between batboy and player in the on-deck circle have direct relevance here. Jim Ryan recalls kneeling alongside Jimmy Piersall while he was carrying on a conversation with a woman in the stands about sewing buttons on his shirt. Bill Turner remembers the day that Clint Courtney, who owned a horse farm in Louisiana, said to him, "See that kid in the stands? He looks like he'd be a good jockey—get him after the game." The result was, in fact, a postseason trip to Louisiana for the kid, if not a career in silks. Another Griffith Stadium story is probably told about every other ballpark as well. Ray Crump's version is about kneeling in the on-deck circle with Jackie Jensen. "A big blonde with a beautiful body walks into the stands, and I says to him, 'Jackie, how'd you like to go to bed with that?' 'I go to bed with that every night,' he says, 'that's my wife.'"

In his first game as a Rangers ballboy, Kim Zeigler violated the customary boundaries between the worlds. Every ball that came his way he gave away to someone in the stands, until his father, the Texas trainer, told him to cut it out. In a later game Kim was embarrassed by a woman in the stands who kept yelling at him that she wanted his hat, finally offering him a kiss for it, to the amusement of fans and insiders alike. And those boundaries were bridged with a certain finality in the case of John Plein in San Diego. As batboy he kept answering the questions about players asked by a certain season-ticketholder named Cathy, until one day she asked him if there was anything wrong with her that he didn't ask her out. Getting over the notion that she was interested in players only, he did ask her out and eventually married her.

In general the batboys' experience at the interface fixes in their understanding the great gulf between the worlds of insider and outsider. As Bill Philips says now, more than three decades past his batboy years, "What I can't enjoy is sitting with people in the stands who just sit and wait between pitches." It is clear that any direct interaction across that gulf is an aberration, like the bombardment of Ducky Medwick that led to his removal from a World Series game or the firecracker thrown by a fan that blinded catcher Sam Narron in one eye. Mudcat Grant must surely have been aware of the particular fan who would always bellow "Sowbelly" at him whenever he pitched against the Senators, but the fan remained anonymous and the player never acknowledged him.

Only by the most egregious and persistent behavior along with distinctive personality can a particular fan actually achieve a place in baseball lore. Perhaps the clearest case is Brooklyn's Hilda Chester, who regularly drew attention to her identity and presence in the Ebbets Field bleachers and who is surely the only fan ever to be instrumental in determining a manager's strategy. (The bizarre incident is told in many places but perhaps best by Pete Reiser in Honig 296–7.) Yet in the fantasy world evoked around baseball in fiction and film, close personal encounters between fan and player are a conventional motif. Lloyd Bacon's *It Happens Every Spring*, Clarence Brown's *Angels in the Outfield*, and especially *The Natural* (both Malamud's novel and Barry Levinson's movie) are clear examples of this unnatural if not supernatural phenomenon. The legendary kindness of Lou Gehrig toward a boy in the stands is sentimentally evoked in Sam Wood's *Pride of the Yankees*. And yet Bill Tofant, without acknowledging that he had seen the movie, remembers when, as batboy in Cleveland, he tried to maintain proper decorum by refusing to take a boy's ball to Gehrig to be autographed during pregame warm-ups, only to have the great player chew him out and send him into the stands so that he could satisfy the young fan's wish.

Art Kusnyer, called "Caveman" or "Cave" for short, spent six years as backup catcher for three American League clubs. But his best stories about batboys originate in his years as bullpen coach for the White Sox. He remembers a kid they called "Haystack" who disappeared in Comiskey Park one day after being sent to bring six dozen game balls to the umpires. Cave searched all over for him, finally found him in the stands with a huge bucket of chicken and several sodas, and sent him running to get the balls. Later Cave found Haystack weeping in the clubhouse and tried to assure him that he wouldn't be fired for crossing the baseball boundaries that one time. "That's not it," said the kid, "I dropped most of my chicken running back here."

Chicago had another batboy, one they called "Bainesy" because he liked to wear a uniform shirt with Harold Baines's name and number on it around town, who violated the boundaries by taunting fans with balls he'd catch during batting practice. The visitors' bullpen was out of the line of vision from the home dugout in old Comiskey, so Bainesy was once sent to peek in and see whether a righty or lefty was warming up. "Lefty," he reported, but a righty came out to pitch. "Well," said Bainesy, "his glove was on his left hand." To avoid confusion the next time he was sent on such an errand, they asked him to get the pitcher's number. His report was "25," the number worn by Wayne Terwilliger, a coach. The pitcher warming up wore number 52. There was much laughter at the batboy's "stupidity," but it never occurred to anyone that he may simply have been dyslexic.

Most ballparks are structured so that the bullpens provide the most intimate glimpses of players for fans. At up-close proximity, fans can engage in personal badinage with players, but boundaries are rarely breached. Jeers may greet the wild warm-up throw or the missed catch, but the context is the awed perspective of the vantage, no matter how close the physical presence. Glimpses into the dugout from certain angles in the stands, however, only accentuate the outside-looking-in aspect of fandom. It is, indeed, from the vantage of the dugout itself that the batboy can see himself as an insider because he can *hear* what is going on, what is unheard and mysterious to those outside—in the boxes no less than the cheap seats.

Four different kinds of revelations are reported by batboys from their dugout experience. First are the lessons of concentration, paying attention to what's going on, knowing whom to avoid and when, and doing one's job. When foul balls get a piece of you, when you run afoul of an embarrassed player or manager, or when an action photo of the play that beats your team catches you laughing at something unrelated in the dugout, you find out very quickly that you've violated the code, and you usually pay for it immediately. But the other three kinds are positive reinforcements of the sacral nature of the game, the sacred mysteries of the insider group.

Where the fan in the stands cannot know what provokes an umpire to take off his mask and advance on a dugout with jutting jaw and pointing hand, the batboy sitting on the bench has thrillingly heard the very words. When a rookie batboy hears the manager apparently talking to himself and then sees players on the field doing what he says ("throw to first" and he does, "pitch out" and he does, "pickoff play at second" and they try it), he soon learns that it's neither coincidence nor clairvoyance but a matter of a coach nearby signaling the play to the field. And when a batboy has the experience of sitting in the dugout through a game with a player or coach explaining the subtleties and nuances of what they are watching on the field, he learns compellingly and with profound immediacy how to view the action and its context in ways that separate him utterly from the ordinary spectator and the fan's appreciation of the game.

Steve Fiffer, in *How to Watch Baseball*, says, "Would that we fans could become historians and eavesdrop on all the conversations that take place during the course of a baseball game" (137). Batboys have that wish granted, though typically they remain in the paradoxical, Keatsian position of the mute historian. But their distinction from fans is internalized as a fixed attitude, not merely a matter of desirable vantage. As Neil Cashen says, "When you sit in the dugout and the clubhouse for years, there's a level of intensity of your involvement in the game, when Robinson is 'Brooksie' and Palmer is 'Cakes,' so that when you're up in the stands, even though you see the intricacies, you don't appreciate it because the involvement and the intensity are missing."

Even in the dugout, some of what goes on is visible to some sections of the grandstands. But once in the tunnel or through it into the clubhouse, the batboy enters a world wholly separate. It is now not the game of baseball but its culture apart from the game. "What you see here and hear here, let it stay here when you leave here." That or some variation thereof is prominently posted in every major league clubhouse, an explicit reminder that baseball has established its own inner sancta.[11] Those who belong in this world accept it as an article of faith, a codified item in what might be called the articles of institutionalization.

Angels batboy Tony Atlas got to play catch between innings with his hero Reggie Jackson of the Yankees. (courtesy of Tony Atlas)

As Mario Alioto, director of marketing for the Giants now, tells about batboying, "It was the clubhouse stuff that was the greatest, not what happened on the field." But sometimes, a batboy has to learn the hard way the lesson that when he is in the clubhouse he can be a fan no longer. Tony Atlas was a star-struck sixteen-year-old when he started working for the Angels, and he gave Reggie Jackson a little poem he had written in school about him: "Action Jackson is his name, / Bold adventure is his game, / On his way to the Hall of Fame." Jackson liked it and tacked it up in his locker. But when the clubhouse man, Dave Howells, saw it, he ripped it down and ripped into Tony: "You don't do that here—we're *not fans!*" Next day he handed the kid a new poem: "Tony Atlas is his name, / Kissing ass is his game, / On his way to the Hall of Shame." The general rule of thumb for clubbies is that you never say even so much as "good game" to a player, because then you have nothing to say when he doesn't have a good game.

Fans in the clubhouse are those who have no place in the game, baseball outsiders who are there by virtue of celebrity in some other arena. Batboys can usually rattle off lists of prominent but star-struck guests who shook their hands in the clubhouse. In Chicago, for example, Jim Sassetti names Jimmy Carter, Jim Belushi, Ken Wahl, George Went, Mr. T, the San Diego Chicken, and the *Sports Illustrated* cover girl, in that order. Mike Rufino and Paul Greco, who were still playing schoolboy hockey, were thrilled to meet Wayne Gretsky in the Mets clubhouse, and they also list Rodney Dangerfield, Glenn Close, and George Bush, in that order. "But," Rufino concludes, "it's the ballplayers who have the greatest impact."

Pat McBride tellingly summarizes the clubhouse attitude to the presence of outsider luminaries: "I'd see the Governor and the Vice President act like kids when they were around Hank Aaron and others. I remember the '75 All-Star Game, when Henry Kissinger was in the locker room, a baseball hat on crooked, his eyes glazed, looking around at Don Sutton, Steve Garvey, Pete Rose, Johnny Bench, Tony Perez, and Joe Morgan. Tug McGraw came up to him with a sandwich, said, 'Baloney, Mr. Kissinger?' and everyone broke up."

I do not mean to say that certain activities of outsider devotees are necessarily foreign to former batboy acolytes. The latter may just as well be season ticket-holders, rotisserie league players, and collectors as any other fans. What I am saying is that the attitudes are distinct, that there is a significant difference between a fan's posed picture with a player, whether subsequently autographed or not, and a personally signed picture of a player alongside a batboy wearing the same uniform. In this context, a personally signed card is worth far more than the card in "mint condition" so highly prized by collectors.

Valued beyond price, too, are memories of clubhouse antics that only true insiders were privileged to take part in, like the frequently mentioned kangaroo courts, where even batboys must on occasion stand trial. Several have mentioned the joys of working in the visiting clubhouse when the Minnesota Twins came to town in the 1980s, the fun-loving bunch led by Kirby Puckett and Kent Hrbek who seemed more "like a softball team" than American League contenders or world champions. Fans of pro wrestling, they would watch it on television in the clubhouse for hours at a time, and then try out the moves and holds on teammates or lucky clubbies. Merritt Riley treasures the New York memory of Hrbek pulling his shirt up over his head and throwing him to the ground, yelling, "Body slam!"

Clubhouses typically become places where club members—players and attendants alike—invent their own games. In the seventies the Yankees played locker room hockey, with a wad of tape for a puck and bottom ends of bats for sticks. Even when Thurman Munson injured his hand playing hockey, the clubhouse games went on. In the 1960s, the Angels locker room was the arena for a game they called clubhouse ball or "sani-ball" because the ball was a rolled-up pair of sanitary hose. It was so popular that several of the former batboys would have reunions and play old-timers games of sani-ball. And one of Jim Schroer's most vivid memories (he calls it "the best one," actually) is from the end of the 1956 season when the Milwaukee Braves came into St. Louis with the pennant on the line, only to have the Dodgers win while the Cardinals beat the Braves twice, the first a tough 2–1 game that Warren Spahn lost on an error by Joe Adcock. Schroer says, "After the Saturday game a clique of five stayed around in the clubhouse drinking beer and some of the champagne—Spahn, Lew Burdette, Eddie Mathews, Toby Atwell, and Bob Buhl. They were playing 'clubhouse ball' with Spahn pitching beer cans to Mathews catching, and I remember Burdette hit one off Buhl's head. Well, before they finally left they splintered all of Adcock's bats and nailed his spikes to the floor."

"Some things happen in the clubhouse you never hear about," says Chad Blossfield, introducing another story about those Braves. Lou Chapman of the Milwaukee *Sentinel*, known around town as "Gumshoe," had apparently written a story that was embarrassing to some of the players. The next time he showed up in the clubhouse, Spahn and Burdette picked him up, carried him into the trainer's room, and threw him fully dressed into the whirlpool. According to Chad, all they said to him was, "Write what you want, but you're soaking wet," and Chapman showed up later in the press box wearing a short-sleeve trainer's outfit.

The media presence in the clubhouse is an annoyance, an anomaly, a profanation, and a mandated necessity. As links between the fans outside and the sacred world inside, they serve the purposes and natures of both—and certainly both the public and the game are nurtured by that service. But to the extent to which they are also self-serving they distort the subculture they mean to chronicle and they delude the public they mean to edify and entertain. It is a clubhouse cliché for a player to pick up a newspaper and say, "Let's see what I said yesterday."

Historically, there are three periods of baseball writing (as opposed to writing baseball).[12] In the first phase, writers essentially wrote as reviewers, looking down at performances from empyreal heights and describing, critiquing, puffing, analyzing, mythologizing, or caricaturing what they saw in their own projected image or from their idiosyncratic or institutionalized vantage. In other words, however much they ballyhooed the material they were spoon-fed by the promoters of the game (to the point where they themselves became co-promoters) they remained separate, a white-collar lens through which to view a blue-collar world. When Ring Lardner added "realism and cynicism" to the mix (Coffin 137) he didn't initiate a new era, he merely lent tonal and tasteful enrichment to the old.

It was when Lardner began to travel with the players, reporting and interpreting from a wholly different vantage, that he helped generate the second era. The "beat writer" traveled, ate, drank, and bunked with the team, and reports were advantaged by firsthand knowledge but disadvantaged by the mutual benefits to subjects and reporters of *failures* to report. While some journalists insisted on keeping their distance to contain the compromise, the whole generation was characterized by an unspoken acknowledgment that the game and the press were symbiotic systems in a common enterprise.

The electronic media changed all that forever, in many ways, and with complexly mixed results. Game stories became largely redundant, or historical reminders, or vehicles for creative interpretations. With universal play-by-play broadcasts and telecasts, the press had no need to present what everyone had seen or at least heard live. Accuracy became an enforceable standard. Game stories were editorially required to contain "meaningful postgame quotes." There are a thousand stories in the naked clubhouse, and each reporter must have one of them.

If the press had to work harder to pursue leads, scoops, exclusives, so much the better. If reporters had to pool their slants, their quotes, their focuses, keys, and highlights, so much the worse. It is no wonder that in such a context, both individual writers in pursuit of distinction and the media collectively in pursuit of comprehensive consensus would alienate players. The more that the reporters knew, the more they aroused a creeping paranoia; an us-them atmosphere had to produce a backlash in the clubhouse subculture. A baseball insider drew back into a comforting sense that he possessed special wisdom and sets of arcana that a media maven kneweth not. Writers who bought into a belief in that gulf became the most respected, and in part their success was derived from the insiders' willingness to share trade secrets with respectful outsiders.

Roger Angell, par excellence, and Thomas Boswell, only marginally less so because of the pressures of producing three or four pieces a week, are the primary beneficiaries of this evolutionary process—and our two best baseball writers. But it, too, can be overly refined (as in the strained side effects of purebred pets). I am thinking of George Will's *Men at Work*, where the insights generated by the process are intellectualized to a faretheewell. (See Chapter 5 below, where an insider's anecdote reflects the subculture's attitude toward Will's work.)

Two tableaux from present-day clubhouses portray the situation graphically. The baseball establishment mandates access. The media may be on the field or in the dugout area up to forty-five minutes before a game, in the clubhouse up to thirty minutes before game time, and back into the clubhouse as soon as a game ends. One tableau is vaguely familiar to the mass audience; we have seen it live in our living rooms. After a big game, there are more videocams, tape recorders, and notepads in the locker room than players. Now cut that back by deleting all the extras, hangers-on, fringe personnel, and celebrities attendant on major events. And imagine only the handful of regulars on the beat for an ordinary midseason game. The men and occasional women who hold the cameras, mikes, and ballpoints are grouped around the designated epicenters of the event, and the story or report is shaped by the dialogue between the groups.

It is the other tableau that I find more revealing. It is the clubhouse scene about four hours before a game. The staff is busy, and some players have arrived early for extra hitting or therapeutic attention from the trainers or some other work-related purpose. As the rest of the club drifts in, so do the working media. Sometimes a reporter will even have an appointed interview with a player. But what typically happens is that the reporters gather in a little circle in a central area in the room. They seem to look around at the players, often spotting a potential target isolated in front of his locker. But even if such a subject is tantalizing, they keep to the safety of their phalanx. And they talk. They joke, they gossip, they trade lies. But they are also at work. They are talking baseball. More to the point, they are determining what the story is to be. And then somehow, before deadline, they write it. Each may write an individual version of it, but they all write the same story.

I suppose I could have visualized that scene or inferred it from the present state of the reporting. Yet somehow it came as a shock to me when I saw it, then saw it again and again. If I saw it in half a dozen clubhouses, I also got verification of it from twenty others. The batboys see it, take it in, joke about it, and largely ignore it—except as they have to circle the pack while completing their appointed rounds. The writers have extensive access to the inside, but they remain outsiders, untapped for membership in the club. It is ironic that from a position of such ambivalence comes the bulk of the way the game, the club, and its world are presented and recorded to the world outside.

In my canvass I found only one baseball writer who began as a batboy, Sid Bordman, who knew the Kansas City clubhouse as a kid before it housed a major league team and then accessed it as a beat reporter when the A's arrived. That background was a tremendous advantage. "Mostly I had learned," he says, "what players and managers think—it was never a mystery in the clubhouse. I learned how players talk, when they meant what they were saying and when they were pulling somebody's leg. More than anything else what I gained from my time in the clubhouse was insight, insight about people, about players, about baseball." The implication is that such insight, such knowledge, such *absence* of mystery, is what separated him from the rest of the corps. That separation is succinctly captured in an observation of Dick Howser, who managed the Royals in the new Kansas City clubhouse Bordman knows so well: "One thing I like about baseball is that you can fool the media a little and the fans a lot, but the uniformed people can't fool each other" (Fiffer 114).

Retired now, Bordman runs the Royals press box during spring training at Baseball City Stadium in Haines City, Florida, and he seems to watch with demystified amusement as the writers pursue their pleasant task.

Rene Lachemann has been a major league player, coach, and manager, but his time in big-league clubhouses began as a Dodgers batboy. His reminiscence of one of the "brighter moments" is particularly appropriate here: "From June that season [1962] when Koufax no-hit the Mets. I'm not usually a souvenir collector but I got one of those game balls and came into the clubhouse for Koufax's signature. He was surrounded by media people for interviews but he looked over, saw me, and said, 'What do you want, Lach?' 'Just wanted you to sign the ball, but I'll get you later.' He stops the interview and says, 'I'll do it now.' He was the classiest guy." Lachemann's story is told in the context of an incident and a player treasured in his memory. For me, it is pointedly instructive about the insider-outsider distinction. The lowest-ranking clubby is nevertheless a club member and a gesture affirming his connection to the ace pitcher takes precedence over the business of commemorating momentous achievement through the agency of the mythmaking media. Sandy Koufax is known as a private person who has often been praised for his consistent graciousness with the media. That distinctive quality is not, however, what made him universally admired in the clubhouse. It was that he always abided by the traditions of fellowship within which every insider was accorded equal respect.

Few players are as accommodating as Koufax. In fact, most of them, at one time or another, will escape the media by entering baseball's sanctum sanctorum, a sanctuary absolutely protected from intrusion by any form of alien life: the trainer's room. Batboys may come and go freely, carrying messages and towels, but press-badge bearers are not allowed. It is a bourne beyond which no member of the fourth estate may travel, an official demarcation between those who belong and those who are at best only adjunct to the club.

When Jim (Doc) Ewell, the late trainer whose almost sixty years caring for athletes began as a minor league batboy in Norfolk, Virginia, invited me into that safest of havens in the Astros spring clubhouse in Kissimmee, Florida, I was taken aback. "Don't worry," he said, "there aren't any reporters around." An effervescent raconteur and minstrel (he'd perform his original ditties a cappella at the drop of the slightest hint), Ewell was a popular guest of Johnny

Carson on "The Tonight Show." But it was neither his engaging anecdotes nor his unfailingly upbeat wit and wisdom that gave me that special tremor of excitement in our extended conversation. It was that he had bestowed credentials beyond the power of baseball writers' associations or public relations offices. Even though it was a day in March when two Astros squads were playing on the road in nearby citrus venues, I was thrilled that he had taken me inside; the jaundiced eye and cynical attitude I brought into the clubhouse from several decades of observation and analysis of the jockocracy were eclipsed in his conscious, benign gesture of acceptance.[13]

Final validation of the distinction made here between devotees and fans, insiders and outsiders, comes from the phenomenon of "batboys" who weren't. Under this heading I include all those winners of batboy-for-a-day contests, drawings, raffles, and auctions; all the one-time substitutes; and all those Tommy Lasorda PR specialties, celebrity batboys. Among the spring-training-only kids, I distinguish between those who serve only on the field, who don't qualify, and those who have earned their spurs by shining the shoes and hanging the laundry. The Povich brothers and Roy Firestone are counted in the numbers of the blessed, but Steve Garvey is not.

Garvey is careful to say that he "did some batboying" from the time he was seven, for the next seven springs around the Tampa area. His father drove teams on Greyhound buses to the ballpark, mostly the Dodgers, but also the Yankees and the Tigers. His father and grandfather were both Dodgers fans, so that Steve felt comfortable with that team. He'd put on his little Ban-lon shirt, blue jeans, and little spikes, and the club would give him a hat and call him a batboy. He shined no shoes, did no laundry, and so was more of a mascot. But he did get to catch for Leo Durocher hitting fungo, to play catch with Gil Hodges, and to know Pee Wee Reese, Junior Gilliam, and Roy Campanella. Garvey says that those springs were a great introduction to professional baseball, that getting to know the personalities on and off the field—even with the "gruffer language"—was a good education and positive experience, but he seems to apply the word "batboy" to himself only with quotation marks around it.

Another Dodgers case is Rob Ogle, Walter Alston's grandson. From the time he was nine he would travel with the club during parts of the summer and remembers suiting up in Cincinnati and helping the batboys, getting the jackets from pitchers from the bullpen and getting batting helmets when the batboys got the bats. Some other times he'd get to sit on the bench, take BP, shag flies, and take second infield; but he had no clubhouse duties. Ogle played a year at class A in the Padres organization and spent five years in the front office of the AAA Albuquerque club, but has been pursuing a more lucrative career in finance ever since.

A third example is Pete Rose, Jr. When his father got the record-breaking hit number 4,192, most newspapers across the country carried the wonderful shot taken by Dick Swain of the Cincinnati *Enquirer* of Pete and Pete, Jr., in Phillies batboy uniform, embracing. Even Roger Kahn, in his collaboration with Pete on *Pete Rose: My Story*, reprints that photo and perpetuates the identification of Pete, Jr., as batboy. Years later, languishing as part-time third baseman for the Frederick Keys, the Orioles class A team, Pete, Jr., had that designation so firmly fixed in memory that several people in the organization suggested I interview him for this project. Everyone assumed he had been a batboy because he had worn that uniform.

The first thing he said to me when the tape started to roll was, "People think I was a batboy. I was never a batboy." And then he went on to say how he had started suiting up and sitting on the bench ever since his father went to Philadelphia. But never, he repeated, was he a batboy. "I never shined any shoes, never did any laundry. Hell, they did mine. Maybe I would have been a batboy if that was the only way I could sit in the dugout. But I never had to, so I never did."

The label persists because it is perpetuated by the media on the principle that once a kid is seen in uniform on the field or in the dugout during game time he must be a batboy. Baseball's PR arm preserves the label, too, assuming that some value attaches to it. Ken Reitz, twelve seasons a National League third baseman, is another designee. "When I was a kid growing up in the Bay Area," Reitz told me, "I worked casually as batboy for my older brother's teams, right up to his college teams, but I was never a real batboy, never in professional baseball."

Reitz, Rose, Jr., Ogle, and Garvey have been authentic baseball insiders. Whatever folkloristic notion of the male Cinderella archetype, ascending to fame from the lowest level of the culture, attaches to these men, as initiates they themselves reject it. But so attractive and powerful is the cachet of belonging, even in the most servile of roles, that the title of batboy is bestowed in public awareness at the slightest suggestion that it might apply or it is actually claimed as a badge of honor by unworthy pretenders. (There are no "batgirls" in major league baseball. The young women employed in a few ballparks to collect balls down the foul lines neither suit up in major league uniforms nor perform clubbies' duties in the clubhouse. There is no pretense of gender equality in baseball; indeed, these women often perform stereotypical roles as dancers or cheerleaders.)

The most egregious case is that of M. C. Hammer, such a megastar that even his assumed name has been shortened to Hammer. Baseball identification is an important part of the Hammer myth. His very name goes back to a frequently observed facial resemblance to Henry Aaron, the Hammerin' Hank who broke the career home run record of Babe Ruth. And it was Charlie Finley, former owner of the Oakland A's, who discovered young Stanley Kirk Burrell doing James Brown routines at the ballpark, in the players' parking lot at that, in the early seventies. He was eleven years old, rap hadn't been born yet, but young Burrell had "been dancing ever since I was born" and doing "Live at the Apollo" imitations for his family since he was three.

Hammer's interviews so regularly rehearse the story that it has become hardened into historical legend (see, for example, *Rolling Stone*, July 1990: 29, and *The Washington Post*, July 29, 1990: G5). It goes like this: Finley was enchanted with him, took him into his private box to watch the ball game, gave him a job running errands in the office, and eventually made him "official batboy" and "unofficial executive assistant" or "honorary vice president" (depending on the version). Some of this is true; some of it never happened. There is no doubt that young Burrell was hanging around the ballpark—two brothers, after all, worked in the clubhouse; no question that Finley made a kind of mascot of him. But he was not a batboy, officially or otherwise.

Steve Maunakea, who was a batboy during those years, has several memories of Burrell: "doing a Michael Jackson moonwalk, dancing for Vida Blue, and giving me my nickname of Charlie Brown. I remember him just playing around in the dugout when his brother Chris was batboying with me and another brother, Louis, was working in the clubhouse. Finley took a liking to him all right. I worked there for years, and I never even met Finley."

Until his retirement in 1993, Frank Ciensczyk was the A's club-

Pas de deux in All-Star tableau: as Jim Rice waits to hit in front of catcher Ted Simmons and a meditative National League dugout in San Diego, American League batboy Tony Atlas (in Angels uniform) runs to pick up bat as Rod Carew turns toward AL dugout after scoring. The NL came back to win 1978 game. (courtesy of Tony Atlas)

house manager, and one of his duties was hiring and firing all batboys and clubbies. Ever since the legend began to find its way into print, Ciensczyk was bombarded with questions about Hammer. Normally generous and enthusiastic in conversation or interview, he has a very succinct response on this issue: "He never worked for me; in fact, I had to run him out of the clubhouse. I'm getting tired of all the people calling me to ask about it. Never happened. Mr. Finley gave him a job upstairs in the office, running errands. Now, his two brothers worked for me, Chris and Louis. Chris was a batboy and a very good one; he was the best kid of the three. Louis was a good kid, too, worked for me in the clubhouse—he's an agent now; in fact, he's Hammer's agent."

Why would anyone who wasn't a batboy want people to think he was, especially someone of the stature of Hammer? It would certainly be easy to borrow an element of identify from a brother, but why would it be desirable? Why does it seem such an important part of the image he wishes to project? The answers, I believe, may be inferred from this whole chapter. Finley may have been the owner but he was not part of the clubhouse community. It is one thing to be an insider who functions as an entertainer, wit, clown, joker, or even fool; but it is quite another to be an outsider acting up to make an impression, to sing and dance his way inside somehow. It is one thing to entertain the troops, quite another to be an entertaining trooper. It is a pleasant thing to be applauded and congratulated by the inner circle from the inner circle, but it is a far, far better thing to be approved and consecrated by being taken into the circle itself.

CHAPTER 3 **Rites of Initiation and Passage**

The legendary Pete Sheehy, whose name has been given to the New York Yankee clubhouse—an honor even rarer than a player's number being retired—began almost six decades with the club in 1927. As the legend goes, young Pete was walking past the closed Yankee Stadium hours before a game when a door opened in the wall, an arm reached out to grab him, and a muffled voice said, "Kid, ya wanna be a batboy?" In some versions, the spectral arm belonged to Babe Ruth himself.

This may sound like a cross between the Lady of the Lake extending Excalibur to King Arthur and the invisible door to baseball immortality in the grove in *Field of Dreams*, and yet the mundane truth is not very far removed. As a kid, Sheehy would often go from his East 96th Street home to Yankee Stadium to sit in the bleachers. One day, Fred Logan, the clubhouse man, stopped him at the gate and offered him free admission if he would help out in the clubhouse. Invited back the next day, Sheehy never bought a ticket again.

In *Baseball: The People's Game* (23–26) historian Harold Seymour tells a similar story about the start of his three-year stint batboying for the Dodgers, 1924–26. In fact, Seymour's brief sketch—being hired, learning about baseball from the inside, and wising up fast among colorful men right where the action was—provides an early model of the standard batboy's story with its formulaic elements of embarrassments, superstitions, surprising incidents, and canny insights. (Seymour got much mileage from this tale. An earlier version appeared in *Sports Heritage* and was itself reprinted in the *Drew Magazine*.)

Basically, there are four answers to the question of how batboys get their jobs: (1) luck—being in the right place at the right time; (2) determination—showing by perseverance that they deserve the chance; (3) merit—winning the position in competition through contests and interviews; and (4) family—being well connected. In all cases, the effect of getting the job is feeling chosen, blessed, and at least tentatively worthy. From the ceremonial tapping to the practical jokes of initiation and belonging, there is a process of attaining membership in the elect, the elite of the sacred world. The quality of these experiences is often routine, mundane, or coarse, yet they mark passages from feelings of awe to feelings of acceptance as batboys embrace what passes for tradition and humor in the self-aggrandizing baseball clubhouse.

Ken Clancy, now an attorney in Phoenix, was a Marquette High School student when he was picked up hitchhiking by Tommie Ferguson, then equipment manager for the Milwaukee Braves. Mahendra Naik, born in Zambia, used to ride his bike to Exhibition Stadium to watch the Toronto Argonauts practice football, and one day he met Peter Bavasi in the stands months before his new Toronto franchise even had a team name. Jeff Sipos, now equipment manager in Cleveland, submitted an essay two years in a row before winning the contest that earned him his first Indians uniform. Bob Elder, later a sportscaster for KEZY and now vice president and general manager of the Anaheim Bullfrogs (roller hockey), stood in line with two hundred other applicants for an interview in a trailer with Angels management. In each case, the man remembering the circumstances speaks with wonderment at his having been chosen. It is not that he was undeserving of the position, but that he still can't quite understand what rationale or mystery produced the choice: baseball has reasons that reason knoweth not.

Tony Atlas, now an Orange County deputy marshal, wrote a letter a week for most of a year before getting a call from the Angels. Patrick Quinlan, now proprietor of the Flatiron Saloon, a sports bar in San Rafael, sneaked into Candlestick Park for sixty games a year, learned his way around, at eleven years old started writing letters to Giants equipment manager Ed Logan, and finally walked into his office a month after the season ended in 1975. Television writer Thad Mumford ("MASH," "Roots," "Different World") ran away from his home in Washington and from college in Hampton, Virginia, to harass his way into becoming a Yankees batboy, the first black batboy in the majors in 1970. (Levine 60, 101–2 reminds us, however, that in the nineteenth century team mascots were often black.) It is not pride in their sheer persistence that characterizes the tone of these men's reminiscences, but exaltation in having their devotion rewarded, the precious few chosen, for whatever reasons, from among so many.

Even those who owed their opportunities to kinship or friendship spoke of their legacy in tones of appreciation and awe. "Baseball," says Donald Hall, "is a game of years and of decades. . . . Baseball is the generations, looping backward forever with a million apparitions of sticks and balls, cricket and rounders, and the games the Iroquois played in Connecticut before the English came. Baseball is fathers and sons playing catch, lazy and murderous, wild and controlled, the profound archaic song of birth, growth, age, and death. This diamond encloses what we are" (*Fathers* 10, 30). Baseball, I would add, well short of Hall's poetic heights, is fathers and sons in the prosaic process of passing along the blessed duties of a batboy.

Managers, equipment managers, general managers, and trainers have often brought sons into the clubhouse to work, but it is very rare for sons of players. One exception was San Francisco Giants batboy Rich Pieretti, whose father Marino pitched in the late 1940s in the American League. Pete Rose, Jr., as explained in the last chapter, is not an exception, though the notion that he was a batboy has wide currency among fans and in the media. But Pete, Jr., belongs instead with the kind of observation made by Mike Wallace, a Rangers batboy in 1973, who stayed on working in the clubhouse, taking over the visiting clubhouse in 1979, moving up to equipment manager for the Royals in 1989 and then on to the expansion Marlins. "Part of the fun," he says, "is watching kids who hung around the clubhouse when they were young make it as major league stars. The Alomars and Barry Bonds, I knew them as kids in Arlington."

The key phrasing here is "hung around" the clubhouse, rather than working in it. Appearance on the field in prime time, in uniform, sitting on the bench or even picking up bats, doesn't qualify. The reality is service in the clubhouse, shining shoes and doing laundry and running errands and getting those souvenir balls signed. The hours are three or four times longer than the time on field and the chores are tedious, but performing the service earns the merit badges, the insignia, of official acceptance into the fraternity.

In Texas, because of the state's strict interpretation of child labor laws, the Rangers have to use boys who can be with their fathers during the late hours of night games. Climate, location, and a tradition of batboys being players themselves also contribute to the need for a large roster of substitutes. In any case, the Rangers have a continuing history of family ties in the clubhouse, beginning with the arrival of Fred Baxter as equipment manager and his son John as assistant in the original migration from Washington. Trainer Bill Zeigler's three sons all batboyed for the Rangers and were blessed in their baseball development by having Ted Williams study and critique videotapes of their hitting.

Rangers equipment manager Joe Macko has seen his own two sons move from batboys to players. Joe was a player himself, got as far as spring training with a big-league club in 1950. In 1972, as business manager of the Dallas-Fort Worth Spurs in Arlington, Joe was offered a choice of jobs in the Rangers organization. He took the equipment manager job to be closer to the field, but it is clear that part of the idea was to get his boys close to the field and be there with them. As an All-American at Baylor, his older boy Steve used wooden instead of aluminum bats to prepare for professional ball, and never mind the statistics. And when Steve made it with the Cubs, their equipment manager Yosh Kawano gave him his dad's uniform number 12. And then the tragedy: a twenty-five-game career at three infield positions, without ever making an error; dead at twenty-seven of cancer. And now younger brother Mike Macko is not going to fulfill the dream, playing his way up the long ladder. He played at McClennon Junior College and then Texas Christian University, with summer-league ball in between, but was never drafted. He got one shot at spring training with the Cardinals, but as one of only three

At an old-timers game, Joe Macko, Rangers equipment
manager, suited up in his old Cubs uniform, also worn
briefly by his son Steve, and posed with younger son,
batboy Mike. (courtesy of Mike Macko)

without contracts among 180 in camp he knew he was there just as a
courtesy. Still, he had a great time and remains grateful for the years
at Arlington Stadium (five summers of batboying whenever his playing schedule allowed) when he got to put on the uniform, go on the
field, and shag flies—an important chore in Texas because of the
long, hot summers. Earning his degree from TCU, he is planning to
pursue a graduate program in physical therapy. And now Rangers
general manager Tom Grieve has seen his son Ben, until recently a
batboy and schoolboy center fielder, chosen by the Oakland A's as
the second player of the 1994 amateur draft.

Baseball is fathers not only playing catch with their sons, but
taking them to the ballpark and getting them jobs as batboys. Broadcasters like Jack Buck, who introduced his sons Danny and Joe to the
Cardinals at a tender age, and beat writers like Shirley Povich, who
moved his sons to Florida schools for spring training where they
could work in the Senators clubhouse, are examples of those who

appreciated the value of the experience. Equipment managers, of course, are in the best position to put boys to work. Take the case of Frank Ciensczyk in Oakland. He not only had four stepsons to employ in the clubhouse and as batboys (Rocky, Michael, Randy, and Stevie Maunakea) but he also found room for the Pieraldi brothers, Mike and Ron, sons of his brother-in-law's brother.

Fathers find all sorts of ways, direct and indirect, to get sons into baseball uniforms, and for all sorts of reasons. The three disparate examples that follow, however, demonstrate the common ground: a profound belief that the experience will be rewarding, uplifting, perhaps even redemptive. Benny Lefebvre's way was hands-on and exemplary. A director of parks in Los Angeles, Benny ran the Rancho La Cienega playground with its four baseball diamonds near Dorsey High School. He told his three sons as well as the six Lachemann boys who were their friends that they would all have careers in baseball. Several of them have fulfilled that prophecy. Rene and Marcel Lachemann and Jim Lefebvre have been players, coaches, and managers in the majors, and Billy Lachemann almost made it as a player. Jim Lefebvre's twin, Tippy, is a pitching instructor at UCLA, and their brother, Gilly, with a law degree and business experience behind him, coached and taught at the high school level before taking his current position at Juvenile Hall in Orange County. When the Dodgers were interested in high school players during those years (the late 1950s and early 1960s), Lefty Phillips and Ken Myers would scout them and sign them, often putting them to work as batboys before assigning them to rookie league teams. And so Rene Lachemann and Gilly and Jimmy Lefebvre were Dodger batboys as a prelude to their professional playing careers.

For the fathers of Jack Hughes and Jay Mazzone, the thought of their sons being players was remote. As a boy Jack was hospitalized for a long time with a brain tumor, and his newspaperman father kept him diverted by having famous people write to him and send autographed pictures. That was how he got started with a lifelong habit of collecting celebrity autographs, pictures, and memorabilia. But even while he was still in the hospital he began to focus on baseball. Then, when he was well enough, he began working at Griffith Stadium, first in concessions and finally, in 1956, as visiting batboy.

Jay Mazzone's physical trauma was even more severe. His hands were so badly burned when he was two that they had to be ampu-

Jay Mazzone, Orioles batboy without hands, and the incomparable Sandy Koufax, together here at the 1966 World Series, were both universally admired in major league clubhouses. (courtesy of Jay Mazzone)

tated. Yet, encouraged by his father, athletics became an important part of his life. Prosthetic devices were designed for Jay with specific tasks in mind: to wear a baseball glove, grip a bat, and throw a ball. And so he played in 8-to-10 leagues, then 11-to-12 leagues. One of the league's sponsors was Mary Dobkin (immortalized in a movie

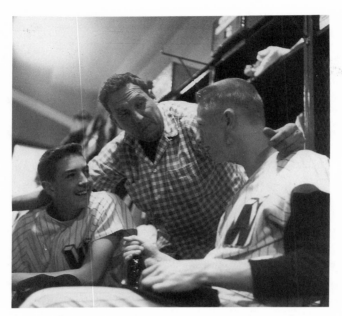

Across the generations: equipment manager Fred Baxter, here with batboys Bob Farmer (l.) and Jim Ryan, was a Senators batboy with Ryan's father when his brother Frank Baxter ran the clubhouse. (courtesy of Jim Ryan)

with Jean Stapleton in the role), and on Mary Dobkin Day in 1965 in Memorial Stadium, Jay Mazzone got to be an honorary batboy. By the 1966 season he had successfully applied for a batboy's job and worked the visiting clubhouse, including the World Series, and also traveled to St. Louis as American League batboy for the All-Star Game. The next season he began six years as an Orioles batboy.

When James M. Ryan worked for the Phoenix Firebirds during the summer of 1989, it marked the third generation of Ryan batboys. James J. Ryan, Jr., got on with the Senators because his father, an FBI special agent, had known Fred Baxter as a boy and had himself batboyed under Frank Baxter in 1924–25. Jim remembers that his father was friendly with Bucky Harris, Walter Johnson, and Goose Goslin, and never wavered from the opinion that Babe Ruth was the best ever: "He never stopped telling about seeing the Babe hit one over the old oak tree completely out of Griffith Stadium." Whether baseball will lead to the FBI for a third generation of Ryans remains to be seen.

We are not talking here about apprenticeship. There is no special art or craft to be learned at the feet of masters. Nor is batboying analogous to a closed union, like Hollywood makeup "artists" or New York City cabdrivers, where the card or medallion is passed down and nepotism is the rule that protects the value of being one of a finite number. It is simply a matter (with apologies to Jerzy Kosinski) of *being there*, of having once been admitted to the inner circle and therefore being privileged to extend membership to others, "legacies," as in college fraternities. That is why sons can bring fathers into the clubhouse, too, as 1984–87 Mets batboy Paul Greco did for his father at Shea, as the Pieraldi brothers did for their father in Oakland, and as Jerry Schroer did in 1955 when he persuaded his father to take over the visiting clubhouse at Sportsman's Park so he could work full-time as the Cardinals batboy (while easing the way for kid brother Jim on the visiting side as well).

Suiting up in a major league baseball uniform is one of the primary confirming processes that betoken acceptance into a sacred or at least private and privileged fraternity. Indeed, often the first sign of big-brotherly welcome a batboy receives is instruction from a player on how to put on the uniform properly, so that the two sets of hose—sanitaries and stirrups—come out right. Suiting up is thus a kind of ritual investiture, putting on the uniform of the brotherhood. Clearly the impact of the event may be enriched when literal brothers are conjoined in the privileged brotherhood.

Quietly but proudly Mark Sassetti remarked to me that when he and his brother Jimmy both suited up as Chicago White Sox batboys in 1983 he thought it was the first such appearance by brothers in the big leagues. I thought then that Chicago, or its south side at least, might be as provincial a place as any other. But I just told him that, no, I had located other combinations of brothers for other teams. In fact, before my random survey was done, I had found examples of sibling batboys from more than half the franchises, a kind of fraternity of brotherhood, reaching back eight decades.

Frank Baxter began as Washington Senators batboy, or mascot, in 1912, and nineteen years later his brother Fred started out in the same position. When Frank died in 1949, Fred, who was managing the visiting clubhouse at Griffith Stadium, moved over to replace his brother as the home club's equipment manager. In turn, Fred's two sons, John and Eddie, served their time as batboys (though both now wear the uniform of the Postal Service—fittingly for Eddie, who was named after The Walking Man, Eddie Yost).

The Cardinals' venerable Butch Yatkeman often says that batboys come in twos, and in St. Louis those pairs seemed often to be brothers: the Bucks, the Risches, and the Schroers, to name a few. Butch also remembers the Scanlon brothers: Don, who joined the navy early in World War II, and Bob, now deceased, who had his choice of St. Louis teams in the 1944 World Series. And then there was Don Deason, who got started with the Cardinals in 1967 because his brother's friend Jerry Gibson was a batboy. (Gibson tells his own batboy story in *Big League Batboy*.)

Friends of brothers, brothers of friends, baseball continues to be a passing on of legacies, like the particular high schools that equipment managers recruit from in Detroit or Chicago, or even a particular suburb. In Minnesota, Steve Labatt says he owed his three years as batboy to his brother's friend who was part of the "Minnetonka legacy passed down originally from Mark McKenzie" (with Clayton Wilson now carrying the baton).

The Minnesota Twins were in fact responsible for the best publicized case of batboy brothers. A contest was held in the spring of 1961, with the winners to be the batboys for the Griffith franchise just moving in from Washington. With *Look* magazine cosponsoring, the Twins promised personal interviews to all contestants, so equipment manager Ray Crump had to fly up from spring training in Florida to interview 326 sets of twins.

Ray recalls, "I eliminated them on several criteria—if they lived too far away, if they were too young, if they were too old, and if they had too much baseball experience. I didn't want kids who wanted to play or watch baseball. I hired Peter and Richard King who lived on a farm, did chores from five to nine in the morning, had never been to a ball game, and wanted the job because if they won it they wouldn't have to do their farm chores. They did well, for four years, but there were no more contests."

Nor are the King brothers the only recent case of identical twin batboys. In Toronto, during the 1988 season, Brad and Greg Grimes kept getting double takes from the players. It became a big game for them to guess which twin was which, and as far as the Grimes boys could tell, it was always just a guess.

Other sets of brothers stand out among the many I interviewed:

Tom and Scotty MacDougal, who suited up together for the Senators in the late 1950s and attained a surviving sense of closeness enhanced by the way people like Minnie Minoso and Ted Williams took them together under their wings; four Cashen brothers (nephews of onetime Orioles general manager Frank) who maintained a serial presence in Baltimore's Memorial Stadium from 1968 to 1982; and another traditional fixture in Baltimore that has survived the move to Camden Yards, the family of Ernie Tyler, who for more than 2,800 consecutive games (through the end of the 1993 season) has retrieved foul balls at the screen and kept the plate umpire supplied with fresh ones, and five of whose sons have been Orioles batboys, including one, Jimmy, who is now equipment manager and another, Fred, who runs the visiting clubhouse.

Finally, I want to cite Gus Tham, who with his younger brother Brad batboyed for the Giants in the late 1960s. Brad, now a business representative for the Teamsters in San Francisco, has talked about how Murph, the equipment manager, "practically raised us." And Gus, who drove a truck for air freight for twenty years after a brief school-teaching stint and now is earning a master's degree in rehabilitation counseling, calls baseball "its own little island" where the Thams learned lessons of "common sense, maturity, how to carry yourself, how to be a man and have fun doing it." But in all that Gus said and later wrote to me, the most impressive remark was about the value of the batboy experience for brothers, the "great opportunity to be with my brother, not just sleep in the same room as so many brothers do, but to suit up together, to do a job together, and all that goes along with it."

Investiture is only the first of the confirming rituals through which batboys experience acceptance in the fraternity of the baseball clubhouse. There are, more strictly speaking, initiations, usually in the form of traditional practical jokes played on the boys. Moments of embarrassment on the field, again usually traditional, may also serve that function. And then there are types of communion experiences, typically being party to the kinds of jokes that traditionally pass for humor in the clubhouse.

Most batboys undergo some version of a wild-goose chase, being sent for some piece of equipment, usually with a specific baseball connotation, though sometimes the generic left-handed wrench, left-handed screwdriver, or some elbow grease (Tom Seaver's favorite). They have been sent desperately seeking buckets of frozen

The Tham brothers, Gus (l.) and Brad, with their nonpareil hero,
Willie Mays (photo by Rudy Tham, courtesy of Brad Tham)

ropes, knuckleballs, sliders, left-handed curve balls, bad curve balls,
and steam. (Pitcher Larry Andersen went so far as to instruct a kid to
go into the sauna with a bucket of water and wait till it turned to
steam.) With rain delays as a pretext they have been sent for the
pitching rubber in the bullpen, for a few feet of white line, for the
thing to roll up the foul lines, or even to cover the wet lines with
toilet paper. Reflecting on these experiences, they attribute the
pranks to players being just kids themselves or to their need to keep
loose. They are taught a valuable lesson to be less gullible and call it
part of growing up fast at the ballpark. "At first," says Mike Mullane, who went through his initiation at Candlestick Park, "you're
just happy they want you to do stuff for them, but when you realize
what they want you just catch yourself and laugh."

There is a consensus that it is all motivated by good-natured affection for the victim, to welcome him fondly into the inner circle of
the clubhouse, to indoctrinate him with its lore, and to let him
know he belongs. In one example I heard, however, that benign inter-

pretation seems to be a view through rose-colored hindsight. Fred Baxter was having trouble with one of his Washington Senators batboys, back in the late forties.

> He was a cocky kid named Pat. He was what I called an angle-shooter. He'd take orders from the players for lunch and then come back from Friedman's drugstore with an extra milkshake that no one had ordered. Someone would finally take it, but the gimmick was that when they mixed it at the drugstore there was always half a shake left over that wouldn't fit in the cup, so Pat would have it before coming back. I never stopped it—more power to him—but I decided to teach him a lesson. He was too cocky.
>
> I sent him up to Baltimore—it was still a minor-league club—to get the bat-stretcher. Of course, I had already briefed Tommy Thomas up there, so when Pat got there Tommy told him he'd come a day too late, that he'd just sent the bat-stretcher up to the Yankees. So he puts Pat on the train to New York.
>
> The kid gets to Yankee Stadium and they won't even let him in. They turned him away at the gates, must have thought he was nuts. He came hangdog back to Washington that night, after spending most of the day on trains, and apologized to me for his failure. And I believe he was not so cocky after that.

Yet Baxter's story of "Pat the angle-shooter" seems an exception to the rule of good-natured humor in these pranks, even in his own clubhouse. Scotty MacDougal, for example, remembers that "Fred loved the bat-stretcher gag, and he had a big laugh when Rocky Colavito got me with it, I think it was in '58. I was familiar with a hat-stretcher, so I fell for it easily." And some thirty-five years after Baxter had his batboy literally sent from Baltimore to New York, the same journey was made, figuratively, for the same purpose by Merritt Riley as a rookie batboy with the Yankees, when Ralph Salvon, the Orioles trainer, sent him from the visiting clubhouse in Yankee Stadium to Pete Sheehy for the old bat-stretcher.

The key to the batter's box is by far the most prevalent of the initiation tricks pulled on batboys. Simple and patently absurd, the joke goes on and on down the years and throughout the baseball world. It turned up in interviews from Texas, Los Angeles, San Francisco, Kansas City, Milwaukee, Detroit, Anaheim, Baltimore, Oakland, San Diego, Chicago, St. Louis, Pittsburgh, Philadelphia, and New York. Anyone who has spent time in the clubhouse is familiar with it and most are willing to take part. When it works properly, the kid is kept on the run among the farthest reaches of the ballpark, though in one reported case Royals pitcher Rich Gale was so much more embarrassed than his victim Dennis Cashen, whom he had sent to the Memorial Stadium bullpen for the key to the pitcher's mound, that when the kid got back to the clubhouse Gale apologized profusely and gave him a T-shirt to make up for it.

The full effect was felt by Steve Winship in Kansas City: "I got to the ballpark early one day for batting practice and I was greeted by Amos Otis, who was getting dressed, getting ready to take some early hitting, it looked like. He asked how my day at school was and all, and then he goes, 'I'm gonna take some extra hitting; go in Howser's office and see if he's got the key to the batter's box.' I said OK, and went into Dick's office, and asked him. He gave a little laugh, but then quickly said, 'No, I think that was left down in the dugout last night after the game. Why don't you go down there and try to find it.'"

Winship was sent all over the stadium, and at each stop someone else picked up the joke and extended it. A member of the grounds crew sent him from the dugout to the bullpen where groundskeeper George Toma had his office. Toma sent him back to the clubhouse to check with George Brett, who told him they were making duplicates in the front office. He then had to change from spikes to tennis shoes to run up to the executive offices on level five, where general manager John Schuerholz's secretary sent him back to the clubhouse.

> By that time, a lot of players were there, and Amos yells over that he wants to hit in five minutes so I better find the key. He and George yell back and forth that each thought the other had it, but George says, "You know I could swear Howser has it. I saw him with it last night. Go on back in there and ask him again." So I interrupted him again and asked if he was sure he didn't know where it was. Dick was all smiles about this time, comes over to me, puts his arm around me, and says, "Steve, there is no key to the batter's box. There's no such thing." Right then I got all red and embarrassed. I just couldn't believe that they were pulling this one over on me.
>
> Here I was, the new kid on the block, and they had me going to everyone in the Stadium for forty-five minutes, almost bothered the executive vice president of the Royals with it. As embarrassed as I was, I went back to my locker, took an old key off my key ring that I had in my jeans pocket, took it over to Amos, and said, "Here's your key to the batter's box. Go take BP." He just busted out laughing. He

and George and everyone who was down there got a kick out of it. That's a joke that we used on all the batboys to break them in on.

In retrospect, Steve Winship completes the anecdote in which he is a victim by referring to a "we" of initiators. The practice is firmly fixed in tradition, no doubt, because it continues to be effective. And the effect is clear in the sentiment that resounds throughout the many tellings of the initiation tales: the batboys accept the clubhouse kidding because they learn that it means they have been accepted.

In a sense, the moments of embarrassment on the field, often described by former batboys as living out their worst nightmares, are themselves like communion rituals—at least when the moments are of a traditional or formulaic nature, when they mirror players' experiences, or when they are experiences which are explicitly shared among batboys and players.

Rick LaCivita, through 1992 a producer of major league baseball games for CBS, says that his experience as a batboy for the Washington Senators was "the thrill of a lifetime, a dream come true." But with the dreams come recurrent nightmares, batboys' fantasies or fears of what might go wrong. For LaCivita himself, the dark side came as a painful shock on Opening Day 1970. The original Senators, transplanted to Minnesota, were revisiting their old home field, and Harmon Killebrew was very pumped up when he homered for the Twins. LaCivita was wearing the visiting team's uniform, and he was very excited, too, when he reached out to shake Killebrew's hand as he crossed the plate. All that positive energy resulted in a broken hand for the batboy.

I would not suggest, even in jest, that injuries to batboys bear the remotest resemblance to those ritual maimings of sacral kings made famous by Fraser's *Golden Bough* (and mixed in with baseball mythology by Malamud in *The Natural*). And yet certain injuries often assume significance when remembered as occasions that allowed the boys to identify with the players.

Getting injured is a sure way for a batboy to get attention, but it is doubly humiliating because on the one hand he shouldn't be noticed at all while on the other he should be able to avoid getting hurt. But many a batboy has been caught off guard and had his nightmare come painfully true. Mark Stowe will never forget the day in Cincinnati when Ken Griffey ran over his toe while scoring a run. And imagine Rene Lachemann's mortification on the one day he neglected to wear a cup in his uniform and was hit where it mattered by a foul ball off the bat of Pittsburgh outfielder Joe Christopher. Or Don Deason's shock one day in St. Louis when he was being so careful of batted balls during Cubs batting practice as he was carrying a bucket of balls in from behind second base that he walked into the path of a throw from Ron Santo toward first base: it caught him right in the head, knocked him cold, and he spent the whole game stretched out in the umpires' room.

The effect of such events is to have the fans in the stands take note of batboys the way they would players and their "bloopers." But then having the players take note as well, however sardonically or tauntingly, is to be made to feel like them because of being treated as one of them. In the familiar ballpark tableau, a ball fouled into the dugout does not discriminate according to the class or age or role of the people scattering. Ron Pieraldi was sitting inattentively one day on the Oakland bench next to Catfish Hunter, who was charting the pitches, when a foul ball caught him on the inner thigh.

Batting practice is the time when most commonly a batboy may identify with players on the field and a time for frequent casual accidents. One day in San Diego, Chris Lehr wasn't quick enough to react to a batting practice drive behind second off the bat of pitcher Bruce Hurst. "It got me in the jaw and neck," says Chris, "but fortunately my mouth was full of bubble gum at the time, and it cushioned the blow. The worst part of it was that Hurst kept apologizing for a week." When Kevin Cashen caught a batting practice line drive in the leg in Memorial Stadium, at least he had the satisfaction of being hit by hard-hitting Orioles third baseman Doug DeCinces.

Bill Philips was paying attention all right, shagging flies during batting practice one day in 1955 in Chicago. "But," he says, "a ball went through my glove and hit me right in the eye. The fans are real close to the field in Wrigley, you know, and they got on me pretty good. I had to be assisted to the clubhouse, got it iced down, but had a big black eye. Big Hank Sauer made me feel better. He shouted out in the clubhouse, 'All these players we got on the DL, now even the fuckin' batboy is on the DL.'"

Steve Labatt's inattention led to injury, too, but not his own. As visitors' batboy in the Twin Cities, he was swinging the lead bat onto his shoulder when he caught Scott Fletcher, who happened to be walking behind him, in the face. The Texas shortstop had to be taken to the hospital for stitches in his upper lip. "And it was getaway day, too," says Steve, which wouldn't seem to make it any worse until you realize that that is the day that tips are left in the visiting clubhouse.

An injury becomes a kind of *felix culpa* for a batboy, who will benefit from it by being treated not only on the field but also (and more importantly) in the clubhouse just like any other member of the club. It is not injury that a batboy fears but embarrassment. What might be called "blooper-phobia" is a built-in occupational hazard of the job. It is as if having the uniform on automatically makes one an object of attention. "Everyone's looking at me," says Steve Friend as he recreates his first day as a batboy in Montreal. "The first time a foul ball went to the backstop, I ran so fast I couldn't believe it. I was only on the field for two seconds, but it felt like an hour. I never ran so fast in my life."

The fear of being watched usually passes with the growing knowledge that, for most fans, batboys typically recede into the structure of the game, like the fungo circles or the grounds crew. But a concomitant fear persists that one could draw attention to oneself by making some mistake. About their initial feelings many batboys say, like Jerry Schroer who worked at Sportsman's Park for both St. Louis clubs in the 1950s, "When I was on the field I always thought everyone was watching me." But almost all of them will echo his next line: "Maybe that's why I got a lump in my throat every time I ran out to catch a foul ball off the screen."

That seemingly innocuous duty often looms menacingly in batboys' fearful thoughts. Tripping, slipping, or missing a ball will not go unnoticed by vocal fans, but it may also result in an umpire's comment about getting on television or a scoreboard message that says, "ERROR BALLBOY." Yet even the humiliation that comes with a sardonic ovation from the crowd may be redeemed by having the players give a standing ovation in the dugout to acknowledge a blooper. The players rarely miss a chance to get on someone. On a hot day in Griffith Stadium, when Bob Farmer ran out on the field to take the warm-up jacket from the incoming relief pitcher, he was mortified to discover the guy wasn't wearing one. No one in the stands noticed, but he couldn't get away with it from the bench.

Speaking of Mahendra Naik, the first Blue Jays batboy, equipment manager Jeff Ross says, "The crowd loved him, this heavy-set Indian kid who always sprinted for balls and bats." But for Mahendra himself that was not a positive part of the experience. "It was embarrassing," he says. "The game should be the focal point. But the team was very bad and the crowd was cheering me chasing foul balls, chanting, 'go, go, go!' The wave started in Toronto, you know, in the horrible old bleachers where you couldn't see anything, and the fans were bored out of their trees. I hate the wave, the Chicken too."

It is because the game is sacred that the essential criterion of a batboy's performance on the field is, like an umpire's, to go unnoticed. And anything that draws attention from the stands or the field or the dugout is bound to be a mistake, one to fear, to regret, and to endure. That is also why the grimmest specter haunting batboys is the fear (or worse, the memory) of interfering with play. To touch a live ball is to risk the curse of the baseball gods and the unanimous derision of umpires, players, and fans alike. Passed balls, wild pitches, overthrows, and fair balls rolling in foul territory have all been handled by batboys instinctively going for the ball. With crowds, umpires, and players all yelling, "Don't touch it," a batboy will sometimes get carried away and throw to a base.

The equipment in a batboy's charge, like his very physical presence, must also be kept out of harm's way, that is, play's way. The rosin bag, the pine tar rag, the weighted bat, the donut, and the bag of used balls must all be removed from the possibility of impeding play, but of course it is the bat, his primary charge, that most concerns the boy. Maury Povich remembers "living out the batboy's nightmare in a spring training game in 1949. There was a play at the plate, with everything coming together—the runner, the throw, the catcher, the umpire, and the batboy. I was so mesmerized by the play that I forgot to clear the bat out of the way. I was just standing there, and the runner slid right through me to the plate. Clark Griffith, sitting in the stands with my mother, said, 'Ethel, this boy of yours is gonna get hurt if he doesn't pay more attention to what he's supposed to do.'"

Gilly Lefebvre remembers being involved in a key play when the Reds were in Los Angeles for a crucial series late in the 1959 season. Vada Pinson was trying to score from second on a single. The hitter had laid the bat down right on home plate, and Lefebvre tried to ease around catcher John Roseboro to pull the bat away just as the throw was coming in. Roseboro shied at Lefebvre's shadow and lost the ball. Pinson scored, said "appreciate it" to the batboy, and Cincinnati clinched the pennant. "Don't feel bad," Roseboro told him, "you were doing the right thing."

A nightmare report from Bob Scherr, a quarter century after the fact, seems to summarize the elements and effects of violating the taboo.

> The Red Sox came in for the first night game of the '64 season, so I'm kneeling down in the Boston batting circle on the first base side. A foul ball is hit over my head, Norm Siebern, the O's first baseman, is running in my direction, the catcher John Orsino is running in my direction, I'm looking up, and I don't know what to do, holding this lead bat; it never happened to me before. I look up, can't see the ball, it got lost in the lights. I got scared, panicked, dropped the lead bat, and ran toward the visitors dugout.
>
> Siebern just about caught the ball but tripped over the bat I had left there. He dropped the ball and was charged with an error. He was OK, nice about it, didn't say a word. But Orsino started screaming and hollering and cussing at me, right on the field. And I was scared to death. I ran across him later in the game, and he mumbled a couple of cuss words at me again.
>
> I'm fifteen years old. When I was offered the job on the O's side a month later, I was scared to take it, didn't want to go over there and take it. And when I did I never said a word about that play to anybody, and no one said a word about it to me. Orsino never said another word.

Scherr, now a politically active Maryland attorney, paused for a moment, then added, "Either he didn't remember the incident or didn't realize it was me that was the visiting batboy at the time." But the trauma lives on for Bob Scherr. Just retelling it, his eyes get the haunted look of someone running for cover.

It is rare for a batboy to cross a player, but one sure path to trouble is to cross an umpire. As Billy Cahill remembers it, from a time when batboys still retained some of the functions of a mascot, he was in the on-deck circle rooting for St. Louis Browns batters—especially his favorites, big tippers like Harlond Clift, Red Kress, and Don Heffner—when he drew umpire Cal Hubbard's attention. "You will stay back by the dugout," Hubbard declared, "and you will quit yer hollerin'." Then Browns trainer Bill Bauman gave Billy a devilish idea, telling him to "shortleg" a few foul balls coming off the screen so that they would roll back toward the plate and interrupt play. He tried it and it worked. "You win," shouted the umpire to the batboy an inning later. "You can go back to the circle, BUT YOU WILL KEEP YER MOUTH SHUT."

Donald James Fitzpatrick ("Fitzie" as Red Sox batboy in 1944 and "Fitzie" still in 1991 just before retiring as Boston's equipment manager) has a favorite batboy story about a kid in Anaheim. Manager Bill Rigney had thrown his cap to the ground in a dispute with umpire Ed Hurley and been chased from the game. When the batboy went to the plate next, he threw *his* cap down, and *he* was chased. The next day, the kid was working as ballboy down the foul line, and the radio he was carrying was blasting loud enough for the umpire to hear. So Hurley threw him out of a second straight game.

Wes Patterson didn't want to attract anyone's attention, but certainly not an umpire's. "In 1986 the Royals got back into Kansas City late from a road trip, and I stayed up all night unpacking them. We'd all gone out for breakfast and then I went to school. I ran cross country and track at high school. At lunch time I didn't eat, I did my workout for track, and when I get to the game I'm dead tired. I was ballboy down the line, and when I sat down for the third inning I fell asleep. I slept the whole inning. The right fielder didn't even ask to play catch. And the umpire, bless his soul, Ken Kaiser, not the fittest umpire in the American League, came down and scared the shit right out of me."

Whether it's the men in blue, the men and boys suited up, or the clubhouse personnel in their jeans, the humor of the baseball subculture seems to run the gamut from the juvenile to the sophomoric. But if men playing or working at a boy's game are lowering themselves to or arrested at a lowest common denominator, the batboys feel elevated when taking part at that level. They may feel privileged when simply witnessing the jokes, self-important when taking part in them, honored when being the butts themselves, or truly blessed when being interchangeable with players in a joking context.

The rudiments of clubhouse humor are embarrassment and shock. If anyone is found to have a weakness, a pet peeve, or a phobia, it is sure to be exploited. Practical joking is universal. Food and drink, tobacco and soap, fire and excrement all are staple elements. Gullibility is a certain target. And pride goeth before a pratfall.

The dugout hotfoot goes back at least as far as 1915, when Hank Le Bost remembers the perpetrator in the Brooklyn dugout: Casey Stengel. The tradition persists, at the hands of such practitioners as Moe Drabowsky, Jim Rivera, Neal Heaton, Bert Blyleven, Dave La-Point, and Roger McDowell. Former batboys are gleeful at the mem-

Asleep on the job, Wes Patterson down the line in Royals Stadium (courtesy of Wes Patterson)

ory of these antics, but the best feeling of all is to have been a victim. It was a highlight of Rick LaCivita's year as batboy, for example, that he was glorified by a hotfoot at the hands of Hall-of-Famer Mickey Mantle.

Shaving cream in the ear or on the cap, various items hung from the back of uniforms worn onto the field, tobacco juice spat onto shoes, spiked shoes nailed to the floor, sleeves cut off shirts and toes from sanitaries—these are standard fare. Batboys enjoy taking part in laughter directed at players but really treasure the identification with the club that is signified by being the object of the laughter. The boys are easy targets, especially of the roughhousing humor typified by Kent Hrbek's trying out new wrestling holds on them, Kirby Puckett including them while making the rounds for his "cup-check" game, or champion A's Catfish Hunter, Paul Lindblad, Dave Duncan, Sal Bando, Curt Blefary, and Rick Munday wrapping them up and tossing them around. "I was their favorite," Rocky

Maunakea says proudly. "They stuck me in a garbage can, taped it shut, and played crank with me—but they also taught me right from wrong."

Mark Sassetti says that "every clubby in America tries to stay away from Blyleven, but sooner or later he'll sneak up and get you. . . . But he's at his best in September, when rookies come up." The implication is that the initiated batboys, at this time of the season, are one up on the tyro players making their clubhouse debuts. Batboys and rookies may be the most frequent targets, since the rule seems to be that any sensitivity, distaste, or fear will be played or preyed upon. Tom Villante may have escaped targeting in the Yankees clubhouse because Phil Rizzuto, acting as a little lightning rod, was a constant butt of jokes, his squeamishness leading to his frequently finding insects in his shoes. (See Blake 30 for another example of Rizzuto as target; see also Howe 66–70 for how the Dodgers abused manager Lasorda with gross pranks.) And Ron Pieraldi describes the A's attitude toward Rollie Fingers: "From Cucamonga, you know, your basic butt of jokes because he's so slow to react. There'd always be this delayed reaction, he'd laugh minutes later when he finally figured it out."

"Locker room topics are the same at every level," says John Mitchell, reflecting about funny business in the Senators clubhouse during their last two years in Washington. "When Eddie Brinkman was around, any time you bent over you could get a bat in the rear." Nor is there much change over time, as John might have learned from his father, whose years as a Senators batboy were precisely three decades earlier. Judge Mitchell, who retired as chief administrative judge of the Circuit Court for Montgomery County (Maryland) in 1992, has one particularly vivid memory of a clubhouse prank. "I was working the visiting clubhouse when the Tigers came to town. I'll never forget this. There was Rudy York in his two-piece blue underwear, a part Indian who regarded himself as a great strongman. Well Barney McCoskey, practically a rookie but already appreciated for a batting stroke which was a carbon copy of Charlie Gehringer's, came up to York and challenged him to a test of strength. 'I'll bet you,' he said, 'you can't stand on a bat—any bat—and lift yourself up.' Rudy, who knew he could lift his own weight easily, said, 'The hell I can't—and I'll use my own bat.' For fifteen minutes he struggled and strained, with everyone laughing, getting more and more frustrated, until he figured out that it couldn't be done."

The tableau of Rudy York's trial of strength is reminiscent of the traditional "three-man-lift" prank. Two players challenge a third to a test of strength, betting and taunting him that he can't lift three men off the floor. The victim agrees to be the third, and then is positioned between the other two in such a way as to be helplessly pinned, which is when he gets every available substance poured all over him. Dave Zeigler remembers an astounded rookie, Pete Incaviglia, getting this treatment in the Texas clubhouse.

It was the Rangers again, on the road in Milwaukee, who got batboy Tony Migliaccio with that one, and it is instructive to hear him tell it. "They were in for three days and they set the whole thing up patiently. The first day, Richie Zisk bet me ten bucks there would be between 30 and 50,000 people in the stands. I tried to collect when there were only about 15,000, but he says, 'I said 30, not 30,000.' The second day there was a similar bet, and I lost again. The third day he offers me a chance to win the twenty back. 'Pick the two biggest guys in the clubhouse and I bet I can lift all three of you at once.' So I get Jim Sundberg the catcher and Jim Ellis the DH, both well over two hundred pounds, and when they have my arms and legs locked, they rip off my pants and pour tobacco, chew, shaving cream, soda, and ice on me, all laughing and having a ball. 'Congratulations,' they said, 'you're now a member of the Texas Rangers.'" That explicit announcement of initiation and membership signals the whole point of a process that is more rite than prank.

The "chew" in that story is chewing tobacco, a persistent but gradually disappearing baseball habit and a frequent ingredient of batboy initiation. Some have even acquired the habit after being introduced to it in the clubhouse. But for many more, the first try was unpleasant enough to discourage any repetition. In recent years clubbies for the Phillies and in visiting clubhouses around the National League have had the added unpleasantness of cleaning up around Lenny Dykstra's locker as another effective deterrent.

John Plein says, "I had been with the Padres for a couple of years—let's see, it was '78 so I was 19—when Doug Rader teased me into trying it. He was one of the craziest guys, I mean fun crazy, and he was a big Red Man chewer. So I took a small chaw and kept it in my mouth for several innings, but I couldn't stand it and had to spit it out finally. Then, a couple of innings later I had to run into the clubhouse bathroom and lost my lunch. Rader had been watching all along, and he walked by and says, casually, 'I forgot to tell you, rookie, you're not supposed to swallow the juice.'"

Rader figures in another tobacco-juice story Plein tells: "Once when he had finished his season managing our triple A club, he was visiting the Padres, sitting in the photographers' area during the game. He had two cups of beer, holding one, the other at his feet. Another guy there was spitting tobacco juice into that cup. Rader finished one cup and picked up the other, and after he takes a sip, the guy says, 'I better tell you I was spitting tobacco juice in that,'—you know, trying to gross him out. So Rader says, 'I thought it tasted a little different,' and drinks it down, outgrossing the would-be gross-out artist."

Jerry Risch, visiting clubhouse manager for the Cardinals, has vivid memories of two debuts. The first was his own as a batboy, suiting up in John Logan's uniform with number 23, for the visiting Pirates. The other, several years later, was thirteen-year-old Sean Roarity's. Sean got started early as a batboy because his father was not only an Anheuser Busch executive but a friend of Tommy Lasorda as well. "So there he was in a Dodgers uniform, waiting for his first time on the field, when Jerry Reuss told him he really needed to try a chew. The kid spent the whole game puking, and we had to suit up the regular kid at the last minute. I'm glad to say it worked out for Sean in the long run. He became a good batboy, and the players loved the way he used to sprint to the plate for the bats."

That memory is itself a conventional batboy's story, one I heard in several nearly identical versions going back to Sid Bordman's from 1940: "One day an outfielder, Arthur (Bud) Metheny, asked me if I wanted to be a player. When I said yes, he said, 'You gotta learn to chew tobacco.' He gave me a plug of Beechnut, and I ended up passed out on the trainer's table. I never saw the game that day. That was my only initiation trick."

Say the word "cakes" around a baseball clubhouse and, aside from being a familiar reference to Jim Palmer, it will suggest two traditional locker room jokes. One is the sour-cake routine, often pulled on rookies during spring training or during the dog days of late season. Part of the postgame spread being cake, one player takes a conspicuous whiff of it and complains that it's sour; a second player inhales deeply and confirms the suspicion of the first; then the next person to stick his nose up close gets his whole face pushed into the cake. It happened to Payton Morris on his first road trip with Atlanta over the July 4 holiday in Philadelphia. To make matters worse, the cake was his, arranged for by his father because he was going to be away for his eighteenth birthday. "But everyone got a good laugh," Payton says, and as the cellar-dwelling club they probably needed it. A decade earlier, in Anaheim, Tony Atlas got it with a German chocolate cake. "I know it's the oldest trick in the book," he says, "but coach Larry Sherry and veteran Willie Davis got me— something to do with keeping loose while winning the division, I guess." First place or last, a team finds the batboy a handy target. Mike Macko adds that not until the Rangers got a kid—batboy or rookie—with the sour cake did he really feel part of the club.

The other cake routine is the common practice of a bare-bottomed player sitting squarely in the cake for laughs. Many bat-boys reported this phenomenon, but a couple gave rave reviews to the performer. According to Jeff Sipos who worked the visiting club-house in Cleveland, the Angels utility player Syd O'Brien, often among the first players out of the shower, had cake-sitting as his specialty. But it was star reliever Sparky Lyle who most impressed his audience, as Pat McBride, now a physician at University of Wis-consin Hospital in Madison, describes the scene in the visiting club-house in Milwaukee: "He did it with perfect aplomb, first the pirou-ette, and then the sitdown in the cake, all in one fluid motion" (and all on the way to leading the league in saves for the Yankees).

It should come as a shock to no one that locker room and dugout humor often smacks of the off-color, the obscene, the excremental, or the just plain gross. Reid Nichols, for example, regaled the Expos clubhouse for half a season with many replays of his dead-mouse sandwich. And Red McKercher remembers the day Willie McCovey first appeared in the Giants clubhouse. The batboy politely intro-duced himself to the rookie, who said, "Aren't you the one they call Red because the hair on your head is as red as a dick on a dog?"

Sometimes the so-called humor relies on the mere use of a "dirty" word, like the punchline of adolescent jokes, but often physical action comes into play. A source from the Red Sox who chooses to remain anonymous tells stories about a batboy who was known as "Crazy Pat" who is now, perhaps appropriately, a schoolteacher. Pat was the kind of kid who would do anything, anytime, anywhere, especially if egged on by the fun-loving stars of the team, Carl Yastrzemski and Reggie Smith. The most outrageous incident occurred in the parking lot at Fenway, hours after a game, when Boston's mounted policemen were relaxing on foot after a long patrol, now that almost all of the crowd had dispersed. Yastrzemski and Smith, taking note of an idle horse's stallionesque equipment, thought it would be fun to see if Pat would literally handle that equipment. Then they watched, their amazement climaxing in hysterical laughter, as Pat ran back into the clubhouse, emerged wearing on both hands the gloves batboys used to buff shoes, and proceeded to masturbate the horse.

George Catloth remembers a routine the Yankees regularly worked on a rookie's first visit to Griffith Stadium in Washington. "They'd hire a little black boy for a buck to stand outside the locker room and holler 'Daddy' at him until everyone around was pointing and yelling. Not all their jokes were in such bad taste. When the old clock was removed from the right field wall, veterans would tease rookies about the clock running slow or fast, and they'd keep trying to find it among the welter of billboard ads." (This story is confirmed by Bob Feller in Honig 275.)

The theme of drinking the undrinkable is a common one in the lore of clubhouse humor. Sometimes it is carried onto the field in the form of vodka sent by a mischievous player to an umpire when the batboy is supposedly bringing water. Wes Patterson tells about umpire Jim Joyce getting caught this way in Royals Stadium, to the great delight of the dugout when he spat it out and screamed. Three years later, on a hot Sunday afternoon in August, with the artificial turf registering 130 degrees, they got him again. "You can't be doin' this shit!" he shouted, but of course they do, and will, whenever the comedy juices start flowing.

Tom MacDougal watched Jim Rivera of the White Sox shake up a can of beer and put it back in the cooler in the visiting clubhouse in Washington. Part of the fun was seeing who would get the jackpot can. Tom liked that joke so much he decided to try it himself when the Yankees were in town. For a long time nobody took the booby-trapped can, until finally Enos Slaughter, all dressed up in a dark blue suit for some special occasion, drew it. First he got soaked, then furious. Nobody laughed at Slaughter, and Tom neither confessed nor tried that trick again.

Garth Garreau describes a variation of that trick from the Polo Grounds in the 1940s. The idea was to uncap a bottle of soda and stick it into the back pocket of the uniform pants. "The cloth is thick," he reports in his book, "and it takes the soda a little while to trickle through, but when it does get through you're left with a clammy, uncomfortable leg.

"Someone gave me the soda-water treatment a minute before we were to go out for the start of the game. I had no time to change. Believe me, I was sore. In that second I felt like throwing up the bat boy job." But the anecdote concludes with the reflection that "if they hadn't given me some of the roughhousing, it would have meant that they didn't think I belonged" (53).

Sometimes what evokes the biggest laughs in the clubhouse are acts of anger or revenge, but often with forms of retribution that plumb the depths of this material. Rene Lachemann remembers the time he decided to teach a lesson to another clubhouse kid who was goofing off during the hard chores of unpacking for a visiting team. The kid was drinking soft drinks out of the umpires' supply, and Lach took a 7-Up bottle and filled it from his own bladder. Unfortunately their boss, Jim Muhey, grabbed the bottle and took a swig before the warning shout of "Don't drink that!" could stop him. "Tastes like piss," he said. The sheepish batboy answered, "It is."

From more than thirty years' experience Fred Baxter vividly recalls two examples of the humor of the old Washington Senators. One involved all-star second baseman Buddy Myer, who fancied Fitch hair tonic and got annoyed when too many people borrowed it on the sly. In his wisdom (his middle name was Solomon, after all) he waited till there was just an inch left in the old bottle, filled it with his urine, and put it back out. It got used anyway, and Buddy dramatically announced to the whole team, "There was this much Fitch, the rest my piss—I hope you enjoyed it."

Fred's other example follows: "Gerald Walker, our left fielder in 1940, had been buddies with Slick Coffman, the reliever, back in Detroit. Slick was traded to the Browns and when they came into Griffith Stadium he came into our clubhouse early and filled Walker's glove with dirt and gravel. Walker was real mad at getting caught by surprise, so he decided to get even. Next day, he came to the ballpark early and sneaked Coffman's glove out of the locker room and took it into the john with him while he took a healthy one. Then he used a sharp stick to fill the glove with it and sneaked it back. You should have heard Slick yell when he stuck his hand in."

Such tales may hardly be amusing for themselves, but in the context of this study they are pertinent. For one thing, the frequency of food, drink, and excretions as staple material in the clubhouse repertoire of humor smacks of basic earthiness, elemental camaraderie, and even ritual communion. Membership in the club is conferred by initiation, and members are made worthy through continuing trials of brotherhood. Old men treasuring what they saw as wide-eyed boys is testimony to its enduring value, not from the content but from the process, because it is this process that validated their privileged presence.

To take an example that will offend no one, not even the most self-important members of the fourth estate, Gilly Lefebvre still chuckles over the time Casey Stengel, managing the miserable expansion Mets, came to the batboy in Dodgers Stadium, put his arm around him, and said, "I'm gonna teach you how to handle the press." Casey escorted Gilly onto the field where several members of the media were waiting for interviews, and there spent half an hour laughing and evading every question by talking around them, double-talking, piling non sequitur upon malapropism, giving the media what they wanted, himself some laughs, and the batboy an amusing lesson.

According to Creamer (*Stengel* 181) Stengel was personally taught that technique by Ring Lardner, who later used Stengel as a *character* in his fiction ("Lose with a Smile" series in the *Saturday Evening Post* 1932). Creamer, whose *Babe* remains a model biography of a mythic/historical figure in any field, closes his portrait of Stengel with a detailed example of the technique in action (316–329). When, in later turns of the gyre, Asinof's book on the Black Sox scandal, *Eight Men Out*, was adapted as a fictionalized film, John Sayles seemed to design his screenplay to emphasize the character of Ring Lardner, whom Sayles then played on screen.

While Asinof's account is justly regarded as the best historical treatment of that tawdry affair, my preference is for Brendan Boyd's fictional version, *Blue Ruin*. In any case, what we have here are examples of how cultural conventions/icons/*topoi* may be matters of infinitely regressive mirrors: life imitating art imitating life imitating art . . . . And this may be strikingly true in regard to baseball. Is it accurate to say that Bill Veeck's Eddie Gaedel (the best account is Veeck's own) begat Philip Roth's Bob Yamm and O. K. Ockatur? Or do both derive from a century-old baseball tradition or a millenia-old mythic tradition? The mirrors don't lie; they only distort—even where it is a *speculum stultorum*.

Gilly Lefebvre's story is a case of the manager and the batboy sharing an inside joke at the expense of people who, however knowledgeable, are nevertheless outsiders (except when former major leaguers). A similar case, a reminder of the young Stengel with a bird under his uniform cap rather than of venerable Stengelese, is a comedy bit without dialogue. It happened when Oakland visited Anaheim for the first time after affecting white shoes with their uniforms. Batboy Leonard Garcia joined the insiders' laughter when, for the Angels' infield drill, shortstop Jim Fregosi (later a major league manager) and second baseman Bobby Knoop (a veritable institution as major league coach) went through their routine wearing *golf* shoes.

Occasionally a batboy gets to be an active participant in the intra-baseball interplay. Steve Winship's example involves a two-day sequence of events on the field in Royals Stadium, with himself first in the middle and then on the receiving end. Amos Otis was out with an injury, so he didn't have to face Gaylord Perry, who was pitching for Seattle. They were friends from their National League days fifteen years earlier when they broke in with the Mets and the Giants, respectively. "Amos took a ball and scuffed it on the concrete side of the dugout, wrote an obscene message on it, and had me deliver it to Steve Palermo at the plate. But Palermo just put it into his pouch without looking at it, and then threw it out to Gaylord when he needed a new ball. Gaylord just laughed and used it. So Amos scuffed another one and wrote another message, but this time the ump saw it and took the joke pretty well.

"Next day I was ballboy down the line, and Gaylord came up and grabbed me in a bearhug, threw me down, and sat on me, with everyone laughing. Amos saw it and called me over to the dugout, telling me to ask Gaylord a question for him: How much longer are you gonna be around? Gaylord's response to that was a second takedown. Then later in the game, when I was warming up with Willie Wilson between innings, Gaylord stole my stool."

Perry was back in the National League when he drew batboy John Plein, taking his privileged road trip with the Padres, into some mischief at Wrigley Field. The pitcher coated up a ball with vaseline and gave it to the kid, telling him to throw it to Cubs manager Herman Franks from about ten feet, to say, "This is from Gaylord," and to run like hell. "I did," Plein says, "Franks gets splattered, curses a blue streak, and then throws the ball over to our dugout where Gaylord Perry is roaring with laughter. You should have seen it." But of course we neither see it nor get it if we are not inside the magic circle.

No clubhouse institution is more emblematic of that inner circle than the kangaroo court, and for a batboy to take part in the proceedings is as close to induction at full rank as he can get. That is why, in the visitors' clubhouse in Minnesota, Mark McKenzie was both embarrassed and thrilled to be summoned as a defendant before the Orioles kangaroo court, presided over, complete with wig and gavel, by Frank Robinson. It seems that during the game, when Frank had had to face reliever Tom Hall for the first time, he had asked the batboy in the on-deck circle what the pitcher had. "Fastball, slider, curve, straight change; the curve breaks away," said professional-sounding Mark. "But he's left-handed," said the MVP. Mark forgot all about that exchange until his summons to appear, but Don Buford defended him and won the thumbs-up sign from the jury of his peers.

Jay Mazzone had no thumbs. His prosthetic devices were designed to help him handle balls and bats. When he started working as Orioles batboy he felt left out because nobody in the clubhouse asked him to do things or run errands. Judge Frank Robinson of the kangaroo court took care of that. He levied a fine on Jay for failing to perform his duty as a member of the club, that is, the jury, by giving the thumbs-up or thumbs-down sign. It was a predetermined judgment, because equipment manager Jimmy Tyler had already prepared a big-thumbed cardboard hand that Jay could tape on and take part in verdicts. From that moment on, Jay was officially included in the community. He had been given the sacrament of clubhouse communion, he was treated by all as a full-fledged first-class citizen of the club, and he felt that he belonged.

To be a participant in the clubhouse court is to be inducted officially as a peer of that realm. Indeed, whenever a batboy is asked, embarrassed, tricked, or cajoled into taking part in a traditional clubhouse ritual, it may be taken as emblematic of a ceremony of induction. He has been initiated into the club and from then on feels entitled to participate as club member in the rites and rights of membership.

CHAPTER 4 **The Calendar of Pilgrimage**

Professional baseball is fundamentally different from other team sports in the nature of its travel. Football teams may make forays on the average of two a month over a sixteen-game season to engage the opposing teams on their home turf, but the total time spent in transit or away from home is a negligible fraction of their season. Basketball and hockey have comparably long seasons, tedious and often meaningless, but they consist of a seemingly endless procession of one-night stands. Among interchangeable Forums and Gardens, whether in Ridgefield or Calgary, the players move in cloned hotels and dressing rooms and stadiums with barely a transient nod at any particularities of place, and spending a mere second night in any one town constitutes the outer limit of a sojourn.

In baseball the travel is fixed in the structure of league play. Baseball teams play *series* of games against opponents, and a so-called road trip is generally made up of a sequence of series. In the period of stable eight-team leagues, each of the four teams of the "eastern division" would tour the "west" by train, over a two-week period, spending three or four days at a time in St. Louis, Chicago, Cincinnati, and Pittsburgh, or in Detroit, Cleveland, Chicago, and St. Louis. Dom DiMaggio calls this the "wonderful sameness" of baseball when he was coming up (8, 43).

It has been argued that in 1876 the "formation of the National Baseball League was partly due to the cheapness and availability of railroad transportation." More broadly, "The new railroads made possible inter-city and inter-regional competition, which in turn heightened interest in organized sports. In 1869, for example, the Cincinnati Red Stocking Club, the first all-salaried professional baseball team, utilized the newly completed Union Pacific Railroad to stage a coast-to-coast tour in which it went undefeated" (Carroll 6). The railroads thereby also contributed to a continental consensus for the rules of the game, as well as a persistence of tradition. They helped make it a hemispheric game as well, bringing it to Mexico, Nicaragua, Panama, Cuba, Hispaniola, and Venezuela, with the assistance of ships of commerce, the Panama Canal, and "individual cultural exchange" (Oleksak 5–17).

The 154-game schedule, with eleven games home and eleven away against each of seven other clubs, provided for a sense of continuity and a degree of familiarity that made the travel much more of a process of visiting known places. A particular road trip, repeated three times a year and year after year, had meaningful and even fixed associations far beyond the play of the games and included the idiosyncratic fields and fans as known and predictable (however comfortable or uncomfortable) entities.

Air travel, expansion, peripatetic franchises, realignment of divisions, and playoff restructuring have changed much of that. And yet baseball hangs on tenaciously to the institutionalized concepts of road trips, "balanced scheduling," series of games at each stop, and even repetitive sequences of series. At the minor league level, where there is even less reason—that is, less competitive significance—to play such schedules, they persist. Perhaps the bus travel and the cost factors have helped to perpetuate such fixed practices, but Major League Baseball must justify their fixity on the grounds of tradition, not practicality and not fairness.

The persisting cycles of travel routes and fixed seasons are major factors, I believe, in the adaptability of baseball for the structures of narrative. The ready-made design serves the fiction of Carkeet,

Hays, Kinsella (*Iowa*), Klinkowitz, Leavy, and especially Roth where the *recording* of the season is what matters. Nonfiction accounts often derive their artfulness from such structuring, as in Dom Di-Maggio, Brosnan, Bouton, Talley, and Halberstam. Okrent structures his finely detailed cameo of the game around a single game. Coover and Charyn, and with somewhat less success Eric Greenberg and Malamud, lift the seasonal structures into more ambitious conceptions or contexts. Most impressively, DeLillo has elevated Okrent's strategy to narrative masterworking.

So hallowed are the routines of road trips that when batboys are permitted to join a team for one they experience it as a kind of privileged voyage, a pilgrimage on well-traveled and amply-legended pilgrim routes, a holy hajj. A voyage to Cooperstown is another such pilgrimage, shared by insiders and fans alike, and the rituals and ritual play attached to induction ceremonies are celebrations of the temporary removal of the barriers that separate the chosen few from the devoted many. The Baseball Hall of Fame thus honors the whole of its appreciative mass world at the same time that it enshrines its special annointees.

In Coover, the ritual aspects of the game prevail in a brilliant performance of narrative resolution on the occasion of a ceremonial contest. The progression has been from art (Henry's invented game) through myth (his narrative histories that grow from the playing of the game) to ritual. In *The Rio Loja Ringmaster*, Lamar Herrin makes the same progression immediately and directly. The first paragraph establishes a literary context when his pitcher-narrator makes allusions to Candide, Meursault, Bartleby, Birnam Wood, and Hemingway. Then he muses that the "real realm" of a hanging curve is "mythology" comparable to "Achilles watching the arrow leap from Paris's bow and watching it home in on his heel. . . . It is the instant that the curve hangs there and not the instant that it is consumed that is the very stuff of myth." With a perfect game working, he quickly associates what he is doing with the ceremonial/festival nature of Aztec ball games, thereby accounting for the novel's title.

Despite the ceremonial/festival Hall of Fame Game, however, the pilgrimage to Cooperstown stands outside the structure of the game.[14] Spring training is another story, a far more significant one for our purposes. The training sites, mostly in Florida but with a substantial minority in Arizona now, constitute veritable shrines, holy sites on which batboy-acolytes aspire and conspire and contrive to descend. For a lucky few, spring training becomes a regular part of their seasonal (festival) calendar, while for many others a single two-week visit is the pinnacle of their baseball ambitions.

One other aspect of travel in baseball, institutionalized to the point of being regarded as a mythic ordeal, is the arduous trek upwards through the minors. Even here, though rare, the experience of a batboy may reflect the values of the whole subculture, because the goal of "getting to the Show" as Ron Shelton's *Bull Durham* and Paul Hemphill's *Long Gone* made so clear, is paramount. Tommie Ferguson, who became, with several major league clubs, traveling secretary, equipment manager, vice president for administration, and scout, learned this lesson from Eddie Stanky in 1946 when, as a sixteen-year-old with a season behind him working in the Red Sox clubhouse at Fenway Park, Ferguson had decided to move over to Braves Field because they would be the first team in Boston to play baseball under the lights.

"Never," said Stanky, the eternally competitive second-baseman, later coach and manager, to the batboy, "never go to the minor leagues. Even if you have to be an usher at the ballpark, stay with the big-league team. That way, at least you'll be there if another opening comes up."

For most of the batboys who have managed to stay on in baseball in one capacity or another, Stanky's policy has paid off, and it's easy to see how seductive a path that way can be. Take the case of Ron Nedset, an aspiring schoolboy player in Milwaukee. Ron got a break during the 1981 strike, when Jerry Augustine and Cecil Cooper, among others, would work out at a school near his home. He got to know them, and through them Bob Sullivan, who agreed to let him help out in the clubhouse, then put him on the payroll when he turned sixteen. From 1983 to 1985 he was the home team batboy and also worked winters at Mike Hegan's "Grand Slam" facility in Milwaukee.

Graduating from high school in 1986 he went on to Phoenix College in Arizona, still hoping to make it as a player. But he would come home summers and continue to hang out at the ballpark, working whenever possible, and working out with the club when allowed. His break came in the summer of 1988, when Larry Haney, the bullpen catcher, had to go home to attend to a family matter, and with the Brewers on the road, Juan Nieves, Teddy Higuera, and Bill

Wegman, who were all on the disabled list, needed someone to catch them at the stadium.

Jim Gantner was one of those who pushed him to go on with his own playing career, to work as hard as he could at it before giving up on it, but Ron found the offer of a job as bullpen catcher irresistible. "That's when I gave up on being a player, and I did it gladly. I was in a Brewers uniform with the name Nedset on the back, and I was making more money than I would be if I were playing A ball. I know I had some talent, but I see too many guys with more talent who never get the breaks and never make it up. So here I am, and here I hope to stay."

Almost unique in taking the route from minor league batboy to major league player is Johnny Pesky. (Ray Oyler, who went from Indianapolis batboy to Detroit shortstop and who is blessed with many of the best one-liners in Bouton's *Ball Four*, is the only other I have been able to identify.) Approaching sixty years in baseball, Pesky spoke with me during a rain delay in Pawtucket where, a month shy of his seventy-first birthday, he was managing the most important Red Sox farm team. He told of growing up in Portland, Oregon, in the 1930s, one of a gang of about a dozen baseball-crazy kids who hung around the Portland Beavers. Their grounds keeper, Rocky Benevento, took a liking to Johnny and got him ("let me," as Pesky puts it, as if he were whitewashing Tom Sawyer's fence) to keep the bullpen and coaching boxes in order, then took him at age twelve or thirteen into the clubhouse as batboy.

Among the fringe benefits of this job was the privilege to use the ballpark and facilities, while the club was on the road, for the kids' own team, called the "Baby Beavers." But Pesky treasures the memory of some of the "nice, nice men" in that clubhouse, including Bob Johnson (that's the late "Indian Bob," younger brother of Roy Johnson, both with lifetime .296 batting averages in their major league careers), who preceded Pesky to the majors by a decade. As a Red Sox rookie, Pesky tripled against the A's and expected some kind of reaction from the older player whose shoes he'd shined many times. But what he got was an amused laugh and a benign remark: "You got around to third so fast I thought someone was chasing you."

Pesky was a young-looking twenty-two when he came up to the Red Sox, and he followed what became a life-long habit, getting to the ballpark early. Johnny Orlando, the equipment manager, would take a look at him and see the kid batboy, not the rising star player (ten years in the American League, .306 career batting average, though losing three full seasons to wartime service), and say, "Grab a brush." Old habits die hard. Johnny Pesky, as a major league short-stop, actually caught himself shining his teammates' shoes. No wonder he has always been regarded by the kids who worked in his clubhouses as particularly sensitive to them and appreciative of their efforts.[15]

About half of the current equipment managers and visiting club-house managers for major league baseball clubs started out in base-ball as batboys. And of those, several batboyed for minor league teams. For Jim Wiesner of the Twins and Mike Murphy of the Gi-ants, it was a case of being in the right place at the right time. Originally batboys for the St. Paul Saints and the San Francisco Seals, respectively, they benefited from the moves of major league franchises into their cities. But the classic up-from-the-minors story belongs to Frank Coppenbarger, the man who in recent seasons has set the Philadelphia Phillies clubhouse in order. Coppenbarger grew up in Decatur, Illinois, and baseball was always the most important thing on his mind. Every day of Little League practice, he walked past the ballpark that was the home of the Commodores, a Giants farm team where Gary Matthews, Don Hahn, John Montefusco, and Steve Ontiveros spent some time. Coppenbarger became batboy in 1967; he was ten and still in elementary school, and his father bought him a little uniform with the number 10.

Coppenbarger remembers how the general manager would sit in the stands, chase down foul balls, and return them to the field, tossing them over the low screen to the batboy. One night one of those balls eluded Coppenbarger and rolled away toward the back-stop at precisely the moment that the pitcher threw a wild one. The balls came to rest about two feet apart, and catcher, umpires, and managers scratched their heads for a long time before the game was resumed with just one slightly used ball in play.

The biggest night of the year at the Decatur ballpark was General Electric night. The company distributed thousands of tickets and gave out many prizes to fans who held the winning stubs. Coppen-barger's cousin from Sacramento was visiting that week, and of course he was there to watch the Commodores, having picked up maybe fifty of those tickets to deposit for the drawing at the game. Naturally, the batboy was the one to pull the winning numbers out of the barrel, and the grand prize went to none other than his California cousin. The gift was supposed to be a fancy stereo set along with free delivery and installation. General Electric reneged on the delivery.

If the club hadn't folded in Coppenbarger's senior year of high school, he might never have left Decatur. There followed two years at Milliken College, the high points of which were visits to Danville, eighty miles away, for baseball. But in 1977 he was back in baseball, working in the clubhouse for the Angels Quad-Cities team in Davenport, Iowa. Ned Berger, now the Angels trainer, was there, and the manager was Chuck Cottier, now third base coach for the Cubs. One of the most impressive sites in Davenport for Coppenbarger was the Unser house, with its batting cage and pitching machine in the backyard. Al Unser had a brief wartime career in the majors, and had managed the Quad-Cities team at one time. Two of his sons, Larry and Jerry, were clubhouse kids working with Coppenbarger, but their brother Del was already an established major leaguer. Now both Frank Coppenbarger and Del Unser are with the Phillies, the latter as director of minor league operations.

Coppenbarger's serious commitment to baseball was demonstrated by his willingness to work the clubhouse for the Angels instructional league team in Arizona, from September through November, for three hundred dollars a month. But when Cottier moved up to the California League club in Salinas in 1978, Coppenbarger went with him. At spring training with the Angels in 1979, they were penciled in as manager and equipment manager for the AAA club in Las Vegas, but Coppenbarger's deal fell through when Cottier signed on with the Mets as third base coach.

The professional relationship with Cottier had meant a lot to Coppenbarger, and they remain close personal friends, but in a sense the end of that direct connection was a break for Coppenbarger. It was at that point that he signed on with the Cardinals organization, running their AAA clubhouse in Springfield, Illinois, and working year-round doing some ticket sales and advertising. During the annual exhibition game with the Cards at Springfield in the spring of 1980, he made a single mention to Butch Yatkeman that if there ever was an opening in St. Louis he would like to be considered for a job in a major league clubhouse.

The following spring that opportunity came, but like everything else in baseball it was delayed by the strike. The job was waiting in St. Louis, but Coppenbarger remained in Springfield, running the clubhouse, playing host among the minor league players to manager Whitey Herzog and general manager Lee Thomas of the Cardinals, who were there almost every day. When settlement came, he could finally move over to the big-league clubhouse, working as one of the assistants to his "hero," Butch Yatkeman. So there he was to experience the thrills of the 1982 season when Whitey's brilliant handling of a questionable pitching staff brought a pennant and World Series title to St. Louis, when Butch Yatkeman got to throw out the ceremonial first ball, and when for the only time in major league history an equipment manager was given a special "day" at the stadium.

When Lee Thomas moved over to the Phillies as general manager, among those he took with him were Nick Leyva as manager and Frank Coppenbarger as equipment manager. It was a long way up for Coppenbarger, an ascent from humble origins that seems a modern American version of folklore's "male-Cinderella" motif. But the comfortable efficiency of the Philadelphia clubhouse in 1990 paid tribute to the lessons he learned along the way, including consideration for the kids who worked there, a healthy respect for baseball loyalties, and the positive model of Butch Yatkeman.

For Yatkeman himself, barnstorming, a now-forgotten aspect of travel in baseball, highlights some of his choicest memories (as it highlights some of the best baseball fiction, such as Brashler, Charyn, Herrin, and Sayles). Cardinals batboy from 1924 to 1931 and equipment manager from 1932 to 1982, Yatkeman takes special delight in recalling off-season fishing and hunting trips with Pepper Martin ("even though I never shot my gun") and the scene of the whole bunch of barnstormers (Paul Derringer, Martin, the Dean brothers, and Jimmy Wilson) sitting around after the games in 1932 and divvying up the take.

In *How Life Imitates the World Series*, Thomas Boswell calls spring training "The Season of Sweet Boredom" (44), and another of his titles is *Why Time Begins on Opening Day*, but Boswell knows as well as anyone that the second week of February, when pitchers and catchers report to begin training, is the real beginning of the new year. In Chaucer's words, "thanne longen folk to goon on pilgrimages."

Jeff Ross, equipment manager of the Toronto Blue Jays, is one of a legion of baseball people who treasure spring training. It is not just the ritual renewal of the new season but somehow proof of continuity, of resilience, of survival. The familiar faces, friendships, and routines reinforce the sense of traditions, which in turn provide a reassurance of permanence in the subculture that is the world of baseball. For Ross, an extra measure of pleasure is provided by his practice of getting kids from the stands to serve as batboys. What often happens, he says, is that the same boys come back spring after spring, like the swallows to Capistrano, to take part in those celebrations of renewal.

Scratch any old-timer (and that includes former batboys) for his best baseball stories and he will inevitably come up with reminiscences that bring back the old itch to get to Florida. In *The Short Season*, David Falkner chronicles the pilgrimage he made when the lure of spring training was too much for a writer to resist. A highly personal account, it nevertheless illuminates aspects and figures of the subculture. His view of Eddie Murray, for example, confirms the batboys' views presented in these pages. And one of the episodes most gratifying to author and this reader alike is the encounter with the late Jimmy Reese (38–45), companion of the Babe, mentor and coach to several baseball generations, and fungo hitter extraordinaire, who began his career as a batboy.

For Fred Baxter, a Senators batboy in 1931–32 under Walter Johnson and later for several decades a clubhouse man in Washington, the thought of spring training takes him back to the time when his wife Doris, later to be mother of two batboys herself, made her first trip to Orlando. The clubhouses then did not have clothes dryers, so there was Fred showing off his handiwork that included three clotheslines full of jockstraps, when Doris banged her head against one and yelled, "Hey! What's in that thing?" And that was her initiation into the concept of cups.

George Catloth, who joined the batboying crew at Griffith Stadium a year after Fred, remembers the two of them going fishing in Florida and, on a slow news day, providing the feature story and picture when Fred ended up with a fishhook in his head. And, typically, that story triggers another, about the time when Casey Stengel brought a bad Dodgers team in for exhibition games with the Senators and went too far with his complaints about the way Beans Reardon was calling balls and strikes. Reardon gave a clear warning—"Once more and it's your ass"—only to have Casey emerge from the dugout with his hands spread wide to approximate the distance a called strike had missed the plate. The umpire turned

Frankly in awe of Eddie Murray, Kevin Cashen knew the slugger to be quite different from the way fans and media perceived him. (courtesy of Kevin Cashen)

to see the gesture and was about to toss him, when Stengel addressed his catcher in a conversational tone about a "fish that big."

Golf was another Florida diversion from baseball. Catloth remembers a clear demonstration of Wes Ferrell's famous temper. A perfectionist, whether on the mound or pitching horseshoes or playing golf, Ferrell one day threw his whole bag of clubs in the lake on an Orlando course and then said to the caddy, "If you go down there for them I'll throw *you* in the lake."

Tom Villante, who batboyed for the Yankees in 1944–45, didn't get to spring training until 1950. He had shown enough promise as an infielder, with Frank Crosetti teaching him to switch-hit and George Stirnweiss teaching him how to pivot on double plays at second base, that the Yankees had arranged for a college scholarship for him. Lou Boudreau had offered to arrange one at Illinois, but Villante was awarded the William P. Coughlin Scholarship at Lafayette. (Coughlin, an alumnus, had played nine years at third base in the majors at the turn of the century.) Villante played two years of varsity basketball, four of baseball, and worked summers for the Yankees, playing summer league ball whenever possible.

Now, degree in hand, he was having his shot in a Yankee uniform at second base, but the first time he took his position for infield drill, a brash twenty-one-year-old named Billy Martin shouted at him, "Hey, move over to short, I'm the second baseman." The same "fresh kid" a couple of days later in Miami Stadium was yelling at Jackie Robinson, calling him an "old pigeon-toed bum." Martin thus helped Villante decide not to spend years trying to make it as a marginal infielder. But it also helped that Villante had sold an idea to United Features for a "My Day in Baseball" column with Joe DiMaggio. Villante "seized the media moment," and by the time the Yankees had swept the Phillies in the 1950 World Series (with Jerry Coleman the regular second baseman, Martin having only thirty-six at-bats all season), Villante was ghosting a Phil Rizzuto column for the International News Service and doing publicity at Batten, Barton, Durstine & Osborn on his way to eminent success in his career.

Spring training, whether in Florida or the Southwest, has often been where would-be batboys have earned their way into clubhouses for the season. John Dykowski performed well for Jim Schmakel in Lakeland in 1989 and landed in the Detroit clubhouse for two seasons. Tony Atlas, having bombarded the Angels with weekly letters for almost a year, finally got a response saying, not now but if you're still interested next year, come to Palm Springs in March and we'll see. He did (taking a couple of weeks off from high school to do so), Mickey Shishido liked the way he worked, and from 1977 to 1981 he was part of the batboy crew in Anaheim. Tim Buzbee had preceded Atlas by two years and got his start the same way. Paying his own way to Palm Springs in the spring of 1975, he made himself useful in Shishido's clubhouse and as soon as there was an opening—right before the season started, as it happened—he was hired.

For Mike Murphy, spring in Arizona became a regular part of his year beginning in 1961, when Horace Stoneham asked him to help groundskeeper Mattie Schwab build the fields for the Giants' Casa Grande facility. "It was like *Field of Dreams*," he says, "building grass and seeing fields grow out of the sand of the desert, Mattie showing me how to make a ballfield out of nothing."

For Wes Patterson, spring training was always more like a pilgrimage for the faithful than a vacation of choice or a busman's holiday. He had started batboying for Kansas City in the summer of 1983 and, seven years later, still working in the clubhouse while waiting for his training to start in the police academy, laments that he has only made it to Florida twice, once to Fort Myers and once to Baseball City—boardwalk and baseball. "It's a different world," he says, "not a hundred percent serious, but a lot of fun, going to the beach and out to dinner, especially when you get to stay with George Brett."

John Nelson has been with the Tigers organization since his batboy years, 1979–82. "I'm a clubhouse man," he says, "it's in my heart." Spring training was always his favorite time because he had authority then, running the visiting-side clubhouse as assistant equipment manager. During his four years in the air force, Nelson would save up his leave time all year in order to take a full thirty days to go to spring training. During his last year in the service, when he got married, that meant forgoing a honeymoon for the joys of baseball in Lakeland. Now, as a minor league clubhouse and equipment manager, it's almost like spring training all year round for him.

Mark and Jim Sassetti, brothers who batboyed for the White Sox, always tried to spend their spring breaks from school hanging out with the club on Florida's west coast. There they got to pal around with players like Ozzie Guillen, himself proud of having once been a batboy for Roberto Clemente. The Sarasota County Fair was a big attraction for them, and Mark describes Guillen "like a kid, playing two rounds of miniature golf and then blowing fifty bucks on video games in the arcades." Jim treasures a souvenir picture taken at the Fair, with Guillen and another batboy posing as "wranglers" while Jim's head appears on the figure of the western "lady."

One night, Guillen got in a batting cage and started putting on a clinic, calling his shots like a pool shark. An old guy standing next to Mark said, "Hey, this guy's good—he might be able to play semipro ball in the Coast League." "Are you a coach?" deadpanned Mark.

"Yeah," said the old-timer, wondering, "What's his position?" "Shortstop," Mark understated about the American League gold glover. "No," said the coach, "he's too small to be a shortstop."

For two Washington, D.C., schoolboys, invitations to work in the clubhouse came because their father was the Washington *Post*'s beat reporter for the Senators. Every February Shirley and Ethel Povich would move to Florida, taking David and Maury out of school and putting them in school in Orlando. "It was so bad," Maury remembers, "that they let us out at noon because we'd already done everything we had to," and their dad had no qualms about asking Clark Griffith to put them to work in the clubhouse.

David worked the springs of 1946 and 1947, his vivid memories of Orlando staying with him during his years at Yale and Columbia Law School, through his almost twenty years as a litigator for Williams & Connelly (the baseball connection having been renewed when the late Edward Bennett Williams, a partner in the firm, became principal owner of the Baltimore Orioles). Off the top of his head, the first thing that leapt from David's recollections was, "Dr. Pepper—that clubhouse was my first introduction to Dr. Pepper." He went on to reminisce about Tinker Field, the Angebilt Hotel, and Berger's Tavern, where his dad hung out with Arch McDonald and other writers; the endless games of hearts; coach Clyde Milan, who had played sixteen seasons for the Senators, at sixty hitting fungoes for hours at a stretch (Milan died during spring training in Orlando in 1953); the toughness of Early Wynn, who was all business even in Florida, believing that every batter was trying to take money out of his pocket; and learning the art of dressing in a baseball uniform so that both pairs of socks and pants all fit right together.

"Clearly the biggest influence on me was Eddie Yost as a rookie. I used to stay with him, doing everything he did, spending hours learning to slide; we'd slide till the skin came off our ass. I'd stand next to him when he was getting coached, next to the cage for batting instruction, learn with him to round the bases the right way, and learn never to flinch at bat or in the field. He was my model as a very hard worker, and I watched him start from nothing, with *some* talent of course, and make himself into a star." Four years as varsity third baseman at the Landon School was David's direct legacy from the Yost model, but clearly the hard-work ethic has paid off in his own career. Yost, incidentally, was so influential a figure for Fred Baxter that his son Eddie is named after him, and Yost was godfather to both John and Eddie Baxter, who eventually were batboys for the Senators (though the Baxters, unlike the Poviches, did not change schools during spring training).

Maury Povich's stints as batboy and ballboy were in 1948, 1949, and 1950, though he had helped out in the clubhouse before that. He remembers being more in awe of managers, first Ossie Bluege and then Joe Kuhel, who were scarier to the kids than the players. But where brother David remembers the Dr. Peppers, Maury remembers the Lucky Strikes and learning in the clubhouse, at nine, how to smoke and swear. Other figures who loom large in his recollection are Early Wynn, Mickey Grasso, and Cecil Travis. Then there was Gil Coan, reputedly the fastest man in the league, but Maury remembers how laboriously every day he'd have to wrap ankles terribly tender from eczema; and catcher Jake Early, whom Maury thought the strongest man alive because he would throw one Povich kid over one shoulder, the other over the other shoulder, and then pick up a third kid between his legs.

A decade later, Maury couldn't get over the teaming up of catcher Clint Courtney and pitcher Hal Woodeschick in Washington uniforms. Each, it seemed, had a phobia about intentional walks: one could hardly get the ball back to the mound and the other could hardly avoid wild pitches. But Povich's perspective by that time had shifted from a boy's field's-eye view to that of a trained media professional. The commentator's vantage may have been anticipated in the boy's eye, though, as when he remembers Babe Ruth's visit to the ballpark in Orlando during his last winter, 1948, with a camel's-hair overcoat and cap covering him from head and shoulders to shins. "I knew he must have been very sick," Maury says, "to be so covered up in the March heat of Florida."

At sixteen, Maury had forsaken the clubhouse for the broadcasting booth. He became a gofer for Bob Wolf, from whom he "first learned the importance of accuracy" for a broadcaster. As "assistant director and stats man I had to keep him up to the minute on factual matters—who was warming up, et cetera." And the work ethic that so impressed his brother got through to Maury as well. In fact, he laments the changes brought to the game by free agency and long-term contracts, because, "in the baseball I remember, nobody ever *didn't* put out all the time."

Roy Firestone, now host of ESPN's nightly "Up Close" show, worked as spring training batboy for the Orioles in 1971 and 1972.

He remembers just showing up at Miami Stadium, then the spring home of the Marlins and the Baby O's, asking Clay Reid for a job, and being hired starting the next day. That night he had his mother rehearse the drive to the stadium. Rehearsal was part of Firestone's way of life; at fifteen he was already a kid comedian working Miami Beach clubs.[16] And playing hookey to work as a batboy, he says, was like running away from home to join the circus.

He was not an athletic child, but an avid fan and collector. Excited at being in the clubhouse with Don Baylor, Don Buford, Bobby Grich, Dave May, Mike Cuellar, and Paul Blair, and thrilled to be sent out for ribs by Boog Powell, he was also so clumsy that he didn't know how to run in spikes and slipped and fell the first day on the concrete ramp to the field. In fact, he had to be shown by pitcher Marcelino Lopez how to put on his sanitaries. (Firestone can't resist doing his Lopez impression: "You no do this this way . . . .")

But it wasn't long before he felt comfortable enough to start entertaining the players in the clubhouse. Ten minutes of shtick before workouts became part of the day's routine, which featured impressions of Richard Nixon and others. Most of the players, but especially Jim Palmer, loved his Earl Weaver impression. Frank Robinson, he says, didn't really approve of the whole idea of clubhouse shtick then, but now gives grudging approval. Brooks Robinson, however, Firestone found to be the most decent and pleasant of guys, one who would ask an awkward kid to play pepper with him. Firestone's son Andrew has the middle name Brooks in Robinson's honor.

One day that first spring, the late Ralph Salvon, the O's trainer, walked up to Firestone and asked, "Are you our new batboy?" "Yes," Firestone said, not knowing what was going on. "And you're the one that tries to be a comedian?" "Yeah," said Firestone, smiling now, but perhaps a bit uneasily. "Well," said Salvon, "you're the worst fucking batboy we've ever had. You got a lot of smarts, kid, but you're a terrible batboy."[17]

It is not surprising that what stand out in Firestone's memory are incidents with a show-biz slant, not athletic performances but pieces of business, material for bits. He remembers traveling on buses with the club, working thirty-five or forty consecutive games, doing the whole grapefruit circuit, and one of his favorite stories takes place on the bus. They were passing numerous low-lying Florida ponds along the coastline and spotted a huge alligator in one.

Curt Motton, a reserve outfielder from Darnell, Louisiana, started telling bayou tales, gator stories in the rural southern black tradition. When he got to the one that begins, "Saw a gator eat a horse once," it was too much for pitcher Pete Richert, whose urban savvy originated in Floral Park, New York. "Cuz," he said, "there's no way an alligator can eat a horse." That stopped Motton for a while, but after giving it some thought, he had a classic response: "Hm, maybe not, but he can *try*."

In the spring of 1990, Firestone went to Arizona to perform for the Orioles "Dream Game" promotion. Now the players were getting *his* autograph on *their* ball, and somehow it didn't feel right or good to him. "It was the greatest feeling in the world," he says, "to go back in the clubhouse and hear the laughter, Blair's unmistakable high-pitched cackle, and hear Boog still telling tall tales. Doing standup again for Palmer and Boog was one of the most pleasurable experiences of my career. A reaffirming feeling came over me, a wave. It's all about the game, the interaction and fraternity of men, being themselves in the clubhouse, away from fans and media. When the press is around, it's always a performance. But this was like getting locked in on reality."

Baseball seems to evoke new ways of distinguishing between reality and fantasy. If the really real is that world in which time gives way to timelessness, and if the clubhouse is like a magic Forest of Arden in the naive, committed, devotional eyes of its batboy attendants, then no wonder that spring training has the powerful grip it maintains. From the perspective in which the Game is all, a purity is attained only when the individual games *don't count*.

In the road trip account of Fred Weisman, every single game is one that matters. Weisman, after more than forty years as a litigator, heads a firm of eleven trial lawyers in Cleveland (including a brother, a son, and a daughter-in-law). But in 1936 nine-year-old Freddie was featured in a Boston *Globe* story headlined "He's the Envy of Millions of Kids Throughout the Nation," with three pictures of him in a Cleveland Indians uniform, including one with Hal Trosky, whose number 7 he shared, and one with his father Lefty, the Indians trainer.

As Weisman tells his father's story, it begins with a tough kid from Chelsea literally fighting his way to the corner of Boylston Street and Massachusetts Avenue in Boston for one of the best newspaper-selling locations in town, where he was befriended by the great Tris

Speaker, then playing for the Red Sox. Speaker told the paper boy that if he ever got to be a manager he would make him his trainer, which I suppose is the kind of thing one would promise a kid without either party believing it completely. But when Speaker took over the Indians as playing manager in 1919, Max David Weisman soon joined the club as trainer, taking the assignment so seriously that he went to night school to learn training techniques.

Fred was born in Cleveland during Speaker's last year at the helm, 1926. (This was the great period of playing managers: during Speaker's tenure at Cleveland, Ty Cobb, George Sisler, and Eddie Collins all managed while playing in the American League, Rogers Hornsby in the National.) But Fred's father, whose manipulation of players' backs was widely known to be as therapeutic as his mother's chicken soup, had become a fixture with the Indians. "She was a very tolerant woman," Fred recalls of his mother, "but she wouldn't let Babe Ruth, whom she called a 'vulgar, rotten degenerate' come into the house." In 1932, Fred's brother was born and given the name Jed from the first initials of the fine Indians outfield—Joe Vosmik, Earl Averill, and Dick Porter. Much later, Jed Weisman would be the Ohio Wesleyan battery mate of Roger Peckinpaugh's son.

Fred's memories of that 1936 road trip include nice touches of father-son togetherness. Lefty, who loved playing games and tricks as much as the horses ("he was known far and wide as a handicapper," says Fred, "so good he left an estate of $400 when he died"), took Fred to a Chinese restaurant in Philadelphia where he persuaded the waiter that the nine-year-old was the owner of the Indians and he the boy's guardian. What's more, he left two tickets for the waiter and his girlfriend at the ballpark to prove it. That was where seventeen-year-old Bob Feller joined the team. "We were about equals intellectually," says Fred, "so we became friends right away." When Feller got his uniform, Fred remembers, he said to Lefty, "My hat's too large," and the trainer shot back, "Make sure it stays that way." One indication that it did was Feller's habit of getting to the ballpark at 9:30 instead of 11 when he was supposed to.

In Boston on that trip, aside from the flattering feature in the *Globe*, Fred had another thrill at Fenway Park. While the infield was being dragged, he ran out to the outfield with Earl Averill and promptly made a nice catch of a fly ball off the fungo bat of pitcher

Lloyd (Gimpy) Brown. Averill told him to doff his cap, and when he did there was great applause from the crowd. But the best part of the trip was that it was the best baseball the club played all year under Steve O'Neill, and Fred was considered a good luck charm. It was especially good for Fred's hero, Trosky, who was on his way to league-leading numbers in RBI (162) and total bases (and errors for a first baseman), runner-up to Gehrig with 42 home runs and a .644 slugging percentage, and a .343 batting average with 216 hits. Fred Weisman has had many wins since the summer of 1936 but perhaps none as gratifying as those he was part of for his and his dad's Cleveland Indians.

A few more representative stories of road trips and their significance to batboys will demonstrate the sacral nature of the experience. Many of them are describing a first experience of travel, so that staying in hotels and eating in restaurants and going out on the major league towns in the company of major league players all takes on an aura of wondrous passage and of communion. And it is interesting how, despite working long hours in one ballpark, they are often overwhelmed by the feelings evoked in others. Fred Mueller, coming east with the California Angels, is awed by "old, old Tiger Stadium, which just reeks of baseball," while Dave Cowart, traveling with the Tigers, called it "a thrill to shag flies in Fenway and stand at the plate looking out at the wall."

Yankee Stadium seems to have the most profound effects, "standing out for the outrageous fans," not the monuments, according to Jim Sassetti. A highlight of Steve Maunakea's time with the Oakland A's was when he "got to pitch batting practice in Yankee Stadium. I felt chills to be where Ruth and DiMaggio played, butterflies. The fans are wild there, not like regular fans everywhere. I couldn't get the ball over the plate, think I hit a couple of guys."

For Tony Atlas, another Angels batboy, the eastern trip produced other kinds of feelings: "The best trip for me was '79, when I had just turned eighteen, to Baltimore, Boston, and New York. Orioles batboy Kevin Cashen took me out with him, and I was shocked when a kid Kevin knew saw us in a club and called him a nigger-lover. Then it was worse in Boston. Rod Carew had warned me not to get into it with fans there because 'East Coast attitudes are different.' Sure enough, another batboy and I were walking to Fenway Park with Willie Mays Aikens when some guy threw a 7-Up bottle from a car at the other batboy, shouting 'nigger-lover' at him. But New York I loved, bright lights, party life, bars with gorgeous women—it was an eye-opening experience."

The glamour and license of life on the road are what impress the batboys, but everything is enhanced—or blessed—because of the company of players. To be looked out for by Carl Yastrzemski and Reggie Smith or by Kirby Puckett and Kent Hrbek or by Brooks Robinson and Boog Powell is to be glorified by association. And it is a free ride to glory. Tommie Ferguson still remembers a western trip in 1947, riding the trains to St. Louis and Chicago: "I was given meal money but I never was allowed to pick up a check. Lunch, breakfast, anything—someone on the team always took care of me." Mario Alioto remembers Jim Barr of the Giants taking up a collection for the kids on their trip to Los Angeles. Rene Lachemann recalls the generosity of the Dodgers: "On road trips the players passed the hat for us in lieu of a per diem, and they were a generous bunch—Sandy Koufax, Don Drysdale, Duke Snider, Maury Wills, John Roseboro, and especially Gil Hodges." And Phil Cline remembers the former Dodger Leo Durocher, when he was managing the Cubs, as being "somewhat distant from the kids, but when we went on a road trip he put the arm on the players to pitch in for expense money for us."

The whole business of paying for things is a lesson in appropriate behaviors that take on the qualities of rituals and taboos. With the Cardinals on his first trip, a twelve-day West Coast jaunt in 1967, Don Deason tried to pay for himself at a lunch counter in San Francisco. Johnny Romano, a ten-year veteran catcher, stopped him, saying, "Don't reach for a check unless you're ready to pay for everyone." But on occasion, the lesson in tradition could have an extra comic effect, as Chad Blossfield recalls about 1956 with the Milwaukee Braves: "We got to take the last road trip of the year with the team, and they gave us twelve dollars a day meal money. In Cincinnati there were four of us kids stuffing ourselves in a fine restaurant when Frank Torre saw us. He was dining with this gorgeous blonde, and of course he picked up our check. He didn't know that we'd each ordered two steak dinners plus strawberry shortcake. Back home in Milwaukee, Torre stands up in the clubhouse and announces, 'Don't ever pick up the check for these guys.'"

The road trip, for some batboys, includes sexual initiation. "That's where I got my sex education," says one, and another recalls Cincinnati as the place where a player fixed up all three traveling kids with a "baseball Annie" named Pearl. The players all knew about it: one came banging on their door, claiming to be the hotel cop, and on the train ride home, the team's star pitcher walked up and down the aisle saying, "Yep, ol' Pearl's got the clap again." Hotel lobbies, not ballparks, are where the presence of groupies is most apparent, and as Mark Sassetti observes, "There's not much alcohol in the clubhouse, either, but lots of it in lobby bars on the road." In the face of these impressions it is even more impressive when a batboy hears his idol, a Hall-of-Fame slugger, through the wall of their adjoining hotel rooms, talking to his wife on the phone late at night, telling her of his loneliness and how he loves her.

Bob Elder remembers traveling to Washington with the Angels and being so obviously hung over at the ballpark that his boss, Ferguson, wouldn't let him suit up as batboy. But poor Jeff Sipos, who got sick on some Cantonese dish in Boston's Chinatown, was presumed to have had too much to drink and fined for missing batting practice at Fenway Park. Kevin Cashen, flying back to Baltimore from a trip west, discovered that two beers were too many for his ninety-pound frame, and when he was seen stumbling off the plane Ken Singleton let him hear about it.

The road is a place to learn things about people by seeing them in a different context. Cashen knew Eddie Murray (both were rookies in 1977) only as a shy guy who didn't deal well with the press. But on a trip to Los Angeles the next year, Murray took him home for dinner, along with Lee May, Pat Kelly, Al Bumbry, and Singleton, and he could see the "moody" star where he was most comfortable, at home. Cashen says, "I was sixteen but looked about twelve, and there I was, a curiosity with five large black major league players going to dinner at the Murray house in Watts. Eddie's five brothers and four sisters were there, and not one of them believed I'd never had ribs before."

Cashen's oldest brother Neil had always thought that Earl Weaver didn't like him because he seemed very distant to him in the Orioles clubhouse. Then, on a trip to Detroit, the manager took him out to dinner and said, "How come you never asked my daughter out?" The favorite trip of another Cashen brother, Michael, included Cleveland, where he was taken "to an all-black disco club by Don Baylor, Kenny Singleton, and Earl Williams. What a thrill. There was no fear in me, not in the company of those three, but in the whole place there were only four white faces, three women and me. On the

Starry-eyed Kevin Cashen relished his time and trips among the Orioles players. (courtesy of Kevin Cashen)

whole, the best lessons I learned in the clubhouse were the positive ones about race relations."

In his understated way, Jimmy Triantas, who was with the Orioles in the eighties, conveys the overwhelming sense of privilege and elevation that comes with this experience. "Road trips," he says, "are a little bit different from working at home. You can catch the team bus with the guys and get there like a half hour before batting practice . . . . And it's more relaxed, you know. They gave me my own hotel room and I could go out to lunch or a movie with one of the players. Everybody's real nice to you, and you get to see so many great towns. Anaheim; Arlington, Texas; Chicago were great towns to go to. Yankee Stadium is a great experience just to walk in. You can feel the atmosphere of all the great players that played there. During batting practice I got a chance to walk out behind the fence and look at all the monuments. It's a great baseball place."

What comes through here is the awe, rather than the solemnity, and a sense of pride in having a place, however lowly, in the special world. Certainly there is no place for solemnity in Ed Baxter's memories of traveling with the Senators and watching Joe Coleman and Eddie Brinkman blowing their duck callers at other guests in their hotel. Nor in Sid Bordman's memory of his trip to Milwaukee in 1942 when the Kansas City team clinched the American Association championship: on the way home they stopped in Chicago for a party at the Black Hawk, "one of the first times in my life I wore a tie." (Incidentally, so enthralled was Bordman with the pilgrimage aspects of baseball that, retired from his career as a newspaper writer, he continues to work in the spring training press box for the Royals in Florida.) Nor in John Plein's most treasured recollection of a trip to Chicago and Pittsburgh with the Padres, when Gaylord Perry and he pulled childish practical jokes on each other, climaxing in a sockless run through the streets and a besieged hotel room. In Graig Nettles's book, incidentally, there is a suggestion that Perry got along better with batboys than with other players: "Gaylord was critical of his teammates, which he always has been in the past. He gets on players who make errors behind him" (106).

As for the awe, it comes in a variety of forms. Tom Villante was with the Yankees when, "on one trip to Chicago, I had a room to myself—except that I woke up in the morning to see a large, hairy-chested man shaving at my sink. It was Charlie Keller, just out of the merchant marines." When Bob Scherr traveled with the Orioles, their broadcaster, Chuck Thompson, would relay on-air messages to Bob's folks that he was having a good time. The good times included sleeping in Curt Blefary's room in 1965 so that the player could evade a bed-check and going to Los Angeles for the World Series in 1966 where Eddie Watt had teased him into believing that Ann-Margret would be his date after he finished batboying the game. For

Batboy John Plein with favorite player, Gaylord Perry, who often got along better with clubbies than with teammates (courtesy of John Plein)

Scherr the awe became a severe case of fear and trembling the time he saw a fight on the plane between pitcher Steve Barber and his coach Harry Brecheen. Manager Hank Bauer broke it up and then proceeded up and down the aisle, intimidating players and reporters alike into keeping silent about the incident. By the time Bauer got around to the traveling batboy Scherr could barely stammer that he wouldn't break the code.

As Steve Friend of Montreal tells it, the road trip confirmed his role as the innocent embarked upon a momentous voyage of initiation and acceptance. Even the most mundane aspects of travel take on magical properties for him, so that in a sense the innocence becomes fixed rather than dissipated. It seems worth listening to him in some detail.

> That [1987] was the year I took my first and only road trip with the guys, to Pittsburgh and New York. It was my first plane ride and I was really nervous, hardly said a word on the bus ride to the airport, though I was sitting with Wallace Johnson, Herm Winningham, and Dave Engle, all players I was pretty close to. It was a chartered flight. The players climbed in, fixed chairs so they could play cards, talk, heckle the stewardess, and all that. A good time. I just sat in the back of the plane with the guys I liked.
>
> I was nervous when the sign came on to tie your seatbelts. I looked around and no one was nervous, no one was tying their seatbelts as we went to the runway. These people travel, always on the road, in the air, for them it's nothing. We were picking up speed and Hubie Brooks stood up and leaned forward, sticking out his arms, hovering around. I loosened up, the flight went well, and the bus ride into Pittsburgh was unbelievable, with singing, the guys in a really good mood, adding their own variations about [manager] Buck Rodgers.
>
> Five days in Pittsburgh, then off to New York. Wallace Johnson was telling me that when they play "We Will Rock You" in Shea Stadium you need seatbelts in the dugout because people in the stands would shake it so much you'd fall off the bench. I knew it was a joke, playing on my anxiety about going to the big city. He said people in the stands would throw switchblades and bring in twelve-gauge shotguns, stories like that, just to make me nervous. I was.
>
> It was the night of a big storm, and flying just above the thunder-heads we could see lightning all around. There was some turbulence but the only one to get a little queasy was Jim Fanning, Expos manager a couple of years back in the time of Warren Cromartie and Bill Lee the Spaceman, now one of our radio announcers. Coming in on New

York the thunderheads cleared a little and I got my first glimpse of the city. I couldn't believe it, all the lights at 2 a.m. I'd never seen anything that big man-made—hard to describe how I felt.

Next day I saw the big difference between working at Olympic Stadium and at Shea. At Olympic, twenty thousand was a good day. No comparison to Shea—the atmosphere, the people in the parking lot with barbecues making a day out of going to a baseball field. They were all there at 3 p.m., four or five hours before the game. Buses stopped beside the entrance, crowded with people wanting autographs. Guards had to push the way through people so we could get in.

On the first day in New York, guys from the visiting clubhouse decided to play a little joke on me. They came over and said I should go see the visiting clubhouse manager and ask him about his mother who is a famous ballerina. I kind of wanted to fit in, and I guess I was kind of innocent, so I went over to see him and started talking to him. Then out popped the question: "The guys were telling me about your mother, a ballerina . . . ." He got mad, just started yelling at me, "You guys are always getting on me." He really rubbed my nose in it, and I felt like dirt.

I went back to the clubbies, said, "What's the deal? He chewed my ass off for that." They said, "You didn't really ask him that?" They were all acting surprised, then said that his mother was crippled, couldn't walk, had been in a wheelchair twenty years, and he was really sensitive about it. For three days then I felt like dirt, and every time I passed the man he'd give me a dirty look.

On the last day I knew I had to go see him, and I explained the clubbies had told me to say it. He said, "What? They didn't tell you? It's all a joke. There's nothing wrong with my mother. It's just one of our tricks—we had one guy going for over a week." I never felt that bad. Hard to believe. They said they only did it to confirm the rumor that guys from New York had no heart.

That little trip brought me closer to the guys—Wallace Johnson who was always looking out for me, Herm Winningham who took me out for my first taste of buffalo wings in Pittsburgh, and Dave Engle who used to go to the movies with me.

Joe Durso has said that "Baseball teams travel like the circus: together, town to town, tied tightly to the night's performance" (Ford, Mantle, and Durso 61). The circus metaphor is itself a baseball convention (see Firestone's use of it earlier in this chapter). Nettles opens the revealing account of *Balls* this way: "Some kids dream of joining the circus, others of becoming a major league baseball player. I have been doubly blessed. As a member of the New York Yankees, I have gotten to do both" (1). In Jim Ewell's experience, the metaphor became literal. He first entered the sacred precincts of the ballpark in Norfolk, Virginia, in 1932, because he followed the Ringling Brothers calliope and then the roar of the crowd.

Yet more meaningfully, it seems to me, the ceremonial aspects of travel with the club serve to reinforce the sacred nature of the subculture and to indoctrinate or initiate the novitiates (rookies, privileged batboys). Baseball travels in a closed circle, and neither innovations in the modes of travel nor expansion to new outposts on the circuit will alter the essence of that experience. That is why the tale of a boy traveling with the Indians in the 1930s sounds so much like that of a boy traveling with the Expos in the 1980s, savoring the legendary places and being blessed by the high spirits of and their own intimate contact with the heroes.

The effects on the hajjis, including their self-celebratory delight in the experience, may be sustained over time—more than half a century in Weisman's case—with all the attributed glow that nostalgia can supply. Fixed in memory as part of indoctrination into a true faith, the sagas of these pilgrimages sometimes come across as tales of old men glorying in the young times that somehow made them feel special, and somehow still do, the afterglow of having made it as accepted fellow travelers on the subculture's convivial tours of duty.

CHAPTER 5 The Central Pantheon

"Gods they were," says Donovan of the artists, artisans, and ceremonial leaders of the lost continent of Atlantis. The resident deities of baseball's clubhouses are similarly sunken from view, though frequently celebrated from a distance or by a perpetuation of mythology. But rarely has so intimate a view as that of the batboys ever been offered for public scrutiny.

A word about methodology is in order here, because this chapter has taken shape in a way distinct from the others. In the first place, I have been given a greater abundance of material from which to draw. Regardless of the questions asked or guidelines suggested to the sources, the responses invariably focused on the personalities, the characters, the very nature of the dominant personages of the clubhouse. Asked for anecdotes, former batboys gave me sketches of people; asked for scenarios, they gave me casts of characters; asked for attitudes and values, they gave me representative figures.

In the second place, however, certain restrictions were imposed on my use of that material. Unlike any other kind of material, much of this was given off the record, "on background," with a guarantee of anonymity and an insistence on retaining the privilege of confidentiality. Readers who turn to *Innocence and Wonder*, then, looking for the firsthand reports on which this chapter is based, will find much of it conspicuous by its absence.

To respect the conditions necessarily accepted, to construct a (defense) mechanism that compensates for my frustrations over these limitations, and to do a semblance of justice to the tantalizing wealth of material so gathered, I have devised the following game plan. The analysis will present *types* of characters. They are drawn from the ranks of the famous, the notorious, and the obscure personnel who dominate the memories of the former batboys, whether they are players, managers, coaches, or equipment managers. Concrete illustrations of the types will be offered, but not (except where explicitly authorized) by designating Batboy A naming Player B. Even where a familiar figure is identified, I have generally drawn from a consensus view of that figure, so that even a quoted remark about that figure may be unattributed because it typically could have been stated by several sources—often in identical language.

As for the typology itself, I have had to resort to invention. The best systems of classification of athletes I know appear in the work of Robert J. Higgs. He first identified eight types of hero: dumb jock, brute, bromide, hubristic hero, bum, darling, natural (folk hero), and absurd athlete. Then, as his dissertation evolved into his book *Laurel & Thorn*, he refined the taxonomy by arranging an expanded dramatis personae under the general headings of Apollo, Dionysus, and Adonis. But these, after all, are figures drawn not from what Robert Lipsyte calls SportsWorld but from Higgs's study of American literature. In *Dreaming of Heroes*, Michael Oriard chronicles with encyclopedic thoroughness the process by which American culture, defined without pejorative connotations as shallow but broad, has necessarily looked to artistic representations of sports to identify, define, and refine its heroic models. "Sport exists," he says, "in a sense, to create heroes, and sports fiction can be viewed from one perspective as a genre that defines exactly who the representative American hero is." But as he goes on from the (I think valid) premise that "American fascination with sports heroes consumes an enormous amount of psychic energy" (25) it becomes clear that the heroes are first identified in the sports and then mythologized in the fiction.

I would argue that the types I identify are the products of a mythologizing process that owes more to the limitations of a creative imagination that reaches for identifiable types and recognizable conventions in narrative components than to any "objective" examination of the real-live persons. According to my construction, the creation, identification, elevation, apotheosizing, and commemoration of heroic figures has more to do with cultural imagination than with history. Cultural history may identify the conditions out of which the heroic figures and their characteristic legends emerge, but it is the consensus of the devotees that identifies the types of leading characters and superimposes that grid on the projected profiles of the heroes they serve and thus *re*-create.

The grid operates in ways similar to the characterizations of dramatis personae in many theatrical traditions. The conventional character types may be called, simply, Miles Gloriosus, Senex, Eiron, Clown, Ingenue, and the like, and no further details are necessary. Playwright and audience, actor and costume designer, all know everything they need to know. Similarly, all a batboy has to hear is the term *Flake*, *Red-Ass*, or *Gamer* used in reference to a clubhouse character, and he automatically associates the type with the person.

One constant assumption underlies the batboys' views of these characters, namely, that whatever they are on the field in uniform or in the public eye as seen through the lenses of the media may be totally illusory. There is the commonly held and firm belief that what they are "really like" is the way they are seen in the clubhouse, the way they interact with the rest of the club off the field, offstage, off-mike, and off-camera, and perhaps most important the way they interact with the clubbies themselves. The heroes are themselves, as it were, when they have no clothes, at least in the eyes of those who serve them—in large part—by caring for their clothes, whether the costumes of their public role or their private wardrobe.

One other constant to be acknowledged here is the universal presupposition on the part of batboys that their function is to serve the players. The opportunity to do so is what brings the boys to the clubhouse in the first place, but that first order of business is reinforced by both the injunctions of the equipment managers and the enacted assumptions of the players. The obedience to assigned roles thus becomes both a fixture of the batboy's self-image and an influence on the labels they assign to others and the categories in which they experience them.[18] A concomitant rule of thumb is that the batboys will adopt the players' views of managers, other management figures, and the media.

The most nearly monolithic personage in this view of the clubhouse is the minor resident deity who presides over it, the equipment manager. He serves the batboys in loco parentis and the batboys respond to him almost universally as a father figure. "He practically raised us" is a phrase I heard batboys echo dozens of times in reminiscences about their former bosses. Moreover, the father-son relationship is suggested by legacies and inbred generations of clubhouse men. From the legendary Pete Sheehy of the Yankees and the equally revered Butch Yatkeman of the Cardinals down to the present, many of the major league clubhouse bosses began their careers in baseball as batboys themselves. Currently that list includes Dennis Liborio in Houston, Mike Wallace in Miami, Brian Prilaman in San Diego, Jeff Sipos in Cleveland, Jim Tyler in Baltimore (along with his brother Fred on the visiting side), Buddy Bates in St. Louis (along with Jerry Risch on the visiting side), Tony Migliaccio in Milwaukee, Mike Murphy in San Francisco, Frank Coppenbarger in Philadelphia, and Jim Wiesner in Minnesota (the last three having served as minor league batboys). Extending back in time, the list would also include Frank and Fred Baxter of the Senators, Ray Crump of the Twins, Leonard Garcia of the Angels, Kenny Bush of the Phillies, Don Fitzpatrick of the Red Sox, and Tommie Ferguson of the Braves.

Like father, like son, each passes on his authoritative admonitions about understanding the nature of the job, about respecting not only the rules but the customs of the baseball clubhouse (including total commitment to privacy), about getting the work done promptly so as to be able to enjoy the perquisites, about maintaining appropriate levels of achievement in education so that the job never becomes a liability by taking precedence over school (that the job is a privilege earned by scholastic achievement and integrity), and about applying themselves to the pursuit of worthwhile careers, whether in baseball, the professions, or law enforcement. To a man, this tutelary deity is seen as practicing what he preaches, and the phrase most often applied to him (other than the one that suggests fosterfatherhood) is "unsung hero."

The monolithic nature of this clubhouse figure serves to maintain the traditions and constancy of the culture and to perpetuate the set of values he embodies and enacts. Players and managers are relatively transient sojourners in any clubhouse while an equipment manager tends to serve several generations of personnel over multiple decades. But none of this is to say that there is no individualism among the breed. They may be stern taskmasters like Fred Baxter or Mark Stowe of Cincinnati, quietly efficient practitioners like Frank Coppenbarger and Buddy Bates (both alumni of the Butch Yatkeman school), or companionable clubmen like Mike Murphy and Dennis Liborio. In Chicago alone, there is a clear contrast between veterans Yosh Kawano and Chicken Willie Thompson.[19] Kawano's devoted presence is as characteristic of Wrigley Field as the ivied bricks, while Thompson's antic nature is a treasure that has carried over from old to new Comiskey Park as well as his concerned fostering of at least one clubhouse attendant who would have nowhere to turn if his time at the ballpark were terminated.

In Detroit, Jim Schmakel stands out in the performance of his protective function; he not only keeps tightly closed the gates of his players' privacy but also shelters his teenage charges from exposure and temptation at home and on the road. Like Baxter and Stowe, Joe Macko in Texas and Frank Ciensczyk in Oakland have supervised their own sons or stepsons in the clubhouse without any deviation from the standard code. The ties of the boys to these men are thicker than blood: it is the relationship of apprentices to masters, including both initiation and performance rites as well as the inculcation of entire belief systems. No wonder these generally unsung heroes are uniformly featured and honored as their disciples nostalgically sing their praises. And when former batboys revisit clubhouses, the traditionally announced purpose is reunion with the chief.

Owners, managing partners, player personnel directors, general managers, and the like rarely descend to the clubhouse level, that is, rarely *ascend* into the consciousness of batboys in their cloistered Olympus. From their perspective, the ultimate authority is vested in the (field) manager, the skipper, the old man. The sense of awe inspired by managers is what most frequently defines batboys' views of them. But so often was their power coupled, paradoxically, with an impression of physical limitations or actual diminutiveness that I began thinking of them as the legendary Seven Dwarfs of baseball. At least that analogue emerged once the descriptions began to fall into a pattern of seven types, but I suppose it would be just as appropriate, given the contradictory natures reported about some of these men, to call them, after Empson, Seven Types of Ambiguity.

The most readily identifiable type, perhaps because the specific label was so generally applied to the examples, is the *Red-Ass*, who habitually acts out his anger in the clubhouse. (It is almost too easy to call him Grumpy, but even though other types to be identified could be cast as Bashful, Happy, and Doc, I will take this conceit no further.) He is a profane shouter and blasphemous screamer, whose favorite attention-getting device is to throw, yank, push, topple, or otherwise dispatch to the floor the players' postgame spread. (Players will get themselves fed elsewhere, and no Red-Ass denies them beverages; the clubbies get to clean up the mess.) Minor temper tantrums will involve merely the projecting of smaller, imperishable, but equally fragile objects. The object, beyond venting, is to get attention. It usually works.

Typically, the Red-Ass is known just as well in public for his antics on and off the field as in the privacy of his clubhouse, so there are few surprises here (except in reverse, where on-field or otherwise public tantrums are contradicted by the "reality" of serene, quiet, sedate clubhouse behavior). Also, typically, it is losing that evokes the rage. It will shock no one to hear that Gene Mauch and Lou Piniella are among those most commonly identified as this type, but one performance of the former is worthy of note. It came after a *win*, a laugher produced by a tremendous offensive explosion by his club. Mauch was infuriated by the celebration in the clubhouse, because it came toward the end of a disappointing season, and he raged at his team, screaming that he had been telling them all along that they were capable of playing at this level. The reporting batboy, who already harbored managerial ambitions himself, says that it taught him not to take any single result too much to heart. As for Piniella, his reputation for "awesome temper" (as more than one clubby calls it) goes back to his playing days. In a typical memory, Piniella "struck out to end an inning. I was working the foul line and tossed him a ball between innings like I'm supposed to. He took it and threw it out over the upper deck."

Hank Bauer, whose belligerence was as likely to be physical as verbal, used the threat of his temper to intimidate, which puts him in some lofty company. Oddly enough, the clearest picture of Manager Red-Ass was drawn around the figure of a revered, hated, awe-inspiring Hall-of-Fame player, Ty Cobb. "He was the worst damn manager there was in baseball," says Eddie Forester, and it was clearly Cobb's behavior, in particular his habit of verbal abuse, Forester was passing judgment on. "Swear at the players, fight with 'em, and everything." If Cobb got mad at the batboy he would banish him from the field to spend the day in the clubhouse, and it could be for something as trivial as not polishing the insoles of otherwise perfectly shined shoes. Still, he appreciated it when Eddie would bring him a gallon of his special brand of orange juice. "Oh, but he was terrible, swear at the players, call them all kinds of names," Forester remembers, going on to tell how Charlie Gehringer, the quietest, friendliest, most cooperative and congenial guy on the club, grabbed Cobb for calling him "a sonofabitch" and told him never to say that to him because he had a mother. If Gerry Walker hadn't intervened, Gehringer would have knocked him cold. "But Cobb was a son of a gun. I said I don't want any part of him. After he called Gehringer that I never did like him. Swear at ballplayers—'sonofabitch,' 'bastard'—I didn't like that. He wasn't treating those guys right."

Clubhouse personnel as well as players avoid Manager Red-Ass, particularly after a loss, but another type they avoid is the *Loner*. This manager enacts the cliché that it's lonely at the top, but he seems to prefer it that way. You don't go near him in the dugout, and you don't cross his path in the clubhouse either. He may or may not be in his office, but you may not know because the door is usually shut anyway. Players may make fun of him, mimic him behind that closed door, but only when they're pretty sure he is out of the building or at least out of earshot. He is typically skilled at delegating authority, like a distant Captain Bligh or Ahab communing only with God or the Whale, while his Mr. Christian or Coach Starbuck takes care of communicating with the crew. In some cases, Manager Loner has the companionship of a bottle, but the best known exemplars of this subtype were rarely handicapped thereby in terms of the results of their teams. I was surprised to find how many of the batboys had nothing to say about the managers they had worked under because they had never had anything to do with them, had rarely exchanged words with them, hardly knew if Manager Loner had even known their names.

The opposite is the case for the managers who may be labeled *Dr. Feelgood*. These leaders make it their business to know the boys' names, even on the road in the visiting clubhouses, so that they can speak to them as people and commend them personally for their work. Respect for others and enthusiasm for every aspect of activity attached to the game, even the most menial, characterize this type of leader. He is a backslapper, but his good humor is contagious and his good feeling for his men and boys is felt as genuine. Al Lopez is remembered as one who "treated everyone, even batboys, as people." Fred Haney and Bill Rigney were also known to wear this label. An incident reported of the latter is exemplary. Rigney would go so far as to ask his Giants batboy, Roy McKercher, his baseball opinions. "I'd always agree with him," Roy says. One day he asked what to do to get both Willie McCovey and Orlando Cepeda into the lineup regularly, and Roy said he didn't know. Rigney said, "Well, I think I'm gonna put McCovey at first, he's a natural first baseman, and play Cepeda in the outfield. Now I want to know what you think and I don't want any bullshit answer this time." The batboy said, "That would be the greatest move in the world." As McKercher continues the story, "The next day after he makes that move, Rig is fired, and on his way out of the clubhouse he stops to say to me, 'It's not your fault.'"

The best example of Dr. Feelgood in the major leagues today is Sparky Anderson. From virtually every clubhouse in both leagues I heard reports of his special managerial quality. He is described as making it his business to deal personally, on a first-name basis, with as many of the clubhouse personnel as he can, and at the same time make it seem like the easiest, most natural thing in the world to do, not a chore or duty but a privilege and pleasure. Where genuine, that is, when accompanied by straight-talking integrity, the behavior of Dr. Feelgood warms the climate of the clubhouse. And when it is accompanied by periodic good fortune and results on the field and in the standings, along with the development of talent that may respond well to positive reinforcment and constructively honest criticism, Dr. Feelgood may have a long and happy tenure in his job.

Other managers, perhaps in admiration of Dr. Feelgood or perhaps envious of the affection, respect, and devotion he receives, make an effort to emulate him, at least to project the Feelgood image. Sometimes this even comes across on camera, on tape, in print, or from the stands as the genuine article. But there's no fooling the limited and privileged audience inside the clubhouse. The masks come off inside when media and fans are not around. The would-be Feelgoods wear the label of *Mr. Media*. They are PR men first and baseball men

Sparky Anderson as Dr. Feelgood welcomed former batboy David Cowart back to the Tigers clubhouse and made his young son Alex and nephew Brian Bigham feel at home. (courtesy of David Cowart)

second. They are readily available, interminably accessible to the media; they play to the grandstands; a gimmick is worth more to them than a well-executed cutoff play.

They will talk about fundamentals to the press, but not to their players. They will talk at length sympathetically about the players, but they have little time for private discussions with those very players. And perhaps that is because their calendars are crowded between games with public appearances or photo opportunities with celebrities. The kinds of reactions in the clubhouse to intrusive celebrities described in chapter 2 are likely to be no different when the interlopers are called "celebrity batboys." As wise as he is to the world of press agentry, Mr. Media receives good press and fans love him for it. In the clubhouse, Mr. Media's name is likely to be Mr. Mud.

The reverse situation is the case with the type commonly referred to simply as the *Pro*. Often colorless, unpopular with fans and uncongenial with the media, he is sometimes assigned the grudging label of "players' manager," a kind of backhanded compliment acknowledging the absence of appeal or value to outsiders. I am not referring here to a subtype that could be called the *Clubman*, the kind of manager who actually hangs out with the players, still sees himself as one of the guys, and rationalizes his ability to lead from that vantage. I do not include him among the prevailing types because, in the first place, playing managers are a tradition honored in history but no longer in practice; second, because such managers are de jure (or soon become de facto) *interim* managers; and third, because such an attitude is in fact regarded as *un*professional in the clubhouse.

The Pro, even if he has been a clubbable player in his career, recognizes that with the office of manager goes a necessary separation from the troops. He has hard decisions to make, and he must make them on the basis of professional judgments. Even when they concern such atmospheric intangibles as "team chemistry," they must be made professionally. He is passionate in his respect for the game, its fundamentals, traditions, cultural values—its "book"— but he is a passionless stoic in the face of hype, hoopla, histrionics, and hypocrisy. He doesn't play to the crowd, he doesn't play the media PR game, and he tends not to play up to upper-level management either. In fact, not playing ball any more, he doesn't play at baseball. It's too serious a business for him. No wonder his image is not a favorite one for fans or media.

It must be said that, like all such taxonomies or systematic approaches to diagnosis, many individuals do not fit comfortably under a single rubric. Some batboys may put a manager in one category while others will categorize him elsewhere. On occasion, a batboy will be perceptive enough to see a particular manager as a mixture of types. Three conspicuous examples of mixed labels that emerged from this survey sample are Whitey Herzog, Earl Weaver, and Tony La Russa. Sometimes cold and aloof, sometimes warm and personable; sometimes a Red-Ass, sometimes a cool Pro; sometimes effusive and engaging, sometimes stoical and uncommunicative; each has been blessed at times by the media with the designation of genius. But I have rejected the notion of a separate category labeled Polymath, because that is the kind of judgment that emerges on sports-talk radio from media and fans rather than from the clubhouse perspective. In the clubhouse, the relative IQ level is ignored, and the composite portraits are taken from elements of other recognizable types.

The image of La Russa as Genius was elegantly embellished when George Will made him one of the primary subjects of *Men at Work*, an intellectualizing exercise par excellence. One former batboy, an intelligent firsthand observer of the game (an experienced insider, in fact), told me he had asked to borrow La Russa's copy when he was done. "Sure," said the manager, "but I'm not sure you'll understand it." He paused, scratching his head, then added, "I'm not sure *I* understand it."

In Herzog's case, while he was often praised for finding a way to accomplish things on the field against the odds, the greatest measure of his genius may have been his ability to compromise or synthesize traditional polarities in order to produce a clubhouse atmosphere that mirrored his own images of the game and a ballclub. He is said to have been able to maintain discipline and be a friend at the same time. He would relax conventional rules such as curfew, but impose radical rules such as time limits for ordinary clubhouse pastimes and distractions and the elimination of postgame spreads, all in the interest of producing a concentrated focus on the business of playing winning baseball. However beguiling or persuasive his behavior might have been in public view, in the clubhouse—within the ballclub—his guiding principle was to show respect by trusting each individual to do what he was supposed to do.

Weaver's Red-Ass rages on the field are still featured in highlight films of baseball histrionics, but a clubhouse consensus has it that many of them were contrived. The occasional outburst inside was regularly assumed to have been calculated to produce desired results from their objects. As voluble as he was on the field, he was experienced as a Loner in the clubhouse, a chain-smoker in splendid solitude plotting his next dramatic confrontation. One batboy, who assumed because the skipper never said a word to him that he didn't like him, had a revelation on the road when Weaver took him out to dinner.

In a sense, then, these mixed-category eminences exhibit the defining trait of the next category: the manager as Misunderstood Maestro. The salient feature of this type is the "reality" of the clubhouse personage that contradicts the public perception. For whatever reason—role-confusion, splintered personality, conscious design, protective or provocative coloration determined by environment, pragmatic behavior for limited but discrete goal-attainment—these men embody the concept that baseball has two worlds, that managers must wear two faces for the faces they encounter outside and inside the clubhouse.

As a player, Leo Durocher was already controversial, aggressive in terms of competition and personality, stirring up attention and animosity. As a manager, however, he settled into a two-faced persona: an obnoxious, brash, loudmouthed publicity hound in public and on the field, but a dedicated professional in the clubhouse. That is, after all, the essence of his most famous line, subsequently the title of his book, *Nice Guys Finish Last*. One batboy remembers him as "somewhat distant from the clubhouse kids" but the one who would "put the arm on the players to pitch in for expense money for us" on the road. Another says, "He had the foulest mouth I ever heard, with a command voice, but he was really good-natured." And a third, remembering him as one of the most generous tippers when visiting St. Louis, says, "He seemed a cold man but he always looked out for the little guys." Stan Strull knew him on a more regular basis in Ebbets Field, but echoes that judgment: "He was aces in the clubhouse and always a big tipper."

Billy Martin is the purest exemplar of this type. The public image he projected is amply delineated in a personality and behaviors that made him prime subject matter for the tabloids. Watching his antics during games from the stands or on the screen, reading or hearing about his contretemps in bars (where, according to Mickey Mantle, Billy was so aggressive he could *hear* someone giving him the finger from across the room), taking in the serialized mock-epic of his relationship with George Steinbrenner, we encountered a tempestuous and troubled personality, tolerated nevertheless for his fierce competitive spirit and his inspired and inspirational successes with unlikely material. And yet from clubhouses around the American League comes an amply documented account of a totally different person.

The batboys' Billy Martin is dependable, consistent, courteous, thoughtful, generous, kind, grateful, and concerned. He might have berated a batboy on the field under the pressure of a game situation, but typically the kid would understand that he had earned the rebuke. Inside, Billy Martin was a pleasure to serve because he would always be appreciative of the service, even for such incidentals as food from a good Italian deli or directions to the most convenient church for Mass. For one who thought of Billy Martin as always in search of instant gratification of earthy, manly appetites, it came as a revelation to hear repeated incidents of his patient willingness to spend hours talking with kids, with equal attentiveness, about baseball or about their personal problems. "One of the most genuine people I've ever known," said one; "a bluntly honest man," said another, "but always a gentleman and considerate in the clubhouse"; and a third, acknowledging that he "could be bizarre," called him "unique, cordial, quiet, and reserved."

The final type of the seven identified from these sources is an antitype. He is the *Manager Sui Generis*, unique whether as an inimitable cartoon-like figure or a finely delineated complex portrait. The caricatured impression one has of Casey Stengel, Yogi Berra, Doug Rader, Wes Westrum, and Don Zimmer (though some would argue that the catchers among these really belong in the category of the Pro) is generally corroborated by reports from the clubhouse. The Stengel who insisted that a batboy accompany him to an impromptu press conference so that he could learn how to confuse, entertain, and evade the media at the same time and the Berra who would typically greet the request to sign a ball with the question "Why?" are, after all, no different from the Stengel and Berra we all know and love. But when a manager develops with a batboy a complex, multifaceted relationship that demonstrates a fully developed human being it is worthy of particular note.

One of the batboys in Kansas City when Dick Howser arrived to manage the Royals was Steve Winship. As it happened, departing manager Jim Frey had lived in a townhouse next door to Winship's father in Lakewood, and Howser moved not only into Frey's position but into his old house as well. Winship met the new manager at Royals Stadium the day after he signed with the Royals in 1981. As he recalls, "He came out to the ballpark early, walked out of the tunnel and right away introduced himself to me and another batboy." Instant acquaintance grew quickly into friendship, especially when the connection as neighbor grew to be at least as important as the connection at the ballpark.

At work, however dedicated Howser was to the game (and he seemed to many to be obsessively focused), he always seemed to have time to play around with the batboy. Steve Fiffer chose Howser as the subject for his chapter, "The Manager: Keeping the Team in the Game," and found him "characteristically collected," "accessible," "pleasant, engaging and forthright" (111–35). Howser took part in the initiation pranks and even joked with Winship during games. Winship eventually found his niche, working for the most part as ballboy down the left field foul line. Whenever he misplayed a ball, Howser along with Rocky Colavito who was on the coaching staff would wave white towels at him from the dugout. "Once," Steve remembers, "the third base ump called time, pointing to the dugout where the manager and coach were waving towels. It's the only time a game was stopped for the signal of a ballboy's error."

Winship remained friendly with Dick and Nancy Howser after he went away to college. By 1986 they were so close that he was their guest at the All-Star Game in Houston. He is wistful, grateful, and sad as he completes the story. "That was the last game he managed before his brain tumor was diagnosed, you remember. After that I'd often spend the night at their house if I could be of use. And I was one of those at his bedside at St. Luke's in '87 when he died. Nancy remains a friend, and I often sit with her at games."

The distance between batboy and manager is great, not so much as a hierarchical matter but as defined by their roles and the rules of protocol. It is far more likely and common for clubbies to be close with players. It is their primary duty, after all, to attend to the players, and they are in daily proximate contact with them. No wonder the batboy often feels he knows the players as well as anyone.

The most common type of player in the batboy's system of central casting is the *Big Brother*, and there are no Orwellian overtones in that designation. This is the player (sometimes a coach or trainer) who makes a kid welcome, makes him feel like part of the club, puts his arm around him or engages in innocent horseplay with him, and takes him under his wing—a phrase that occurred with insistent regularity throughout the interviews. The Big Brother is the guy who shows a boy how to put the uniform on properly and models for him appropriate behavior on the road, in hotels, and in the restaurants he takes him for meals. He is the player who, as pitcher Jeff Parrett did for Steve Friend in Montreal, spends long hours talking after games in the clubhouse and invites him to be his "son" when the Expos have a family day for the team.

Big Brother may more often than not be among the younger players, but he comes in every age group. Bobby Knoop, for example, was

Dwight Gooden, a Big Brother to Paul Greco, played whiffleball and shot hoops at a Greco family barbecue. (courtesy of Paul Greco)

identified as one who took kids under his wing as a young Angels player and who still does so as a coach in his fifties. On occasion, a very young player will be more comfortable among the clubbies than among veteran players, for example, seventeen-year-old rookie Bob Feller, who was close to a twelve-year-old batboy.

There are more pitchers identified as Big Brothers than players at any other position. Batboys speculate that that's because they only work every four or five days and so have more time to develop relationships with clubbies, because they are not under the same day-to-day pressures as regular position players, and because pitchers and batboys are companions shagging flies during batting practice. Utility infielders form the second largest group in the Big Brother category. They are often at liberty to sit next to a boy in the dugout, sharing observations about the game—and life—as they contemplate what they see on the field and in their world. But some Hall-of-Famers are included among the type. Joe Morgan, for example, was always the kind of Big Brother who would toss the keys to his convertible to a kid brother to use on a date. George Brett and Gaylord Perry, among others, have engendered a considerable legacy of affection from boys with whom they spent time in the clubhouse, hung around on the road, and shared recreation time on off-days or during the off-season. And it is Big Brother to whom a batboy may turn in times of trouble to find consolation. In the visiting clubhouse at Yankee Stadium, pitcher Pete Vuckovich eased Paul Gonoud's grief at losing a friend in a car accident by sharing intimate details of his own youthful escapades.

Another type of "relative" who shines brightly in the batboy's remembered constellation of the clubhouse family is the *Dutch Uncle*. This is the player who with stern affection makes sure that a batboy learns a hard, useful lesson. Recognizing or hearing that a boy has experimented with controlled and dangerous substances, he will take him aside and tell him, "Son, please don't kill yourself. That stuff's no good." When a kid comes off the team plane after his first road trip and is having trouble walking straight, Dutch Uncle will let him know in no uncertain terms that such behavior is unacceptable. When a batboy shows up at the ballpark wearing the unmistakable signs of a hangover, Dutch Uncle will embarrass him by public recognition of his condition, making repeated drunkenness unlikely because not worth the combined price of humiliation, headache, heaves, and sweats. Or he might give the wayward boy a sardonic grin and say to him, "How're you doing, son? I can play two today, can you?"

Dutch Uncle may be called upon to give instruction in ethics, politics, education, diet, or "safe sex." Many a batboy has been chastised for the inappropriateness of a political gesture in the clubhouse (particularly if associated with some aspect of the "Movement" or any form of social change, not to mention rebellion). In some cases, the lesson must be weighed against the circumstances behind the teaching. One batboy remembers his disappointment and surprise when a player he had been close to and respected came back to visit after being traded and told him, "Don't get married." But the batboy had heard about the player's messy divorce and so could separate this cynical observation from the valuable previous advice he had received from this player.

Dutch Uncle's lessons about baseball values and appropriate public (on-field) behaviors are heartfelt and stern. Bill Tofant remembers how Lou Gehrig impressed upon him the importance of courtesy to fans, modeling that behavior after Tofant had been unnecessarily abrupt and perhaps somewhat arrogant. And Bill Busch got a chewing-out from Joe Adcock, who had seen Bill shake his head in disagreement with an umpire's call on a ball hit down the line in San Diego. That gesture went unnoticed by the umpire but not by Adcock, who let Busch know later that it was not his place to express such judgments. If you're in uniform you're not a fan, and the fact that the ballboy may have had the best view was not an acceptable defense.

Dutch Uncle may appear in unlikely form, like Jim Piersall in a Red Sox uniform in the visiting locker room at Griffith Stadium. Jack Hughes was a twelve-year-old batboy when Piersall came into the clubhouse early one afternoon and found him perusing a girlie magazine he'd found in another Red Sox player's locker. Piersall grabbed it out of Jack's hands, threw it against one wall and the kid up against another, saying, "I don't want to see you with this kind of stuff anywhere anytime." Later during the same series, Piersall knelt with the batboy in the on-deck circle and told him he was going to hit a home run, and promptly did. But it was the Dutch Uncle routine that makes Jack Hughes say, "The player who made the most profound impression on me was Jimmy Piersall."

If Father Figures, Big Brothers, and Dutch Uncles are types readily available to boys from their own models of family configurations, the other figures among the dozen or so types of players that emerge from batboys' stories of the clubhouse seem to originate in legendary, traditional, conventional, and assumed associations with the baseball world itself. Whether the boys bring certain expectations with them into the clubhouse or learn the designations once they are there, they seem to be able to identify the types readily. They may be consciously looking for a Mentor, for example, or hoping to encounter a genuine Flake, but they are also able to recognize and label the Hollow Hall-of-Famer and the Prima Donna as quickly as if imprinted with the characteristics of the taxonomy.

The *Mentor* is distinct from Big Brother and Dutch Uncle in that his role is not familial but tutorial. And his curriculum is baseball. Sitting next to Big Brother on the bench, a batboy might talk about their plans for the evening. Next to Dutch Uncle, he might find the topic to be the errors of his ways the night before. Alongside the Mentor, he will hear about plans for the next inning, comments on play or strategy of the inning before, and analysis of the situation immediately at hand. Gilly Lefebvre remembers Ron Santo taking

Mentoring on the field: Rocky Bridges gives infield point-
ers to batboy Billy Turner. (courtesy of Jim Ryan)

time to talk with him and give him hitting lessons. Mike Mullane
remembers Bob Brenly for teaching him fundamentals of catching
and hitting. And Jimmy Triantas is still overwhelmed by the memories of sitting next to Terry Crowley in the dugout: "He'd tell me
things about the game. He sorta had baseball ESP and nine out of ten
times he'd be right."

Big Brother and Dutch Uncle make the batboy's life more rewarding in general and at large; the Mentor makes his experience more
special in particular and in the privileged confines of the dugout or
clubhouse. Taking advantage of the opportunity and the eager audience to pass along the intricacies of inside baseball, the Mentor
makes the batboy aware of nuances, sensitive to rhythms and
trends, and appreciative of the possession of arcana. The gift of
Dutch Uncle is maturity, of Big Brother nurturance, and of the Mentor illumination. They are the magi of the batboy's emergence.

The three types of players discussed above are identified by batboys as a result of direct experience. In the cases of all the following
types, the identification is made as a result of observation. Certainly, the observation may be of attitudes, attributes, and behaviors

that impinge directly on the batboy, but even that direct experience produces a kind of distancing that allows the batboy to fix a label from his repertoire of known types. The Gamer provides a clear example of how an observed type becomes a grid that may be superimposed on isolated incidents.

Gamer is a term of such universal approbation in baseball that clouds of clichés cluster around it. "Some kind of competitor," "he comes to play," "he plays hurt," "he does the little things to help his team—the things that don't show up in the box score," "he'll run through the fence (brick, steel) to get the ball, through anyone to get the extra base (or score the run)," and in every way "he shows up every day" "with his game face on." The Gamer is a "ballplayer's ballplayer," a "get-down-and-dirty" performer, who "plays hard to win" and "gives 110 percent." He'll "take one for the club," "give himself up," "never stop digging (or hustling)," and "there's no quit in him."

These are clichés not only of language but of thinking as well. The batboy knows that baseball values require him to admire and praise the Gamer. But to get in the Gamer's way is for the batboy to get in harm's way. Failure to match the Gamer's competitive mood, pace, dedication, and determination is to risk his wrath. Any on-field gaffe that impedes the Gamer's performance will bring down that wrath. And if attitude and atmosphere in the clubhouse don't match what is appropriate to events on the field in the Gamer's eyes, his wrath will be accompanied by a communicated contempt for the miscreant clubby.

Over and over again, I heard about incidents of embarrassment on the field, when batboys made errors of omission or commission that evoked censure and rebuke from Gamers. And the slightest intrusion on the hostility of a Gamer in the clubhouse after a tough competitive loss often elicited disproportionate outbursts. Yet instead of feeling guilty or shamed, instead of being humiliated or hurt or reflectively angry, what the batboy will feel—either because he knows he's supposed to or because it is an effective defense against those negative, anxious, or self-loathing feelings—is pride in and admiration for the competitive spirit of the Gamer.

Invariably the batboy will conclude by saying that a day or hours or even minutes after the offense, the Gamer will act toward him as if nothing had happened. (Outstanding examples are offered about John Orsino in Baltimore, B. J. Surhoff in Milwaukee, and Steve

Rogers in Montreal.) In the Gamer's eyes a mistake hurts the club, but the Gamer knows it's worse for the club to hold a grudge. "He said that to you?" or "He did that to you?" one asks the batboy after the reported incident; and he replies, "He forgot about it right away. That's the way he is, he wants to win so bad. He's a gamer. So I forgot about it, too." He laughs when he reports what the Gamer said or did to him, and one wonders why, if the incident was so forgettable, it's one of the first things he remembers as he reflects on his whole batboy experience.

It is a source of pride to the batboy to acknowledge the Gamer's mastery of the fundamentals of the game. At the same time it is a tribute to the batboy's own appreciation of the little things, of the value of selfless effort over self-aggrandizing style, of what is admired by those inside in the know over what may be adulated by spectators and television watchers. Take for example the champion Mets of 1986, winners of 108 games, with such stylish, charismatic figures as Keith Hernandez, Ray Knight, Darryl Strawberry, and Gary Carter, along with once and future stars George Foster, Kevin Mitchell, and Howard Johnson, plus a rotation of Dwight Gooden, Ron Darling, Bob Ojeda, Sid Fernandez, and Rick Aguilera (top four in winning percentage in the league, three of the top five in earned run average, and two of the top five in strikeouts), and Roger McDowell and Jose Orosco in the bullpen (forty-three saves between them). In all the Olympian glory of this colossal clubhouse, the two players idolized by the whole group of batboys that season were Wally Backman and Lenny Dykstra, two down-and-dirty Gamers. (Is it coincidental that the decline of the Mets began with the departure of these two in 1989? Unfortunately, the subsequent ascendancy of the Phillies has been accompanied by Dykstra's transformation into a Flake.)

The *Flake* is probably the most immediately identifiable type, in part because so many different sets of credentials are admissible. The most common of the subtypes under the umbrella heading of Flake is the Jokemeister. He is a practical joker, a clown, an observer of no boundaries. All clubs have them, and every clubhouse has its legends about them—even though their jokebags are likely to be full of tricks tried, true, and trite. The limited range of imagination rarely extends beyond the burning of shoelaces, the tossing of burning newspapers into bathroom stalls, the surprising presence of shaving cream in unlikely places, the naked sitting on ceremonial cakes, the pushing of gullible faces into baked goods, the hanging of embarrassing equipment on uniforms worn unsuspectingly onto the field, the nailing or knotting or cutting of dress clothes in the locker room, and a variety of pranks involving bodily functions or excretions. Add to this farcical inventory the initiation rites discussed in chapter 3, and you have a compendium of the standard devices.

From the batboy's perspective, it is a mark of honor to be victimized by the Jokemeister, to be chosen as a subject worthy of his attention, to be tapped by the hand of the divine fool. But it is also a matter of pride to be cannily aware of the risk at hand and to avoid it. A third source of pleasure is to have witnessed the embarrassment of others, not only in the sense that there is a universal audience to laugh at a pratfall, but in the honor felt in being part of a privileged audience. The tone of the reminiscence is that of achievement, whether the report is about having been "got" by Moe Drabowsky or Bert Blyleven or Roger McDowell, or having dodged being got, or simply having borne witness to someone else being got. The brighter the star brought low by a trick, the higher the achievement for the witness.

The prevalence of uniform parts as the stock in trade of the Jokemeister suggests a traditional association with a clown or fool in motley. Indeed *Clown* and *Fool* are alternative epithets for *Flake*. Casey Stengel is remembered for lifting his cap to allow a hidden bird to escape. McDowell entertained by wearing different masks or walking on his hands with his uniform on upside down. Another trait or privilege of the traditional clown/fool is that he is free to say anything at all to anyone at all. (The wise fool in Shakespeare, a conventional character type in the Elizabethan theater, perhaps in direct lineage from the *Eiron* of classical Greece, and the court jester are prototypes of this clubhouse role.) This behavior, too, earns the designation of Flake in the clubhouse.

There are several other sorts of offbeat behavior so honored—in the breach of appropriateness: the genuinely bizarre, like the keeping of paraphernalia for voodoo worship in the locker room; the exceptionally moody, an exhibiting of extremes which suggests that trainers should keep supplies of lithium along with liniment; the preternaturally slobbish, making John Landis's *Animal House* seem like the nest of a relatively prim primate; and the peculiarly abstract, suggesting out-of-body presence anywhere but in the locker room with the rest of the club. The last three sets of characteristics, incidentally, match the descriptions of Len Dykstra in the Phillies

Batboy Tony Atlas took his job seriously, but Mark (The Bird) Fidrych was ever the Flake. (courtesy of Tony Atlas)

clubhouse, where no one seems to know what he's doing or might do next, where his "head is at," what he's talking about, or why the floor of his locker either is or requires a spittoon—until he puts his game face on and his game mouth and mind in, that is, until he takes on his original shape as the Gamer.

The two adjectives generally applied to the Flake are *crazy* and *weird* (*character* and *nut* are other frequent epithets, for players like Bobo Newsom, Bill Voiselle, and Fergie Jenkins, and for Charlie Grimm, who as a player kept everyone laughing and retained the epithet "Jolly Cholly" into his managing years), but these words are always uttered with approval, admiration, astonishment, or even awe. What is interesting in the context of this study is the resemblance of the Flake figure, in the batboy's view of him, to the traditional Trickster of mythology. It is only when all of the subtypes in the configuration become evident that the full picture emerges, but when it does we find a composite portrait of that ubiquitous god. An unpredictable and ungovernable shapeshifter, he may do or say or be anything, and no sanctions apply to him. He flouts conventions, and he tests the limits of tradition itself. He provides farce, but he also engenders fear. With his crazy behavior and weird ways, he keeps everyone and turns everything "loose," and to be touched by him—whether blessed or cursed—is to be marked with distinction. But he is also to be avoided, rather like Coleridge's archetypal artist with his flashing eyes and tossing hair inside his circle of magic.

Only two types of clubhouse characters, it seemed to me as I kept hearing about them, give batboys more pleasure to remember than the Flake. In both cases, the thrill of pleasure is heightened by the fact that only insiders can know the identity of individuals who qualify for these labels. In fact, both are primarily based on the misperceptions of the public about them, though the reversal or refutation of the image is positive in one, negative in the other. They are the Media Misnomer and the Hollow Hall-of-Famer.

The *Media Misnomer* is the player equivalent of the manager as Misunderstood Maestro, and his number is legion. In part that is because, as a media re-creation, baseball provides a cast of thousands, and it is virtually a media requisite that many in the cast wear black hats, and that they, in turn, get the most attention because, as everyone knows, they are more interesting than the All-American Jack Armstrongs of the game. In part, it is because in the natural course of publicly scrutinized athletic events, players will behave differently on the field, before the public, and in interviews with the media, from the way they behave with their peers, other club members, or their families. And in part, I believe, that is because the batboys take enormous pride and pleasure in being able to say, "You only know the bad boy image portrayed in the media, but in the clubhouse I know the guy as a prince among men." Every batboy says it every chance he gets, and every batboy has at least one example of the type.

The examples come from every level in the hierarchy of players, but they have one thing in common: public perception as projected or reinforced by the media. In fact, batboys often attribute the public misperception to the players' lack of cooperation with media people, who in turn turn on those players. Ted Williams, probably the prime example, had stormy relationships with fans and press alike, but is extravagantly praised for his generosity, concern, and regard for clubhouse personnel. The late John Donovan liked to tell the story of his camel's-hair coat, a gift to the pennant-winning Red Sox of 1946. When the Filene's tailors came to the clubhouse to take measure-

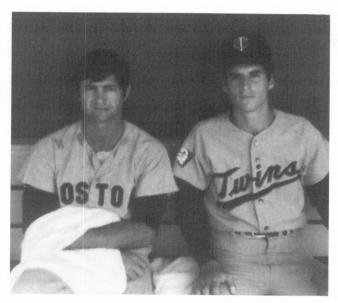

Mark McKenzie in dugout with boyhood idol Carl Yastrzemski. Grim competitor on the field, Yaz was great fun for
clubhouse kids. (courtesy of Mark McKenzie)

ments, Williams refused to stand for his until all the clubbies were
included in the package.

His successor in Fenway's left field also got a bad rap from some
fans and writers who found him to be too moody or too narrowly
focused on playing hardball in every way. But the kids who dealt
with Carl Yastrzemski at home and around the league remember
him as a congenial, fun-loving companion who, along with Reggie
Smith, made the Red Sox of those years an engaging club. And then
his successor, Jim Rice, was regarded in some quarters as a dour,
sulking troublemaker, but not in American League clubhouses.
From New York to Kansas City come reports of his genuine friendliness.

It is hard to find positive portraits in the media of Roger Maris,
Pete Incaviglia, Curt Flood, Eddie Murray, Steve Carlton, George
Foster, Alex Johnson, Cliff Johnson, Amos Otis, George Hendrick,
Jim Palmer, or Dick (Richie) Allen. Most of them were notorious for
avoiding or denying interviews. "You just don't know the real men,"
say the batboys, who provide incident after anecdote demonstrating

Mickey Mantle, with batboy Tom MacDougal, was easy for snapshots but difficult for autographs. (courtesy of Tom MacDougal)

the warmth, generosity, dignity, congeniality, and thoroughgoing professionalism of these men. Even Ty Cobb finds a supporter among former batboys in Jack Hughes, who is full of praise for Cobb's kindness toward him as he pursued his quest for a souvenir—though in all fairness to the image, this occurred decades after his playing and managing days.

Then there is the already ambiguous case of Mickey Mantle, viewed as moody, childish, temperamental, and inconsiderate at least as often as generous, gregarious, and spontaneous. As visiting batboy in Oakland during Mantle's last season, Mike Pieraldi says that Mantle taught him "about strength and inner character, achieved and maintained at great cost—that's what being a pro player is all about. It was the biggest thrill to see Mantle up close, kneeling in the on-deck circle with him. I saw him hobbling on bad knees but giving his all to baseball."

Finally, not to exclude the fringe player from this category, there is the example of Chris Brown, a backup third baseman who got "bad press" in San Diego. A Padres batboy says, "They said he was too laid back and wasn't nice to the fans. There was even a suspicion that he faked injuries, but I can tell you that he was really nice to clubhouse kids." What may be inferred and is occasionally made explicit is the significance attached to generosity. Players who are reluctant to share their time with writers or fans often give freely of themselves and their worldly goods to the lowliest baseball personnel. They will even go out of their way for batboys, taking them to dinner and movies on the road, attending their graduations and weddings and their children's christenings, taking time to visit their sick relatives, and in one case playing whiffleball at a backyard family barbecue. But the one constant feature of the Media Misnomer is that he is always generous with his tips.

The *Hollow Hall-of-Famer* is the mirror image of the Media Misnomer, but he appears much less frequently in batboys' reminiscences. Still there is equal relish in puncturing the balloon of a lofty media-generated public image. This player is widely recognized as an exemplar, appropriately humble about his stardom, appreciative of others, congenial and cooperative. But the batboy knows him as aloof (not only from his teammates but especially from the staff that serves him) and directly experiences the echoes of his hollowness.

The Hollow Man is skilled at public relations, and sometimes enters the PR field after his playing days are over. Hall-of-Famer or all-star, he can get the votes, but he doesn't fool the clubhouse attendants. He may be urbane, articulate, and friendly, like Dave Winfield in his three-piece suit and with his alligator briefcase, but the batboys find his friendliness empty because unaccompanied by gratuities. Mike Schmidt gives good interviews, quality presentation, and the public image of a model citizen, but has nothing left to give in the clubhouse. He talks the talk of the baseball club but off camera he walks the walk of solitary, moody splendor.

Flashy and outgoing on the field, Tony Fernandez is persona non grata in the clubhouse. Batboys find him to be dedicated to maintaining his exclusivity, wanting to perform his own routine while being left alone. In itself, this would be acceptable, but it seems to those reporting to reflect the kind of self-centeredness that drove Fernandez to pursue records for triples regardless of game situation or team concerns—which is why he also holds records for getting thrown out at third. In a less affluent era, Enos Slaughter and Red Schoendienst distinguished themselves for their miserliness, while hale-fellow-well-met Johnny Lindell could behave with a touch of sadism to a batboy. What looks like dedicated professionalism on the field or back-slapping good nature in public is experienced in the clubhouse as one kind of meanness or another.

The flamboyant Denny McLain, long before his public image was tarnished by antisocial and criminal behavior, was universally despised in baseball clubhouses. No matter how much he asked to be done for him, he never gave anything back. "There's only one player I'd ever badmouth, that no-good bum Denny McLain," says Fred Baxter. "I'll tell you the kind of guy he was. One day he was denied entry to the team parking lot—he'd given his ticket to some bimbo—and he lied to [owner Bob] Short about it and had the parking attendant fired. When he was traded he left town owing me sixty-seven bucks, and he never paid. I got even, though. I kept his golf clubs, gave them to my son."

Another Hollow Man is the sad case of Pete Gray, the one-armed outfielder for the Browns in the war years. Seen (and exploited) as heroic, and clearly a figure likely to engage the sympathy of a public enjoying his triumph over limitations, he was known in the clubhouse as a bitter, angry man with neither a gesture of kindness nor a word of good cheer for anyone.

Finally, with personal reluctance and considerable hesitance, I include in this category the revered name of Willie McCovey, the most popular San Francisco Giants player ever, surpassing such beloved stars as Willie Mays, Orlando Cepeda, Juan Marichal, and Will Clark in Bay Area affections. Without meaning to undercut such regard or to demean the man, I include McCovey because he turned a different face to the club from that which beamed on the Giants fans. The ebullient performer, who somehow also managed to convey the character of a gentle giant, was known in the clubhouse for his deadpan humor and sardonic wit. Generous but demanding, he was best known for his moodiness. "Same old Stretch," says Mike Murphy who still sees him occasionally, "still moody as hell. I learned to stay away from him when he's moody, and he seemed to like you more the more you stayed away. I learned to know his moods, to stay away and let him make the first move."

The *Prima Donna* is closely related to the Hollow Man, but may have some elements of the Flake as well. The crucial distinction is the fact that the eccentricities associated with the Prima Donna are known or at least commonly suspected by the world at large. He is a larger-than-life figure, and his every characteristic, perhaps especially his volatility, achieves legendary proportions. Half a dozen examples emerged as sketches from the interviews, and one was delineated with great detail.

A couple of temperamental pitchers qualify here: Guillermo Hernandez, whose insistence that he not be called "Willie" was as vigorous in the clubhouse as it was in public, and Dock Ellis, whose sometimes overpowering performances on the mound were matched by towering rages in the clubhouse. One batboy says, "He treated me worse than I've ever been treated in my life. He'd berate me and everything he'd say to me was foul."[20] Going back to the Yankees of 1935, one finds that the departure of Babe Ruth did not mean an absence of egregious behaviors in the clubhouse, not with "fancy-dan" Ben Chapman calculating his own batting average and pitcher Pat Malone, who was known for urinating into the fire of the pot-bellied stove that stood in the center of some clubhouses.

There is no surprise at finding George Bell, Rod Carew, Rusty Staub, and Kirk Gibson identified as Prima Donnas, batboys thereby confirming media-generated impressions. Bell's "arrogance" is the salient feature that "rubs people the wrong way" in batboys' reports, though "on good days he was one of the nicest players." Should a ballboy down the line assigned to play catch with him between innings, however, accidentally throw the ball away from him, Bell would stand, hands on hips, and stare at a boy who would dare commit such an unacceptable error, then pick up the ball and throw to someone in the bullpen. In Carew's case, a batboy who recalls the kind of clubhouse pettishness that would lead a troubled, talented, brilliant, "pouty" rookie to refuse to sign balls would come to justify the temperament of "the most misunderstood player in the game—battered childhood, bad marriage, and all that."

As for Staub, he seemed to cultivate the Prima Donna label both on the field and in the clubhouse. His bat was never to be placed in the bat-rack, and if he grounded out the batboy had to meet him at the base line with the bat so that he could carry it back to the dugout where he'd continue to hold it in his hands. "He had to have new sanitaries every day or he'd pout and cry," says an American League batboy, while a National League clubby reports the same, adding, "We learned that whatever Rusty wants, Rusty gets, and that whatever Rusty says is right." Gibson couldn't have cared less what he was called. Called "my least favorite player" by one batboy, "a bitter, angry man who was never satisfied [and who] would throw his cleats at us if he didn't like the way we cleaned them," he was also called "another great guy" who would "fire guys up by talking loud and being funny, but he'd get angry at himself and swear so that the crowd got on him." A third Tigers batboy who liked Gibson heard from his equipment manager that Gibby just never liked batboys, which allowed the kid to say with some pride that "he seemed to like me, talked to me like a normal person." Sometimes it takes more than one evaluation to encompass the ambivalence that is the legacy left (and perhaps courted) by the Prima Donna.

An illustrated dictionary of these terms would have to have the entry for Prima Donna accompanied by a picture of Reggie Jackson. Not since Babe Ruth has a figure of such enormous proportions emerged from the baseball world, one with the power of personality that demands attention to the legend as much as to the history. Virtually everyone interviewed whose path had crossed Reggie's in a clubhouse had a story to tell and a strong opinion about him. (See Tullius's chapter, "Reggie! Reggie! Reggie!" 306–19, for some players' views.) Batboys loved him; batboys hated him. He treated them like brothers; he treated them like bums. Both extremes of that polarity could even be experienced by the same person, depending on which Reggie suited up on a particular day.

Some batboys remember idolizing Reggie until they encountered him in the clubhouse and were subjected to his "rotten" treatment of them. Others remember extraordinary acts of generosity and kindness. "A very bad guy, who thought the world revolved around him," says one. He constantly ordered the kids around, calling everyone "Junior." But he made it a point to remember the names of some, like one who stumped him on a trivia question and another who amused him with a smart-ass remark. (Asked politely to sign a couple of balls, Reggie said, "You can take those balls and stick 'em up your ass," but when the boy answered, "As long as you sign them first I'll put them wherever you want," Reggie laughed, signed, and never forgot that White Sox clubby.)

Ron Pieraldi tells a story demonstrating the regal generosity of the larger-than-life hero. Years after his tenure as an A's batboy, Ron went to a car show at the Cow Palace in San Francisco where one of Reggie's prize cars was being shown. Taking questions from the crowd, Reggie was obviously enjoying his cameo appearance as an automobile maven. Ron raised his hand and asked, "Are you still using that Adirondack 288 RJ?"—a question that sounded as if it might have been car talk but was a reference to the model bat that Reggie had used to earn the name Mr. October. Reggie recognized Pieraldi and made a big production out of it, introducing him to the crowd as Oakland's former "great award-winning batboy." (Contrast this scene to Jim Ryan's experience with Mickey Mantle at a souvenir show in Phoenix, where, handed a photo of himself with Ryan in uniform and asked if he remembered him, Mantle dismissed him with a "just the batboy" remark.)

In his one season as an Oriole, Reggie left very vivid memories in the Baltimore clubhouse: "a chameleon who could go from nicest guy to really ignorant in a flash"; "so into his own self-importance that it felt like I was his personal servant"; "very affected, taken with himself, aware of his celebrity"; "one of the nicest guys in baseball . . . always congenial"; "always playing mental games with people, even with fourteen-year-old kids." The ambivalence of witnesses is present in testimony from other clubhouses as well. From Oakland, "He could be grouchy, but he'd sit down and talk with you, too. He could be aggressive, and then he'd come back and be sweet." From New York, the same batboy who marveled at Reggie's generous gesture in giving him a signed bat had his Jackson card tossed on the floor when he asked Reggie to sign it. From Milwaukee, the one batboy I found who had become a priest said that Reggie was a "very intense" player who would "take his frustrations out in the clubhouse."

Forgiveness may come not only from an understanding of pressures or from heroic achievements, but also from quiet acts of genuine kindness that may be extravagant, though private. Batboy Thad Mumford, for example, told Reggie in New York about his grandfather being ill in Washington. And the next time the Yankees were in the Baltimore–Washington area, Reggie spent an hour visiting the old man in the hospital. In the visiting clubhouse in Minnesota, Reggie became so friendly with batboy Mark McKenzie that he served as godfather to his daughter and was present at her christening. When the child died at two, Reggie dedicated his five hundredth home run to her. Later, at his own request, he became godfather to the McKenzies' twin sons. The Prima Donna may be characterized by the difficulties of dealing with him, but that is a function of his "star quality," which he displays on and off the field, a charisma that exaggerates both positive and negative personal traits and is exhibited in the characteristically gigantic nature of his exploits.

Prima Donna plays Godfather: Reggie Jackson went out of his way to be present at christening of former Twins batboy Mark McKenzie's daughter in 1982. Jackie Marie is held by her aunt, Peggy Piwaica, alongside Reggie, flanked by parents Linda and Mark. (courtesy of Mark McKenzie)

If instability is the hallmark of the Prima Donna, the Pro is seen by batboys as reliable and consistent, one who takes everything in stride. The behavior of the Prima Donna may be rationalized as artistic temperament, but the Pro's life and lifestyle are matters of craftsmanship and solid citizenship. This character type has the widest application among the batboys, and the descriptive terms associated with it include *dignity, leadership*, and *gentlemanliness*. Several all-star squads could be manned by players who exhibited those qualities and were designated as Pro by batboys. The roster includes Tommy Henrich, John Pesky, Tom Seaver, Johnny Bench, Gil Hodges, Roy Campanella, Al Kaline, Don Mattingly, Norm Cash, Frank Robinson, Robin Roberts, Richie Ashburn, Eddie Mathews, Jesse Barfield, Joe Morgan, Minnie Minoso, Pee Wee Reese, Jim Kaat, George Brett, Roy Sievers, Dale Murphy, Ernie Banks, and Jackie Robinson.

Stan Musial draws frequent recognition in this category, always a gentleman, always a credit to the game, and always a big tipper—which to the batboy may be the most impressive feature of all. Thurman Munson is often identified as a model Pro, as are Alan Trammell, Lou Whitaker, Gary Gaietti, and Al Bumbry. Gil McDougald was so admired that a batboy named his daughter after the player's daughter, and Don Baylor is remembered for the friendliness that went along with his generosity. It wasn't always the stars or aces of the team who were held up as models by the batboys and thus named as Pro. Jim Barr is remembered as the one who took up the collections for Giants batboys in the 1970s, Larry Bowa and George Vukovich who were admired in the Phillies clubhouse in the 1980s, and Bud Black who was grouped with George Brett and Bret Saberhagen as exemplars in Kansas City. But star quality is often associated with the Pro, who is often team captain or presides over kangaroo courts. Ron Santo, for example, is remembered as an "exceptional person," admired for his "consistency" and "the fact that he never took his own emotions out on others"; Cal Ripken, Jr., for being a "genuine all-American type"; and Tony Gwynn as "a good guy with a great attitude and work ethic"—a direct quotation from more than one interview, so that it may qualify as "the book" on Gwynn.

This roster would not be complete without the name of Harmon Killebrew, called a "genuine good person" and "great human being" by batboys. Since he was also named by a batboy as his particular "hero," Killebrew might just as well serve to introduce the next, final, character type: the Pro raised to the level of All-Pro, whom I call by a name not used in the clubhouse. He is the *Ego Ideal* of the subculture; that is, he is the player who is internalized by baseball insiders as the embodiment of the most admired values.

The Ego Ideal sets the standards of what the batboys would aspire to *be*, whatever goals they pursue in what they choose to *do*. They would want to achieve the dignity of Joe DiMaggio, the modest dedication of Charlie Gehringer, the gracious acceptance of greatness of Sandy Koufax. They would want to match the model of manliness of Nolan Ryan, the good-natured thoughtfulness of Rocky Colavito, the achievement through effort of Eddie Yost. They speak of the "genuine goodness" of Buddy Bell and also see him nostalgically as an avatar of the good old days of the game. They speak of the extraordinary, unfailing generosity of Hank Greenberg, who is remembered all around the old American League circuit as "the

Ego Ideal in the clubhouse, Nolan Ryan with batboy Mike Macko (courtesy of Mike Macko)

gentleman of all time" (see, for example, Barney McCoskey's report to Ira Berkow in Greenberg's *The Story of My Life* 130).

No matter how much pleasure they take in correcting the frequent outsider's misperception from the inside, they seem to take equal delight in confirming the universal view of fans and media alike of Brooks Robinson. "It's true, that's what he's really like," they would say. Jay Mazzone may have put it best when he said, "Brooks and his wife and his kids are the Ozzie and Harriet type of people. Always were and always will be. It doesn't matter where or when you run into them, it is always the same. You never heard him say anything bad about anybody."

Ultimately, there is Willie Mays. Over and over again he was identified as the greatest ever. There would follow an eyewitness report of a play that only Mays could make and then it would be matched by an anecdote demonstrating Willie's warmth, generosity, loyalty, good humor, and evenhanded friendliness encountered in the clubhouse or on the road or somewhere outside the confines of the club or the game. In short, the player nonpareil is also the embodiment of the values and qualities aspired to and embraced throughout the subculture. In the batboys' eyes, Willie Mays at the same time stood above all others and stood shoulder to shoulder with even the lowliest member of the club.

Supplying the material for this chapter, batboys present themselves as the mythographers of the clubhouses, the repositories of lore and tellers of tales. Above all, they are the delineators of the subculture's heroes. In a setting where the preponderance of the population is made up of clearly identifiable heroic or character types, the batboys take pride in separating the genuine from the mistaken impressions of a hero-worshipping but iconoclastic mainstream culture (and its media) outside. What they know is the measure of their value in being in the know. And since what (whom) they know—the main body of the club membership—consists mainly of larger-than-life figures with whom they associate freely and intimately, it is no wonder that the batboys experience their inculcation profoundly and embrace their allegiance strongly and lastingly.

CHAPTER 6 Ritual, Service, and Ethos

Among the hoariest of jokes in my father's repertoire, acquired during a youth largely spent as a vaudeville claqueur, was the one about the man who had the worst job in the circus. The hours were long, the pay was peanuts, and he had to follow along after the elephants and clean up their mess. Why do you stay? he would be asked. Why don't you do something else that's not so hard, that pays more, and that doesn't stink so bad? What, he would answer, and leave show business?

Why would anyone who knows what the job entails want to be a batboy? As Paul Wick told Bob Wolf for *Batboy of the Braves*, a batboy is a laundry man, a shoeshine boy, a waiter, an errand boy, a ballplayer (shagging flies during practice), a janitor, and a messenger. The hours are long, the pay minimal, the tasks menial, the indignities many, the prospects of advancement extremely scarce and limited, the perquisites peripheral, and the whole atmosphere of the job stultifying, boring, dead-ended, demeaning, and devoid of significance or cultivation or uplift. Well, because it might be the only possible way to get into baseball.

To listen to batboys talk about what they do is to hear a job description uttered in tones of pride and cherishing that belie the actual content of the report. There is also an undertone of amusement and affection, suggesting a self-imposed spell that goes with the batboy's emotional attachment to the whole subculture of the clubhouse. As a result of this process, drudgery becomes ritual and menial tasks do take on meaning. The clubhouse procedures are repetitive, enduring, and conventional, and all the rules, habits, and routines have become institutionalized or rationalized as superstitions or, more important, as traditions.

It is with good-humored bemusement that former batboys described their duties to me. Beyond the uniformity of the content of these reports, in fact, it was the unanimity and conformity of the *tone* of the descriptions that was most impressive. When, out of 170, there was a single dissenting voice, it came as a jarring surprise, though I could regard it finally as the exception that proved the rule. It came from a young man in Detroit, Tony Antonio, who had the good grace to come out to the airport to be interviewed while I was waiting for my next flight, rather than meet me at Tiger Stadium.

Tony told me, "The first couple of years were fun, but then I lost interest. I was surprised at how much time was spent on cleaning clothes, toilets, and shoes. I liked being there but not doing all that stuff." His family was disappointed when he quit, in part because he inherited the job from his cousin Dave Cowart, but he "learned that I could make more money cleaning rugs." The "good guys" he remembers were "all good tippers too." Such bottom-line thinking is highlighted by his concluding remark. "What did I learn? Nothing much, really."

Tony Antonio is remarkably open and frank about his values. He simply never bought into the system, never subscribed to the notion that dollars earned in one context could be worth more than dollars earned elsewhere. Traditions and cultural ethos be damned, a dollar is a dollar and work is work. Having rejected the premise that there is something special in the closed world of the baseball clubhouse, values that may be learned, earned, and conferred (but not quantified), Tony's conclusions are valid and unarguable. But for his clubhouse peers (and presumably for his family as well) there is a presumption of inherent value in being there, in accepting on faith what must necessarily go unmeasured, in serving for the sake of belonging, in participating in an experience that is its own reward, and in earning perquisites of quality that are more precious than a sum of salaries. A pearl of great price it is, in itself, to become a member of a baseball club.

Even the lowliest of boot-camp assignments, latrine duty, is spoken of with good humor, acceptance, and self-deprecation. In several cases, that very chore carried with it a special privilege. It was the occasion of being present, unwittingly and unobserved, when there were closed-door meetings in the clubhouse. These stories are told with wide-eyed wonderment, the memories still fresh of how, because they were cleaning showers and sinks and toilets, they got caught behind those doors when the rest of the world was locked out. And what they heard of those sessions was such potently privileged communication that they trembled not only in the fear of being caught listening but also under the burden of bearing sacred secrets.

The quality of the experience is easily captured in the memory of it, but the remembering batboy never unburdens himself of the substance of those exchanges. The bathroom also became a place of sanctuary where players went to smoke once it was banned from clubhouse and field. Fred Costello says that at Candlestick Park batboys were offered a fifty-dollar reward for turning in players for smoking in the bathroom, but he never turned anyone in, "although other players would tell me who was doing it and try to get me to turn them in." So the code of silence extended all the way to the latrine.

Every routine chore in the batboy's job description may evoke a memory of experience charged with meaning. Stories, of an apparently conventional nature, seem to be associated with every aspect of the job description. The abject servility of shining shoes, for example, is rehearsed for every batboy who has a subsequent playing career—encounters on the field with players whose shoes they had shined. There are also the eccentric variations, like the shoeshine that changed the course of a World Series (see the prologue). And there was the time when Bob Short came into the Senators RFK clubhouse with Hubert Humphrey, who characteristically shook hands with everyone, including a batboy who was so excited to shake his hand that he didn't realize it was covered with shoeblack. In Milwaukee, as Mike Doyle tells it, the clubhouse kids made a speed competition out of the shoeshining. One day in the visitors locker room, one of them mistakenly used pine tar instead of the liquid polish, because they came in similar containers. The Giants found their shoes all glued together with pine tar, and Doyle says he can "still hear the Alou brothers swearing in Spanish when they found them."

A batboy's typical workday (the day of a night game) may be broken down into several segments: pregame (itself subdivided according to specific routinized procedures), game time, and postgame. Going over the drill for each segment, we may identify some stories associated with them. Many of those interviewed shared details of their routine assignments, with the most comprehensive reports being those of Wes Patterson of the Royals and Jimmy Triantas of the Orioles, both of whom served for several years during the 1980s. As we go through the routines and chores, however, the conventional anecdotes relating to them will be derived from many sources.

The pregame period falls normally into three segments, the first leading up to batting practice, then BP itself, and finally the period from the end of BP until the umpire's traditional cry of "Play ball!" The first segment may well be the most hectic of all, beginning around 3:00 or 3:30 when the batboys arrive in the clubhouse (after school) or perhaps earlier during the summer months. Patterson describes this time as "runnin' around with my hair on fire." Running errands is the generic phrase for much of this activity, and it is during this time that most of the initiation pranks described in chapter 3 take place. It is a significant time, laden with meaning and value in the batboys' memories.

The errands include mail call, the batboys performing the lowliest bureaucratic function of messenger. Mail is sorted and brought to players' lockers, press releases and stats on other clubs to managers and appropriate coaches. Roy McKercher remembers the day his own stack of mail rivaled that of Willie Mays. It was during the Giants' first season in San Francisco, and Roy had been flown back to New York to be the "mystery guest" on "What's My Line?" That brief appearance, briefer than might have been expected because Arlene Francis guessed his occupation almost at once, generated a lot of fan mail for the batboy, and Mays first teased him about stealing the player's mail—or his thunder—saying, "Why'd you put my mail in your locker?" and then, "One TV show and you get more mail than I do." To share for an instant a small part of the experience of being Willie Mays and then to have Mays acknowledge that sharing are two complementary contributions to the sense of wonderment in the tone of McKercher as he describes the moment three decades later.

The dry cleaning machines are emptied of clothes during this early pregame period, and the batboys see to it that all laundry is distributed properly and fresh sanitary hose laid out in the lockers, which have all been straightened up awaiting the arrival of the players. One of the boys will usually have the daily assignment of tending the umpires' room, cleaning it up, shining their shoes, hanging their underwear and T-shirts from the night before, and setting out fruit, sandwiches, coffee, sodas, and ice for them.

It is a frequent observation that most umpires are overweight, and several batboys account for this condition as a product of the men in blue being on the road throughout the season, eating hotel and clubhouse food, so that providing them with some healthy alternatives is a concern. When John Plein was a Padres batboy in the 1970s, he took particular care to avoid making junk food available to the umpires. Their job is "tougher than a player's," Plein says. "If they were sick, I took care of them, got the doctor, ran to fill prescriptions." He took this part of his assignment so seriously that he began to lobby for the umpire's attendant to be a separate job. The campaign was successful, and Plein has held the job since 1981.

Mickey Morabito, now traveling secretary of the Oakland A's, is another who "became a big umpire fan" during his years as New York Yankees batboy in the early 1970s. Above and beyond assigned duties, Morabito would often drive the umpires downtown after games and even take them out to dinner. His observations about the change in umpires' attitudes, how they have become more confrontational over the years, comes from a privileged vantage. (In Gerlach, a dozen umpires, including Beans Reardon and Shag Crawford, tell their own stories.)

One of his specific memories concerns the traditional value system in which boundaries of baseball procedures are clearly defined. In the Yankees scheme, one batboy was assigned to handle the phone near the home dugout connecting the field with the press box. Mickey was asked to check with the umpire, for the official scorer, about a play at third base. He started to run out toward Jake O'Donnell, who'd made the call, when the home plate umpire stopped him.

"It was Frank Umont, a gruff crew cut guy," Morabito says, "and he says, 'Where the hell you goin?' I told him, and he says, 'God-damn it' and walks back, grabs the telephone, and starts screaming, 'You guys are watchin' the game up there, do your job up there, and don't be askin' us for help.'" When Morabito calls himself an "um-pire fan" he may in part be referring to their function in maintaining appropriate boundaries.

One constant of the umpire-room detail is the delivery of the six cartons of game balls. There the umpire scheduled to call balls and strikes for the game rubs up every ball with specially prepared mud from the bed of the Delaware River. Many batboys reported this ritual, taking special delight not only in their intimate knowledge of this piece of baseball arcana but especially in being a witness to the rite or having had the umpire instruct him in the proper procedure.

Preparations for batting practice primarily involve the orderly movement and arrangement of equipment. This process may begin as much as an hour before BP if any of the players want to take some extra hitting. (And as we have seen, this is another common occa-sion for initiation pranks.) If the batboy has a field assignment for the game, he may want to suit up before BP because he could have little time to do so during pregame preparations. Once the equip-ment is in place—bats, helmets, catchers' equipment, pine tar, rosin bag, donut, weighted bat, towels, batting practice balls, water jug, and Gatorade, all in its proper place and order—and the players begin to take their swings, some of the most cherished moments in batboys' memories come to pass.

Standing around the batting cage, batboys may rub shoulders and share in idle conversation with managers, coaches, players, and each other. Jimmy Triantas recalls the day that he and his buddy Norris Jones were there, watching the Orioles batters, especially Eddie Murray hitting them out from both sides of the plate, and they were laughing about a camping trip they had taken together. Murray came around the cage and asked what they were laughing about. "When we told him," Triantas says, "he joined in. I remember looking over in the stands and seeing some kids just staring at us. At that point I realized how good I had it—me and my best buddy and Eddie Mur-ray kidding around behind the batting cage, while other kids could only stare."

While the players do their stretching exercises, batboys may often be seen playing catch with coaches or each other, but when batting

Extra batting practice for Jeff Kunkel means batboy Mike Macko plays "soft-toss" with him. (courtesy of Mike Macko)

practice itself starts they take up various stations of duty. One is behind second base, where the assignment is to fill buckets with balls retrieved and tossed in from the field and then to deliver them to the mound for further use. On many clubs this is a chore nominally assigned to starting pitchers not scheduled for that game, but they customarily contrive to get clubbies to do it for them. What the kids must concentrate on in that situation is not getting hit by thrown or batted balls, but when they are hit they are not likely to forget it. (A few examples are reported in chapter 3.)

By far one of the most cherished privileges of being a batboy, at least as their stories are conventionally told, is shagging flies during batting practice. In places like Kansas City and Texas, where the temperature is likely to be in three-digit figures during BP through-out much of the season, the players count on the clubbies to do a lot of the shagging. Regardless of the climate, it is during this activity that their awe at the players' skills is most directly experienced, but it is also a time when their own worth is authenticated, when they experience a validation of their membership.

In Detroit one of the kids got hurt shagging flies, so that privilege was lost to Tigers batboys, which made it all the more thrilling for Dave Cowart on his road trip to Boston to be shagging flies in front of the Green Monster in Fenway. Bob Farmer, an outstanding high school, college, and semipro player, says that he learned the difference between baseball at various levels the first time he was in the field for BP at Griffith Stadium. "There came a drive off Minnie Minoso's bat and I charged in for it; it carried so far over my head it hit the wall. Later a Jim Lemon line drive went past my ear so fast my life flashed past too."

Dennis Liborio remembers shagging flies in Tiger Stadium, on the road with the Red Sox, prior to the game that would decide who made the playoffs in 1972. He called off rookie pitcher Don New-hauser on a ball that flew twenty yards over his head, but he attributes the double misjudgment to the tension of a crucial game. The classic story of a batboy's meaningful experience shagging flies, however, has been told by Gerald Rosen, first briefly in his fourth novel, *Growing Up Bronx*, then in expanded form as "Dreams of a Jewish Batboy" in Jerry Klinkowitz's *Writing Baseball*. On his one day as a substitute batboy for the Giants in 1954, he found himself in center field in the Polo Grounds fifteen feet to the left of Willie Mays. Instinctively he moved for a ball hit between them, yelled "I got it," and made a graceful catch as the great Mays turned away. Only then did he realize the enormity of what he had done, but after a moment of unease he "began to feel as if I were glowing, as if I had been alleviated by moon gravity and somehow all the organs and tubes which filled my body had been magically transmuted into a diamondlike light" (*Writing* 54).

Ritual, Service, and Ethos   149

A peak moment for the batboy: Mike Macko pitches batting practice. (courtesy of Mike Macko)

Rosen speaks of leaving the Polo Grounds that day with "a sheaf of memories" that would stay with him for a lifetime, but no longer with the dream of becoming a big-league player. His story has an epilogue worth telling, passed along to me by Jerry Klinkowitz. It seems that Rosen was working on final copy for his first book with his editor in her Brooklyn Heights apartment when Miles Davis dropped by to see her. When Rosen suggested she tell him to bug off, he became "the only person in history to call off *both* Willie Mays and Miles Davis."[21]

The crucial element of these ballpark experiences is the thrilling opportunity for the batboy to perform, in uniform, on the same field, alongside major league players. However routine the drill, the performance elevates and exalts him. On rare occasions or in some rare circumstances, a batboy may get to participate directly with players in exercises demanding a higher level of skill, like taking part in infield practice, playing burnout or pepper, even pitching batting practice. In Boston, the owner of the Red Sox made it a regular practice to play pepper with the batboys every day. Dennis Liborio remembers protecting Tom Yawkey's right side, with Vince Orlando at his left. "I'd be wearing a first baseman's mitt and a batting

Member of the club, batboy Merritt Riley warms up alongside all-star Wade Boggs. (courtesy of Merritt Riley)

helmet—like Dick Allen—and Mr. Yawkey had a Ty Cobb model glove about the size of his hand. He always wondered how I could catch the ball with that big thing." It was fun, but the best part was that "every month he'd give us fifty to a hundred dollars for playing with him." In San Diego, John Plein enjoyed playing pepper with Bob Davis and Willie Davis, especially when some Padres pitchers would join them and get frustrated and embarrassed when a batboy was better than they were at it. In San Francisco, Bob Fenech was pretty good at it, too, but could never get the bat out of Willie Davis's hands. "Catch ten balls in a row and you can bat," Davis used to say, but if Fenech got up to eight Davis would smash one through.

At Candlestick Park Patrick Quinlan was running an errand into the visiting clubhouse where he met Willie Mays, then a Mets coach. Later, on the field, Quinlan played pepper with Mays, and remembers it now as "sheer heaven . . . the greatest moment in my life." Mays, in fact, often gratified a clubhouse kid by playing catch with him before a game. His very last game as a player was in a Mets uniform in Candlestick, and it was Mario Alioto he asked to play catch with him. Mario was so nervous, he says, that it felt like Willie was throwing two hundred miles an hour while the fans were giving him a tremendous ovation. Across the Bay in Oakland, Mike Pieraldi's memory has both pleasure and pain involved. He was delighted when Brooks Robinson asked him to play catch, but ended up with a badly sprained thumb when Robinson fooled him with a knuckleball.

Kenny Bush, who wanted to be a player, started batboying for the Phillies right at the start of his teens. He kept doing it for eighteen seasons, and though he never made it as a player—he couldn't hit— his fielding was good enough for him to play shortstop during second infield drills. Larry Shenk, who does PR for the Phillies, reminiscing about his early love of baseball, says, "I used to go early to games at Connie Mack Stadium and used to be there when they'd take infield practice, and there was this kid taking infield during second infield—it was Kenny Bush—and I'd envy him and wonder how he got to do that." Now he knows that it was part of Kenny's recompense for being a batboy for so long.

In every one of these reminiscences a common theme appears, that of the thrill of taking part in these ritual practices as an equal, a full celebrant among celebrities and the envy of all who behold them. Steve Winship remembers Rickey Henderson as the worst burnout player, who threw so hard at him from fifteen feet that he once broke the webbing of Steve's glove. Tony (The Flea) Simokaitis and Kurt Schlogo say that Tony Pena and Jose Oquendo were the worst when they were with the Cardinals. They would throw the ball as hard as possible from fifteen feet until someone quit; "they're crazy."

While the lucky ones are on the field during batting practice, others are performing a variety of duties in the clubhouse: cutting up fruit, preparing the postgame spread, keeping the locker room clean, packing bags if it's getaway day, picking up dirty clothes, shining coaches' dress shoes, seeing to the managers' needs, even getting some players' cars washed. But when BP is over, the pace goes into overdrive. In order for players to relax up until game time, the clubbies rush madly to deal with clothes, equipment, and refreshment for them.

But after a frantic hour, there's about a half-hour lull. Often this is the time when batboys try to get the players to sign balls in the universal PR activity of the trade. Many players find this tedious and perhaps infra dig, and so the tradition of batboy forgeries has grown to be part of the job description. Legend has it that it began when Charlie (The Brow) Di Giovanna began signing for the Dodgers manager Burt Shotton, who was suffering from a palsy that made it too difficult for him to sign the balls himself. Over time, it became de rigueur for each batboy to master a certain number of signatures, including those of visiting players. In Washington, Tom MacDougal practiced for hours to get the Mantle and Berra hands down pat and signed hundreds of balls for those two stars, who hated to do it themselves. In Anaheim, where Bob Elder handled the Mantle signature, Mantle once told him, "Hey, you're a better signature guy than the guy I got in New York." Elder was proud of his "letter-perfect" signature, but his favorite story about signing balls is about the time that Rod Carew said he didn't want to be bothered when Jim Fregosi was passing two dozen balls around for signatures, until Harmon Killebrew, who rarely said anything in the clubhouse, handed them back to Carew, saying, simply, "Sign 'em—now," and he did.

It is during this lull in the game's occupation that some of the oddest chores are imposed on batboys. Roy Firestone enjoyed running out to get a mess of ribs for Boog Powell. (Appropriately, Boog now sells his own brand of barbecued ribs behind right field in Camden Yards.) At Wrigley Field, Rich Eberle used to have to run out and get Ron Santo hot dogs and hamburgers from outside the ballpark—until manager Leo Durocher caught him. "I hope that sandwich tastes good," Durocher said to Santo, "because it cost you a hundred and fifty bucks."

The pregame lull is the time for many of those errands relating to the kinds of activities that Bouton's *Ball Four* and other such books have reported to the partial tarnishing of the all-American game. It is the time of notes carried to women in the stands, of room keys discreetly deposited in eager hands, and even of money forwarded for other kinds of action. Mark Sassetti remembers that during one season when the A's were in town to play the White Sox the Illinois Lotto had gotten up to $42 million and players were handing him twenty- and fifty-dollar bills to buy tickets for them. Jose Canseco peeled off two bills from a roll of about fifty hundred-dollar bills, and Sassetti ended up buying $480 worth of quik-piks at the Greek liquor store on Halsted Street.

Occasional betting in the clubhouse is usually limited to NFL pools in the early fall, Kentucky Derby and Indianapolis 500 pools in May, or small-stakes card games, but there is the occasional plunging exception. Paul Gonoud tells the following story about Mickey Rivers (whose horse betting was just one of his colorful off-field activities) visiting Yankee Stadium when he was with the Texas Rangers. "One day he comes in with a hot tip on a horse. Some guy in the bleachers gave it to him, number two in the third race. Mickey gives the tip to clubhouse guys, players, everyone, and collects money and sends me out to the Meadowlands with several hundred bucks to bet it all on the nose. So I bet it, number two in the third, and he runs out. Turns out, the tip horse was running at Yonkers. Actually, it didn't matter, because the right horse ran third anyway."

There is a broad general consensus that the game itself is the easiest time for batboys. Tony Pastore adds that it is the easiest time for players as well and maybe the least important thing, just "one thing they do in a working day" that might include benefits and chores for the Players Association in addition to taking care of their bodies and their financial affairs. Like many others, Pastore says, "For me, I can't wait for the game to start, so I can rest a little."

During the game, the primary requirement is to attend to the basic details of his particular assignment. The job title itself implies tending to the bats, having them in order, getting them into the batters' hands, replacing them promptly if cracked, and retrieving them promptly to keep them out of the way of play. Mistakes are costly in this last regard, but there are other considerations for this most elementary of duties. Batboys have to know how and when to take the bat from the hands of a player who has struck out, and they have to learn special rules like the "Reggie rule": keep your eyes open and be ready to duck because that bat could fly anywhere. A career that totaled 2,662 strikeouts made that a vital rule to obey.

Hank Aaron struck out only 1,383 times to go with his 755 home runs, but Gilly Lefebvre remembers how "he went bananas when I tried to take his bat" after he fanned. Wherever Rusty Staub played, batboys had to cater to his fetish, never putting his bat in the rack and making sure he had it in his hands to carry back to the dugout to hold between at-bats. In at least one case, to take the hitter's bat required an act of genuine heroism: it was batboy Gus Tham who took the bat/weapon from Juan Marichal's hands when his attack on John Roseboro had initiated the melee.

Batboys must develop a feel for the rhythms of the game so that they can anticipate both the action and the pauses, to be in the right place—either out of the way or right there to do the appropriate chore. Meeting the relief pitcher at the right point between bullpen and mound to take his warm-up jacket requires delicate timing, and so does stepping out of the dugout to catch the one-hop toss of an infield practice ball when a new inning is about to start. A good batboy will learn how to judge which fouled balls may be kept in play and which should be tossed out, and he will never delay a game by failing to keep a ready supply of new balls in the plate umpire's pouch.

As many have observed, the measure of a good batboy is like that of an umpire: if you don't notice him, he's done a good job. Still, several have been distinguished by their efficient speed in doing their routine chores. Mahendra Naik, for example, in the early days of the expansion Blue Jays, would get more applause for his hustle from Toronto fans than the players got, which was a source of chagrin to him; he wasn't supposed to get attention. At the other extreme is the Orioles batboy, Ivan Crayton, whose languid efficiency in setting out and retrieving pine tar rag, donut, and weighted bat each inning occupies the inter-inning interval so slowly and so fully that it has become a remarkable sort of somnambulistic spectacle in Camden Yards.

When batboys are caught up in extraordinary circumstances, attention is inevitable. Chad Blossfield with Nippy Jones's shoe-polished ball in the World Series and Merritt Riley with George Brett's pine-tarred bat are obvious examples. But slighter occasions, as when Gerald Rosen had to run on the field with a cup of eyewash for Ted Kluszewski, may lead to batboys entering, in Rosen's phrase, the "sacred fraternity of 'The Televised'" (*Writing* 57). At one time, the ritual celebration of batboy greeting home run hitter at the plate became such a staple photo opportunity for newspaper immortality

Joining the "sacred fraternity of 'The Televised,'" batboy Tony Atlas is interviewed before a "Game of the Week" by Jim Hill of CBS. (photo by David J. Hopley, courtesy of Tony Atlas)

that league rules were instituted to remove the minor actor from center stage.

Perhaps no moment of on-field intimacy is more rewarding to a batboy than professional conversation in the on-deck circle. Mark Stowe was impressed with Pete Rose's intensity during a game. "You didn't talk to him or break his concentration, and he said little on the bench. But in the on-deck circle, he'd hand the donut to the batboy and tell him when he was gonna bunt." In San Francisco, Bob Fenech liked to ask hitters to name the toughest pitchers they had faced (Koufax and Gibson were the consensus answers), but one day Ron Hunt of the Mets ignored the pleasantries to send Bob for a new bat. There wasn't another one of his in the dugout so Bob had to run to the clubhouse. By the time he got back, Hunt had hit a home run with the old bat he didn't like, but yelled at the batboy, "Where the hell was that bat?" and then used the new one next time up.

It is a gesture of professional respect when a player asks a batboy

Joe Kuhel of the Senators waits to congratulate Buddy Lewis, who has homered in 1937; next in line to shake hands is batboy George Catloth. (courtesy of George Catloth)

in the on-deck circle about the pitcher. Gilly Lefebvre says it happened often, but that when he told Joe Torre that the Dodgers pitcher had nothing but "heat," and Torre struck out three times that day, the player didn't laugh when the batboy asked, "What happened?" Mark McKenzie had mixed results from his on-deck conversations with visitors in Minnesota. He endeared himself to Reggie Jackson by tipping him that Jerry Koosman liked to throw a slow curve and then follow it with a slower one. Jackson went to the plate and froze on the slow curve for a strike and a 2-2 count, then sat back and waited for the slower one that he hit into the seats. But during the same season McKenzie's careless remark to Frank Robinson about Tommy Hall's repertoire of pitches resulted in a summons to Robinson's kangaroo court.

During the game itself, some clubbies remain inside, rarely even keeping up with the progress of the game. But even while attending to clothes, shoes, buffets, and general cleaning, clubbies may find themselves at a privileged vantage point: they can see the temper tantrums of players removed from games or of managers ejected. Some of those performances have taken on the trappings of heroic feats of anger in the witnesses' memories, as locker rooms are trashed, uniforms are soaked or burned, and whole buffet banquets are violently rendered inedible. And sometimes, as Wes Patterson says, "a clubhouse guy gets to play psychologist or group therapist. Here I am, making five bucks an hour, and I'm sitting next to Mark Gubicza making a million, but who's been knocked out of a game. And I'm telling him to relax, calm down, and if I'm lucky I cheer him up."

The postgame scene in the clubhouse is often described as resembling the John Landis movie *Animal House*. Of course, before the batboys get in there they have to clear all equipment from the bench, and once the field lights are turned off it's hard to find the odd contact lens case left in the dugout. Then there are whole new sets of errands to be run, messages to deliver to friends in the opposing clubhouse, to family or friends waiting outside, and the like. Umpires also require attention. When the players are showered, fed, dressed, and interviewed—in whatever order—and the clubhouse is left to the clubbies, often around midnight, then batboys can relax. They get to eat whatever food is left, but there are uniforms to clean and hang up, shoes to shine, dishes to wash, and lockers to straighten out.

Even the routine chores of the postgame period can have their fringe benefits in intimacy within the baseball family. John Mitchell gets to drive with Frank Howard to the airport and lives to tell about it and return with the big man's car. Another batboy will find a large amount of money in a visiting player's locker, race to the airport to return it, and come home with a fat tip. Another will find Roger Clemens's wedding ring and reach him with the news just before he boards his plane in Chicago. Still another will open the door to a frightened player who has rushed back to find his missing stash of drugs and witness his relief when the clubhouse man takes him aside to return it without acknowledgment of its contents.

It is common practice for some players when they go on road trips to leave their cars in the care of batboys. They have to have them washed and gassed up when the team returns home, but in the meantime they have free use. Several have wonderful memories of driving to their proms in a star's convertible, Joe Morgan's Cadillac getting repeated mention. And inevitably there are the mishaps. For Kevin Cashen it was a friend accidentally ripping the top of Larry (The Hawk) Harlow's Monte Carlo; he not only told Cashen not to worry about it but tipped him two hundred dollars for the season. For Don Deason it was smashing the front end of Lou Brock's Dodge Daytona into the parking lot wall shortly after getting his license. Brock laughed and said, "Don't worry about it. I own the dealership."

Best of all, on occasion, players and coaches may sit around for hours drinking beer and swapping sagas while the batboys are privileged to sit and listen. Billy Turner and Bob Farmer still remember the feeling of being truly blessed to hear Rocky Bridges tell his tales into the small hours. John Nelson calls Steve Kemp a "throwback" for the way he would hang around the locker room talking baseball. In both Texas and Cincinnati, Buddy Bell is remembered the same way. Going back a little further, Scot MacDougal recalls, "Billy Martin and Cookie Lavagetto were two guys who'd visit with you for hours in the clubhouse after games." Gilly Lefebvre identified clubhouse man Jim Muhey as "one of the great storytellers in the game, along with Dick Stuart and Stan Musial," but Mike Murphy bestows the palm for best baseball storyteller of all on Steve Bilko, a journeyman first baseman whose ten seasons among four teams (two in each league) gave him a cast of thousands for his tales.

One of the most impressive results of this whole study has been the unanimity of values expressed by former batboys as they attempt to assess the lessons learned from their experience. Almost to a man they spoke of the "work ethic" they learned both in the clubhouse and by observing baseball men and especially the players they admired. Then there was a pairing of two apparently contradictory tenets. One is an egalitarianism based on the two principles that even superstars are human beings who put their uniform pants on one leg at a time, and that every person who has ever been employed in any capacity in the clubhouse is a full and equal member of the baseball confraternity—an insider where all outsiders are absolutely excluded. The other is an appreciation of hierarchy, based on the notion that the way to maintain the treasured sanctity of their special world is for every person to take care of his assigned role, to be a team player, to sacrifice for the club, and not to overreach. (Michener 102 cites Al Rosen's articulation of the principle that baseball is not a democracy.)

Hierarchical egalitarianism is not unique to baseball, nor is it necessarily an oxymoronic construction. The Round Table, after all, had its King Arthur and its heroic elite, and Olympus had its rigid internal hierarchy although all its denizens were of the eternal elect. Indeed, the whole feudal construct, the degrees of Masonry, and categories within halls of fame all give the lie to the apparent intrinsic contradiction. What seems to be a unifying characteristic of all these groups is the high value of keeping the faith, of maintaining an allegiance to the code of the group, which includes protecting its secrets, so that *any* contradiction may be dismissed as something that cannot be understood by the uninitiated.

So it is with baseball. The allegiance to the game is an abiding article of faith, but it is not translated into hanging on as a *fan*. Fans, by definition, are *outsiders*, so that former batboys often express their discomfort with sitting in the stands, their unwillingness to mingle with the unwashed, the unblessed who never carried a rosin bag to the mound or shined a pair of major league spiked shoes. The basic loyalty is not to club, team, franchise, or even personnel, but to the game, to the ways, values, and attitudes that characterize the subculture.

As these men extrapolate their batboying lessons to the world outside and to their later lives, they have trouble articulating much beyond a nostalgic longing for a way and time that has been left behind. But it can translate very loosely to a kind of "conservative" patriotism in which what they admire as "American" is what they cannot readily find in the society they inhabit. Perhaps that is why so many of them end up in law enforcement, and why they say things like "Baseball is the door to the world of men" and "If every kid in America could be a batboy, America would be a better place."

On rare occasions, an insightful observation is reported from one who has managed to achieve the perspective of an outsider. Tony Atlas, for example, says that he wouldn't want his son to be a

With shared patriotic pride, batboy Dave Cowart and Tigers catcher Lance Parrish doff their caps to salute for the national anthem. (courtesy of David Cowart)

batboy—and not just because it would limit his ability to participate in baseball as a player. His own mother, Tony says, if she had to make that decision again, wouldn't let him do it. She claims that the environment of the Angels clubhouse changed Tony's value system, and not for the better, when he got too close to the cars, the money, and the women. And Tony agrees, at least on one issue. "I wouldn't want my son to learn, as I did," he says, "to treat high school girls the way players treat women, often as objects but a hazard of being a groupie."

It may be an inevitable negative side effect of a men's club that women are demeaned, but it takes a rare club member to acknowledge that as a problem or a liability. Over against that effect, however, is the frequently reported positive lesson of tolerant racial attitudes, a value that goes hand in hand, in batboys' experience, with lessons of teamwork and mutual respect. "I use that now—mutual respect—in my work as a police officer," says Kansas City's Eric Winebrenner. And Jerry Schroer, who owns and operates a nursing home company, says that his experience in Sportsman's Park at the time when blacks were first being accepted in the majors has made him "extremely sensitive to bigotry ever since."

The virtues associated with being a "red-blooded American man" are thus particularized in the clubhouse ethos as object lessons for batboys. As a result, even Mike Pieraldi, who describes himself as the "last of the counterculture batboys—or maybe the first," has some positive feelings, mixed though they may be with notions about alternatives, about the value system. When Mike wore a black armband into the clubhouse in mourning for the victims at Kent State, he was shocked out of it by the first player who saw it and said, "Are you in sympathy with those people? They all shoulda been shot." And when Bobby Kennedy was shot while the A's were on a road trip, after the team came home there was simply no discussion of politics at all in the Oakland clubhouse. But for all that, this self-styled "Abbie Hoffman of baseball" says, "I learned healthy attitudes from players: to do your best to give it your best shot, to set goals, and that trying and failing is better than not trying," because for them, after all, baseball is not just a game but their life.

Scot MacDougal, now a business entrepreneur, says that sports are a great teacher of discipline, that he learned the lessons of hard work and perseverance from ballplayers. Bill Turner, now a district court judge, says the lessons were dedication and teamwork and that if someone is paying you a dollar, to give them a dollar and a quarter of effort. And Pat McBride, a doctor, says that he always appreciated the positive feedback from players who called him the "Charlie Hustle of batboys." The primary pre-med lessons, according to Dr. McBride, were that hard work pays off and that life could be good if you enjoyed what you did.

Throughout this chapter detailing the chores, lessons, and values taken on and taken in by batboys, we have seen them play two general roles that have also become fixed in the fiction and mythology of baseball. As neophyte or acolyte, we have seen them as the lowest of the low, but elevated by the whole set of totems they serve. And as silent witness or audience, we have seen them exalted by what they have been privileged by their very presence to see and hear.

Jeff Millar and Bill Hinds, the canny satirists of the comic strip "Tank McNamara," once depicted Donald Trump seeking to relieve financial pressure by borrowing from Jose Canseco. In return for the loan, Trump accepts the ultimate humiliation of serving as Canseco's batboy. And in a climactic demonstration of the ignorance of arrogance, Trump—wearing the uniform designation "BB" and carrying a stack of bats—says, "For God's sake, I don't *know* what 'the pine tar rag' *is*."

In "The Day the Walrus Hit .400," Louis Phillips has a character say, "I'd be lucky to end up as a bat-boy in Siberia" (71), an indication that that would be the lowest position on the lowest totem pole in the game, while also implying that it's still in the game and that anything outside is unthinkable. In Lawrence Ritter's *The Glory of Their Times*, Sam Crawford, speaking from the vantage of almost a century ago, says that "those old Baltimore Orioles didn't pay any more attention to Ned Hanlon, their manager, than they did to the batboy" (227). And that assumption of "lowest" is echoed by the use of the word "even" in David Halberstam's report of the meticulous care taken in negotiating the deal that brought Fred Sanford to the Yankees: "Never had George Weiss checked out a deal so carefully—he even questioned the St. Louis clubhouse boys and the St. Louis reporters about Sanford's personal habits" (231). But to link the clubbies with the beat reporters is to conjoin two wholly different orders of mythology.

As a corollary to the position of lowliest rank among those who serve the club, batboys are also in position to hear the sacred secrets, to absorb the mythology, and to be witness or audience to their performance or recitation. I am reminded of the prisoners on the chain gang who are blessed to sit at Dragline's feet in Donn Pearce's novel *Cool Hand Luke*, hearing the epic exploits of their hero from his chronicler. A first-person narrator both records that chronicle and testifies to its value for him, while in Stuart Rosenberg's movie version that quality is dramatized in the closing sequence as George Kennedy's Dragline fulfills the requests of his captive audience to perform his narrative remembrance of Paul Newman's Luke and therewith ennoble their existence with some mythological, or at least mythologized, value. It may be more to the point to allude to *One Flew Over the Cuckoo's Nest*, where it is Ken Kesey's artifice to have his narrator, Chief Bromden, adopt deafmute and chronic catatonic poses *so that* he will be allowed to witness and absorb the elements of the story he is narrating.

Fred Haney called the batboy's privileged position "the most dazzling vantage point of all. . . . In him lives the spirit of baseball, a

sport scientific, fascinating, and, above all, human" (Wick ix).
Haney also insists on the importance of the position, one of "pride
and envy." Indeed, that special vantage translates into mythology.
Only the batboy in *The Natural* knows the secret of Roy Hobbs's
magic bat, Wonderboy. In Jerry Klinkowitz's *Short Season*, the story
"Nicknames" shows how only the batboy can report—as in this
case he does verbatim—what he has heard from "just a yard behind
the screen" (80). And when Sam Jones, in *The Glory of Their Times*,
tells how Ed Barrow got him from the clubhouse checkers game to
the field for pictures, it is the batboy who is the necessary go-
between (227).

W. P. Kinsella's fictional treatments of baseball generally have a
structure of fantasy within fantasy. In such an arrangement the inner mythology of baseball can be conflated or confused with fans'
musings. In *The Iowa Baseball Confederacy*, a nostalgic fan rein-
vents himself as a historical mascot/batboy, who then becomes a
heroic participant in the epic playing out of the fantasy game. In
Daniel Stern's *Rookie of the Year*, this fantasy of a young fan as
Cinderella pitching hero with magical (that is, orthopedically freak-
ish) powers is depicted in simpleminded innocence (just as it was in
Lloyd Bacon's *It Happens Every Spring*, with a college professor as
adolescent naif with magical chemical powers). Perhaps the ultimate fantasy is *The Kid from Left Field*, Harmon Jones's 1953 movie
remade for television by Adell Aldrich in 1979, in which an eleven-
year-old becomes a batboy in midseason and club manager soon
after, dazzling all with his knowledge of history, trivia, strategy, and
technique.

In Kinsella's story "How I Got My Nickname" (*Thrill* 50–51),
however, there is implicit acknowledgment that such folktale na-
iveté is somehow a violation of baseball tradition. The narrator is
caught by the batboy "staring wide-eyed at the players and the playing field" and responds by curling his lip and sticking out his
tongue. Even the enacted fulfillment of the narrator's fantasy is
disgustedly rejected by the knowing batboy, whose observation of
the boy-fan's transient glory is, "Take a picture, it'll last longer."

At the end of a working batboy's day, the fortunate final role of
story-hearer is the one that encapsulates the whole worth of his
position. There, listening to the legends and lore of the game, as told
by such chroniclers and bards as Rocky Bridges and Steve Bilko, he

takes in the mythos of baseball. And in his devotion he embraces its codes and values. Having been rendered worthy to become a part of it all, he then has it become an essential part of him. As story-hearer, Mike Mullane concludes, "I learned that the clubhouse is a shrine, and I was living out a fantasy being there."

CHAPTER 7 Queer for the Yard

"I always saw baseball as magical, larger than life," says Mike Mullane, taking advantage of a break in his classes at St. Mary's College to reflect on his batboy experience.

> And those feelings were just enhanced as a Giants batboy. I was so in awe that first day I couldn't speak—the grass of Candlestick Park seemed like a magic carpet.
>
> It gets in your blood, you know, becomes a part of your life and you never want to give it up. It's also a job, a tedious one with long hours, but whenever it would start to get to me I'd tell myself that I'm where a million others would love to be. I was a seventh grader then, and the first week in June I asked for the Friday night off so I could go to my school dance.
>
> When the players heard that, they started kidding me, taunting, saying, "What's the matter, aren't you queer for the yard? Aren't you queer for the yard?" I was upset at first, misunderstood what they were saying. But then I realized two things—they were asking me if

my love for baseball didn't come first, and they were letting me know by teasing me that way that they liked me and accepted me.

Rick Merschbach had a Cincinnati version of Mike Mullane's story. Going to his high school prom, he dressed in the Reds clubhouse after an afternoon's work. He took a lot a razzing that night, led by Joe Morgan, but when he left in his tux to pick up his date he was driving Morgan's green Cadillac with the white top folded down.

As a business major in college, Mullane hoped for some kind of front office job in baseball. Meanwhile, having outlived his batboy years, he continued to work for the Giants as bullpen catcher, traveling with the team during the summer. "Baseball is more than a game," he says. "It's a way of life. The clubhouse is a shrine, and for me to be part of it is living out a fantasy. There's a passage in Roger Kahn's *Good Enough to Dream* that really hits home. It says that baseball is the door to the world of men. That's just what it has been for me. It's a comfortable, safe feeling, sitting around any clubhouse in America with baseball people, talking, just talking. If that's what it means to be queer for the yard, then I am."

Mullane, a young man in his early twenties, has thus summarily articulated many of the themes of this study, especially in his illustration of the perception that it is the world of the clubhouse that lends a special magic to the game. At least, to play on Con Conrad's phrasing, some call it magic, but I call it love.[22] Over and over again I heard the same sentiments echoed among my sources, in a variety of tones, and enacted in various ways. What comes through with virtual unanimity is that, though their feeling for baseball may not have changed as the result of being batboy, it grew and intensified. In this chapter, more than elsewhere, it seems to me important to quote my sources verbatim, to allow the lover to express the intensity of his feelings in his own language. The familiar, echoing phrases themselves will do more to capture the essence of the feelings than any summary or analysis could.

"If every kid in America could be a batboy, America would be a better place," says teamster Gus Tham. Bill Turner agrees. Now a judge in Montgomery County, Maryland, he says, "If I were offered a job today to be a batboy for a month, I'd take it in a minute. It was a fantasy job, a dream come true. I could have pinched myself."

Clayton Wilson, a junior marketing major at the University of Minnesota when interviewed, sounded just like Mullane. "I was

Jim Ryan, Bill Turner, and Bob Farmer (l-r) played ball together and batboyed together. Still in close touch with one another almost four decades later, Farmer is a police officer in Maryland, Turner a judge, and Ryan an FBI man in Phoenix. (courtesy of Jim Ryan)

always in love with baseball, caught it from my three older brothers, I guess, and I was a Twins fan since age five. Now I'm just hoping I can do an internship with the Twins as part of my degree."

"I ate and slept baseball before I became a Senators batboy," says Jim Ryan. "Played every day after school till dark, all day summers and weekends. Bob Farmer, Tom MacDougal—both also became Senators batboys—and I played baseball at Pinecrest Field every free moment. The batboy experience changed my attitude not at all. I still love the game. It was the best job ever." Active with the FBI in Phoenix, Ryan continues to maintain his baseball contacts, particularly during spring training.

In Chicago, the Sassetti brothers share that feeling of love and commitment. "I don't know what I'd be about if I wasn't around baseball," says Jim, five years a White Sox batboy. And Mark works a regular forty-hour week that takes him to Wrigley Field as a Pepsi rep on a schedule arranged so that he can carry on in the Comiskey clubhouse.

Frank McNulty was the most publicized batboy of his time by virtue of posing for one of Norman Rockwell's most famous *Saturday Evening Post* covers in 1948. A couple of years later he was featured in a *Sport* Magazine story headed, "Everybody Envies the Batboy." "And why not?" McNulty muses, reminiscing about those days. "To sit through a pennant-winning season is an experience like no other. It feels like destiny has taken over, everything preordained to work out right. Amazing things would happen for the Braves in '48.

"In Chicago, the lead had shrunk to a game or two, and we lost the first game of a doubleheader and then were losing the second. I remember that Jeff Heath hit a drive over rookie Hal Jeffcoat's head. Jeffcoat hit his head on the ivied wall and Heath, who'd normally take two and a half days to run around the bases, had an inside-the-park home run." It was an interview with a comptroller in Framingham, who happened to be a baseball nut and zeroed in on McNulty's World Series ring, that launched a successful business career for the former batboy, who is now president of *Parade* magazine.

It is no surprise that in some cases the personal feelings are so strong that the former batboys insist on keeping them to themselves. The relationships they value are treasured in a chosen privacy, even when baseball continues to be part of their lives. In Baltimore, for example, equipment manager Jimmy Tyler balks at sharing any of his batboy experience. "I don't have much to say," he says with cordial understatement. "They are all good memories, but I like to keep them to myself."

Cleveland's Bill Sheridan, for many years the visiting clubhouse manager in Memorial Stadium, happens to have been batboy for the champion Indians in 1948, and his attitude echoes Tyler's, only more aggressively. "I don't like to talk," he said. "I don't share. I keep my stories inside; they're mine." But the patient interviewer is rewarded with some comments anyway.

"I still love baseball," he said, as if reluctant to acknowledge the feeling. "But I don't like the way it's changed. I remember Joe Gordon and Kenny Keltner and Early Wynn," he added, as if today's players are not in the same league or worthy of the same regard. Then, after a reflective pause, "We used to have what we called 'getaway pitchers.' I bet you never heard that one. Games were played in two hours, an hour and forty-five minutes—fastest games you ever saw, because it was getaway day and they had a train to catch. No," he says, the jealous lover till the end, "my memories are my own."

The stories of love affairs with baseball are often tinged with regret and sustained by memorabilia, souvenirs in the original nostalgic sense of the term. To walk downstairs in Jack Hughes's suburban Maryland home (address unlisted because of his fears for the security of his treasures) is to enter a museum-like time capsule. Two full rooms are crammed with pictures, programs, bats, balls, gloves, and anything that might bear a baseball autograph.

"Baseball has been central to my life," Hughes says. "I worked around the stadium for sixteen years, mostly in concessions, but in '56 I was visiting batboy for the Senators." His lifelong habit of collecting celebrity autographs, pictures, and memorabilia began when, as a boy, he was hospitalized with a brain tumor. It was how his dad kept him diverted during the many slow months. He soon focused on baseball and specialized in the Yankees, his favorites. Prominently displayed now are pictures of himself with Mickey Mantle and Whitey Ford, taken at Cooperstown after their induction into the Hall of Fame, events that Hughes had promised to witness while he was shining their shoes eighteen years before.

"I have two regrets in life," he says. "Twice I failed to follow up on opportunities that might have kept me in baseball. First, I could have gone to Minnesota with the club when Griffith moved the franchise. Despite a lack of specifics, I was offered a job with them. Second, when I finished college at Mount St. Mary's, I could have gone to graduate school in sports management at Ohio University. And then, maybe . . . ." The sentence is never finished, but the wishful look is clear. Hughes has fashioned a successful business career, mostly in public relations, and now spends leisure time not just with his family and his golf game and his memorabilia but also as a volunteer seller of season tickets for the Baltimore Orioles. The torch burns brightly still.

Ray Crump did go to Minnesota, but only after being told he couldn't have the equipment manager's job with the new Washington franchise. "I was ten years old when I was hired as a visiting

At the Baseball Hall of Fame in Cooperstown, Jack Hughes keeps his promise to Mickey Mantle and Whitey Ford. (courtesy of Jack Hughes)

clubhouse boy in 1949," he says. "I got fifty cents a day, and it cost thirty-four cents carfare to get there and home. But I loved it. It was like going to a boys' club for me.

"I was the youngest batboy at the time, wore number 97 on my uniform. Bucky Harris gave me that number. Calvin Griffith—my only boss—retired number 97 when I left the field for the clubhouse, and that was a guy who didn't even want to retire Harmon Killebrew's number." When Crump left the Twins clubhouse a few years ago, he "retired" to a baseball souvenir store and museum across from the stadium. He is not at all unwilling to advertise his baseball background and connections, but as far as his best batboy stories are concerned, well, he's working on his own book.

Tom MacDougal finds all the interest and excitement about cards and shows and autographs to be "comical." Talking about how much he loved being a batboy, he says, "Every day was like a first trip to Disneyland; it was the most fun time of my life. But all my baseball cards are personally signed to me by players. They're dog-eared and wrinkled, therefore 'worthless' or 'valueless' to collectors. To me they're invaluable."

One souvenir that got away from the MacDougal brothers was the Opening Day ball that young Scotty brought to President Eisenhower for his signature. Ike was glad to sign the ball, but neither Tom nor Scot will ever forget what happened next. Calvin Griffith took the ball out of the president's hand, said, "You don't have to do that," and then, turning to the batboy, "Beat it." It is small consolation that the boy had already been obliged by the vice president. "To Scotty, your pal, Dick Nixon," reads the souvenir ball.

The souvenir ball that Bill Turner treasures is unique. It is hand-painted in four brilliant colors and signed by the artist, pitcher Russ Kemmerer, who presented it to Turner, inscribed with a personal message, when he finished his tour of duty as Senators batboy.

Merritt Riley's room in his father's house in Levittown has several personalized items of memorabilia. Most prominent is a blow-up of the famous George Brett-Billy Martin pine-tar-bat incident, with the batboy right in the middle. The photo is signed by all those directly involved. But it is in the utility shed behind the house, in a trunk locked as securely as Jack Benny's vault, that the mother lode of Merritt's memorabilia is found—his collection of signed bats. When I visited Riley, he was working as a bartender at the Canterbury Ales in Oyster Bay, just a relay throw from the site of the Avianca plane crash. His father is a retired policeman, and Merritt was waiting for admission to the police academy. He has since become one of New York's finest, patrolling the Brownsville section of Brooklyn, but at the time he was also considering the possibility of going to Joe Brinkman's umpire school. "For three years," he says, "I did nothing but live baseball. I was a celebrity among my friends, and it was a tough transition after. I regret that I didn't try to open any doors to a possible career in baseball." And then, trailing off with the wistful look I'd seen so often in others, "Maybe going to umpire school . . . ."

What can happen when the love affair has run its course and a forced separation occurs? If there is a chance for reconciliation, doesn't the former lover often pursue it? Can't absence make the heart grow fonder? Can the relationship be redefined and accepted, even if there are limitations imposed and conditions attached? Can a chief's favorite ever settle for the role of second squaw in the tepee? What about, Can't we still be friends?

Take the case of Patrick Quinlan. "I loved being Giants batboy, especially being around players who loved what they were doing. It was heaven. The greatest moment of my life was meeting Willie Mays, when he came back to the Stick as a Mets coach. I not only got to rap with him for twenty minutes, but I played pepper with him and slapped five." When he moved to Los Angeles and began a career in restaurant management, Patrick couldn't stay away from the ballpark. "Well," he says, "at first I'd manage to get to sixty games a year at Chavez, but it wasn't the same, and I gradually cut back. But I missed the feeling of somehow being part of the game. So ten years after I hung up my uniform in 1979, I jumped at the opportunity to go into business with my brother in San Rafael." They run the Flatiron Sports Bar, a place with eleven television sets, three big screens, and a satellite dish. "It's not exactly like being there, but it's as close as I could get, and I couldn't stay away."

"I couldn't refuse," says Thad Mumford about the time in 1982 when new Yankees manager Gene Michael invited him to suit up in pinstripes again. Mumford had batboyed at Yankee Stadium when Michael was the shortstop, two years he remembers as being "one huge goosebump." And now, plying his trade as screenwriter on the West Coast, Thad still plays ball for a semipro team in Los Angeles.

Patrick Quinlan's bubble burst when he could no longer batboy for the Giants. (courtesy of Patrick Quinlan)

Johnny Boggs is another who couldn't refuse the invitation and became one of Tommy Lasorda's "celebrity batboys."

I was a ballboy in Ted Williams's first year as manager of the Senators, 1969. But my most vivid memories of batboying come from the post-seasons of '77, '78, and '81. I was twenty-four years old and already married when I went down to Philadelphia and suited up for the Dodgers. I got to play pepper with Pete Rose, who called me 'the banker batboy' (which I was, I was working for a bank at the time) and promised me one of his bats as a souvenir. He came through, too.

It was exhilarating, a fantasy, and it brings you back down in time to be living out fantasies. . . . One friendship I made through baseball was with Steve Garvey, who also started out as a batboy, and it has blossomed into an important business connection. Now, working out of San Diego, I'm Tony Gwynn's agent, and I still have tremendous enthusiasm for the game of baseball.

"I couldn't stay away," says Cleveland's Jeff Sipos.

> I was hooked on baseball as a kid. . . . I loved playing, watching, and—
> being a Clevelander—getting frustrated by it. I'd get a rush seeing
> games on TV, hearing Jimmy Dudley on radio, even spring training
> games.
> I finally got to batboy on the visiting side in '71, then the home side
> in '72. And for the next five summers, while I went to college at
> Bowling Green, I worked on the ground crew. I even went to spring
> training for two weeks every year—couldn't get it out of my blood. I
> drifted after that, had no direction for a few years, and when things
> were at their lowest in my life, in '81, I started hanging out in the
> clubhouse again. In '83 I got the job as umpires' attendant, then be-
> came assistant to Cy Buynak, the equipment manager, in '84, and I've
> been there since, happily.

The Indians' move into their new stadium in 1994 involved a shift in
clubhouse assignments: Buynak now runs the visitors clubhouse
and Sipos is the Indians equipment manager.

"I couldn't stay away," says Mario Alioto in San Francisco.

> I'd been working in the Giants clubhouse and as a batboy for seven
> or eight years when I turned eighteen in '79. So I left for a few months,
> working as a bank teller, and then started college at St. Mary's. But it
> was no good. I was too homesick for the ballpark. Then Eddie Logan
> retired as equipment manager, Murph moved from the visiting club-
> house, and when Eddie Brinson, who was in line to succeed Murph,
> was hit and killed by a drunk driver, I was offered the job.
> Once I was back in baseball, college was fine. I ran the visiting
> clubhouse for three seasons, got my degree in business administra-
> tion, moved up to the front office, and now I'm director of marketing.
> But I'll tell you one highlight of my college career: I once traded a
> Phillies cap for two bottles of cabernet sauvignon, to Von Hayes, of all
> people, and three years later he ends up in a Phillies uniform.

Tony Migliaccio juggled his high school playing career in Mil-
waukee with his job as Brewers batboy. Even in junior college at
Central Arizona, he came home summers to work in the clubhouse.
But when he started at Arizona State and then transferred to the
University of Wisconsin at Milwaukee, it looked as if he was
through both as player and clubby, until equipment manager Bob
Sullivan died suddenly at forty-three and Harry Dalton offered Mi-
gliaccio the job. "I was one semester short of my degree, but I was in

the right place at the right time and I couldn't stay away. I said yes to the job and so long to college."

Tommie Ferguson faced a similar decision in 1954. Back in Boston after two years in the service, he had thought about becoming a newspaperman and been accepted at Xavier University to study journalism. But his heart was still in baseball, in the Braves clubhouse to be precise, even though they had moved from Boston to Milwaukee. He proudly wore his 1948 World Series ring and had been sustained in Korea by the regular packages of peanut brittle and *The Sporting News* sent by Bob Elliott, "Mr. Team" of the Braves. Indeed, he had received his "Greetings" from Harry Truman in 1952 just as he was loading equipment into a station wagon for the trip to spring training in Bradenton.

It took a newspaper writer to arrange Ferguson's reconciliation with baseball. Hy Hurwitz of the Boston *Globe* wrote a story about him and called John Quinn in New York on his behalf. So Ferguson became equipment manager in Milwaukee, though he still made his home in Boston and sold neckties in a Boylston Street haberdashery during the off-season. That's where he was in 1961, now married to Petey ("the only Irish girl I could find in Milwaukee"), when Bill Rigney and Fred Haney walked in with Gene Autry to offer him the traveling secretary job for the new Angels club. (Haney had managed the Braves in Milwaukee. Ferguson says, "He gave me the biggest break of my life—a marvelous human being, always making little people feel important.")

Ferguson went on to serve the Seattle Pilots, then the Milwaukee Brewers for fourteen years as traveling secretary and vice president for administration. Since 1983 he has been scouting for the Phillies, living in southern California, and spending a month every fall on Cape Cod.[23] "My decisions were easy for me," he says. "I chose the Braves over the Red Sox in '46 because they were first to play under lights in Boston. Being a batboy was a perfect job for a kid, the clubhouse a great teacher of human nature. Then '48 was my perfect year: I graduated Brookline High, lettered in hockey and baseball, went on a western trip with the Braves, got to the World Series, got a big enough share to buy a car for my parents, and had my first butterfly girl, you know, just to look at her gave you butterflies. How could you break away from a world that gave you all that?"

Red Willis and Billy Cahill are two others whose return from the service was back home to the old ballpark. Willis had been a Tigers

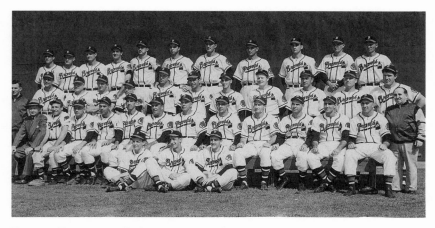

Tommie Ferguson called 1948 "my perfect year," in part because the Boston Braves won the National League pennant. He's the batboy on the right, and he stayed in baseball. Charlie Chronopoulos, in the middle, is Chief of Police in Tyngsborough, Massachusetts. Frank McNulty, on the left, who posed for Rockwell's "The Dugout," is president of *Parade* Magazine. (courtesy of Tommie Ferguson)

batboy for four years before his army years, 1951–53, stationed mostly in Alaska. Back in Detroit he did whatever was available, running errands, reading turnstiles, until he started selling tickets in the late 1960s. As director of ticket sales, he would say, "It got in my blood, and I couldn't stay away." Retired now on disability after a stroke, he still communicates the same message.

Cahill batboyed for the Browns from 1937 to 1939 and then went into the service. As soon as he got out, he came back to Sportsman's Park and caught batting practice for the Browns through the 1949 season. "I always loved baseball," he says, "and I still do. I'm a retired man now, but one uniform is still hanging in my closet—not the army one, the baseball one."

Given their choice, many of these lovers of baseball would never leave the sacred precincts of clubhouse and ballpark. For John Nelson, for example, his four years in the air force never even constituted a time away from the game and the Tigers clubhouse. "It's in my heart," he says, explaining why he saved up thirty days leave each year to spend at spring training, even his last year in the service when he and his bride went to Lakeland instead of on a conventional honeymoon.

Nelson's title with the Tigers, when I first interviewed him, was Administrative Assistant to the Vice President for Office Operations. That may sound like a euphemism for errand boy and handyman, but having "fallen in love with the clubhouse job," he was just waiting for an opportunity to run a clubhouse and had sent his résumé to every potential expansion franchise. By the spring of 1992 his diligent devotion had paid off—he had become the Tigers minor league equipment-clubhouse manager.

Looking around the decaying charm of Tiger Stadium in 1991, Nelson could see several prototypes of his own attitudes. I've already mentioned Red Willis in the ticket office, but "Tiger Joe," the security guard, has been around even longer. And then, about every other day in the grandstand, he could see Eddie Forester, who followed his batboy years with fifty-three more in the grounds crew, and at age eighty-eight still could not stay away.

The attitude of these lovers is eminently romantic. Their language is filled with words like *magic, dream, fantasy, devotion, heroes*, and *starstruck*. A stubborn unwillingness to be torn away may be equated with hanging on. In San Diego, for example, Mark Thomson followed his two batboy years by working in the clubhouse assisting the equipment manager, while his decision to move on to college from junior college awaited an assessment of possible baseball jobs, "if not clubhouse, maybe PR." He had at least two good Padres models for his devotion, Bobby Alldis and John Plein.

Alldis was a batboy from 1981 to 1985, then stayed on to help with the club's video system, while working a full-time job in a newspaper advertising department. He would start at 5 a.m. so that he could get to the ballpark by 2 p.m., so reluctant was he to give up his connection with the game and relationships with people like Tony Gwynn, Andy Hawkins, Dick Williams, and Goose Gossage. Now in a different field and no longer with the Padres, Alldis finds time to coach high school baseball. Plein's batboy stint ended in 1979, but he stayed on to work part-time with the grounds crew, lobbying all the while for the umpires' attendant to be a separate job. He won his case in 1981 and held that job while working as a bonded carrier in the corporate advertising department of the *Union Tribune*. "I had to buy a house less than a mile from Jack Murphy Stadium so that I could work both jobs," he says. Plein now has his own business as a licensed insurance adjustor, which makes it easier for him to accommodate his continuing ballpark service.

After his batboy days in Milwaukee, Ron Nedset chose to stay on with the club as bullpen catcher rather than try to make it as a player. "Everything I've done for the first time in my life had to do with the job of being batboy—first beer, first cigarette, first chew, first time with a woman—and players were in on it all. I just want to stay in baseball somehow, maybe college coaching." It is no coincidence that he singles out Rene Lachemann as someone he looks up to, who "was really good to me." A career baseball man (player, coach, manager), Lachemann too began as a batboy.

For the luckiest ones the love is reciprocated. Take the case of Charlie (The Brow) Di Giovanna, who spent fifteen seasons in Dodgers clubhouses in Brooklyn and Los Angeles, on the road and on tour in Japan, all but the last few as batboy. When he died in 1958, at age twenty-eight (rheumatic fever had damaged his heart as a child), he was eulogized in *Coronet* magazine by Dick Young, who focused on the warm laughter that surrounded his presence in the clubhouse. As the practice of getting signatures on balls became a regular part of the batboy's duties, it was The Brow who perfected the benign forgeries that spared the players and inspired generations of clubhouse hands. *Coronet* named their batboy-of-the-year award for Di Giovanna, and Roy McKercher, the first San Francisco Giants batboy, was the inaugural winner. He remembers The Brow as "the best loved of the batboys."

Another fortunate suitor is Mike Murphy, who worked the 1958 and 1959 seasons as batboy on the visiting side in San Francisco.

> I got to meet such great old stars as Stan Musial and Bill Mazeroski. Everyone kind of liked me. They called me "Bobskin" or "Junior" because I looked like Bob Skinner, very thin, skinny, whittly like Bob, and I couldn't catch a ball out there either, like Bob, so every time I see Stan he still calls me "Skins" or "Skinner."
>
> I've worked all my life around baseball and I love baseball. I go to special events for baseball, and I do special things for kids for baseball. I try to keep emphasizing to my batboys about playing baseball and then going on to better jobs after they leave. And that means getting an education. I've been running a clubhouse since we moved into Candlestick Park, in '60, and I've always tried to bring my kids up to be good citizens. I wish there was a million clubs, give a million kids the chance to be a batboy.
>
> I've had a couple of rough kids, like Brad Tham and his brother Gus, and Pieretti, and Bob Fenech. We were all wild, tried to drink with the ballplayers, but I would tell them, I did all that but you've got to go on

On closing day in 1950 Stan Strull wore the Brooklyn home
uniform while Charlie (The Brow) Di Giovanna suited up for the
visiting Phillies. The beloved Brow was in Dodgers blue or clubhouse until his death. (courtesy of Stan Strull)

to a better life, get an education for yourself. Don't slip back, like
Mario Alioto, who worked as a batboy and had a chance to go to St.
Mary's but wanted to hang around the ballpark. Now he's director of
promotions for the Giants and has done a good job, as he did as a
batboy and in the accounting office, but he had to go back and finish
college to get where he is now.

Still, hanging around the clubhouse may become a way of life. In
St. Louis, Kurt Schlogo batboyed on the visiting side in 1982. Tall

and well-muscled, with curly blondish hair, Kurt looks like a player, especially with a plug in his mouth (he claims he chewed before he was ever a clubby), but he hangs on in the hope of someday getting a job as visiting clubhouse or equipment manager. Joe Dunn in Philadelphia has the same ambition. A batboy for several seasons through 1987, he continues to work as a clubby while applying for every opening that comes up, and has had the experience of running the clubhouse for the St. Lucie Legends in the Senior League.

Veterans Stadium in Philadelphia houses several models of former batboys whose devotion to baseball kept them inside the game: equipment manager Frank Coppenbarger, whose story has been told in chapter 4; Mark Andersen, now assistant trainer for the Phillies, fifteen years after starting as batboy; and perhaps most instructive, memories of Kenny Bush, who managed the visiting clubhouse until 1991. His private room at the back was like a place out of time in contemporary baseball, an anachronism with pinups of nude women and ashtrays full of cigarettes smoked down to the shortest of nubs. Bush was a Phillies batboy for eighteen years, a major league record. As a boy he had sold newspapers around the ballpark and got to know everybody. "At twelve or thirteen, in '49, I got the chance to be batboy, and I been there ever since, starting at two dollars a game. I wanted to be a player, and I took infield, but I couldn't hit." While he was still in the game, but not without a sense of bitterness coloring his nostalgia, he could say, "It's a different game now. Money makes the difference. You got to cater to 'em, babysit millionaires. I remember Robin Roberts, a super guy, and Ashburn, a gentleman. My most vivid memory is '64, a bad year, the year of our September collapse." As a batboy approaching thirty at the time, perhaps Bush's regrets have something to do with that season being a last shot at glory on the field.

Of course, not all rejected suitors settle for less intimate relationships just to maintain a connection with the love object. And that is the other side of the coin, the pain of departure from what has been an engaging or consuming passion. "I loved it, loved being part of it," Steve Maunakea says, "and I still love it. I would still play if I had the chance. But I might go to three or four games a year now, and I just can't watch it—it really hurts too bad."

In Chicago, some thirty-five years after his batboy experience, Bill Philips has an explanation for a similar attitude. "The nuances of the game are what make it interesting and romantic. The allure

Striking the classic batboy's pose in 1955, photo-
genic Cubs batboy Bill Philips got to endorse Wilson
gloves in a *Sport* Magazine ad, while two pages away
Stan Musial endorsed Rawlings. (courtesy of Bill
Philips)

comes from understanding all that, so I can't enjoy sitting in the
stands with people who just sit and wait between pitches. For example, I'm friendly with Dick Stockton, a very knowledgeable sportscaster, but he said he had to learn many intricacies from working in
the booth with a former player, Hawk Harrelson."

In Baltimore, Kevin Cashen says that he doesn't go to games
much, simply because "he doesn't know any players anymore." His
older brother Neil, whose main baseball interest these days comes

from rotisserie leagues, is more explicit. "Oh, I'll go to four or five games a year, as a social thing, but it's not the same. Sitting in the dugout and the clubhouse for six and a half years there's a level of intensity to your involvement in the game, when Robinson was 'Brooksie' to me and Palmer was 'Cakes,' so even though you see the intricacies from the stands you don't appreciate it because the involvement and the intensity are missing."

"Baseball is its own little island," says Gus Tham. "I don't get out to the ballpark much. It's just too difficult to sit in the stands as a fan. Especially in the first years after I was batboy, I couldn't take it." Implicit in his image is the notion that the island is a magical one, and that the spell doesn't extend to the stands. For many, the process of reducing the level of enchantment is too painful. And it is not surprising to hear the batboys equate their feelings to those of players who experience hanging up their uniforms as a kind of dying.

"Most guys," says Milwaukee's Tony Migliaccio, "leave the game bitter. They feel they could play another season or have another job. Coop [Cecil Cooper], for one, a great guy, comes to the ballpark from time to time, but he won't come in the clubhouse." That describes batboys as well as players. The Orioles' Jay Mazzone, one of the most celebrated batboys because he performed his duties without the benefit of hands, might bring his kids to a few games a year but makes no contact with clubhouse, dugout, or bullpen. He shows no bitterness, just a resignation that the time he suited up was a separate time, and over with, and there is no point of contact anymore.

Roy McKercher offered several reasons for not going out to Candlestick Park these days. "I don't like fighting the crowds and the weather," he says, and then, more reflectively, "and besides I was spoiled by being on the field. I understand what people go through when they have to quit playing. When I left, after being a batboy for four years, I was devastated. Any success I've had [as a basketball official and deputy sheriff in San Mateo] I attribute to the Giants organization. But when I left, a big part of me was left behind."

McKercher speaks in the phrases of a faithful lover, a true believer in the kind of magic that touches the heart. And he speaks for many. Clearly, the majority of former batboys never get the chance to stay in the game. The faint of heart leave early, intimidated by the odds, pursuing other professional goals (or loves), frustrated by the drudgery, or driven by hormones. (White Sox equipment manager Chicken Willie Thompson, when speaking of former batboys he's lost track of, says they're all "out chasin' fat girls.") Former batboys have gone on to distinguished careers in law, medicine, business, religion, politics, publishing, engineering, architecture, journalism, broadcasting, advertising, education, and even show business. But setting aside those who have managed to maintain some career connection with baseball, I found that the one profession that attracts by far the most former batboys (around 15 percent in my limited sample of 170) is law enforcement. It is almost as if "queer for the yard" suggests *Scotland* Yard to them. From chiefs, detective lieutenants, and FBI men to deputy sheriffs, airport guards, marshals, and patrolmen, former batboys often seem to be wearing or carrying a badge. (In Philadelphia, from 1935 to 1938, Hal Kelleher pitched in some fifty games while also serving the city as a police officer. The Phillies finished last or next to last in those years.)

The numbers are too striking to be coincidental, and I tried to elicit explanations from the subjects themselves. Jim Hackett, who rose through the ranks to become chief of detectives of the St. Louis police with the rank of lieutenant colonel, supposed it was because a lot of police are around the ballpark and then said, "It's the same type of job anyway, dealing with people."

Charlie (The Greek) Chronopoulos, chief of police of Tyngsborough, Massachusetts, says, "What seems really funny to me now after more than thirty years as a police officer is that in all my ten years hanging around the ballpark and in the clubhouse I never thought of doing police work." On the other hand, for Eric Winebrenner, a police officer in Kansas City, and Steve Labatt, a deputy sheriff in Minnesota, the lure of the ballpark was just a temporary attraction because they were already committed to becoming officers of the law.

Mike Murphy says, "I got good experience working, hanging around baseball. But it's just seasonal work for most people. Off-season I still do some police work, helping to keep kids off the street. And I always try to put my kids, my batboys and clubbies, in law enforcement. It's a good choice. It's year-round, never have to worry about it, civil service, just keeps you going."

What they do not acknowledge and perhaps do not even recognize is how much alike the worlds of the clubhouse and the precinct are. Beyond the ritual investitures of uniforms, the inner sancta of private rooms, and the initiation rites of acceptance and brotherhood, there is also a code, a tacit loyalty oath, an *omertà*. When the relationship is terminated, when police officers have to hang 'em up, they react in ways that echo the reports we've heard from ex-batboys. They try to hang on in some capacity, they go into related work like security (sometimes, coincidentally, ballpark security) or private investigation, they hang out on the fringes of the police beat (the familiar police bars, diners, clubs), or else they distance themselves as far as possible from the world they treasured while they had a role to play in it but cannot tolerate when their usefulness is over. That is, they go fishing.

When we listen to batboys and police officers talk about their careers, we hear tones of pride, wistfulness, regret, nostalgia, occasional gratitude, and sometimes bitterness. In other words, we hear what we might expect to hear from someone whose deep emotional involvement in a job is nurtured by the special world and place in which the job is performed, but who often has difficulty in putting his feelings for it aside, integrating them in a mature self, and moving on.

We hear what it felt like to be one of the guys. And underneath those revelatory tones we sense something else, the rooted similarities of the lure of the bats and the badges. When men's lives are devoted to boys' games, acting out or somehow fitting into the pre- and early-adolescent fantasies of ball games and cops-and-robbers, then to give them up is to acknowledge the end of youth. Old men in uniforms, whether dress blues or road grays, are pathetic reminders of the security once felt by being part of a special group, protected and nurtured by a devotion to the maintenance of itself as special. Baseball nourishes these feelings in many ways, including its unique custom of having the coaches and managers, however anomalously decrepit, suit up in the same garb as players (not to mention batboys) decades or generations younger.

Where are all the *young* men gone? Gone for jocks and soldiers every one. The recognition of mortality comes with greater force when maturity itself has been long postponed. The longer it takes to graduate from the brotherhood, to put away the childish things—the raiment, trappings, equipment, accoutrements of the game—the stronger will be the pull to stay or the shock of having to go. That is one reason that stories of former athletes have such appeal for writers and such poignancy for audiences.[24]

The old soldiers telling their war stories in Ritter's *The Glory of Their Times*, Honig's *Baseball When the Grass Was Real*, and Heiman, Weiner, and Gutman's *When the Cheering Stops* sound the same clarion notes with the same rumbling subtext as our aging batboys: What a time we had when we were part of the game. No one can know what it is like who has never had the privilege of being there, rubbing shoulders with the Hall-of-Famers and the other greats and all the regular guys, belonging to the same club and belonging in the same clubhouse. And every time we hear them talk about their introduction to or initiation into "the world of men," we understand them to mean men who, by managing to carry on as boys in the most privileged of boys' clubs, kept a world outside the world for the rest of us to admire, envy, applaud, and deeply long for.

EPILOGUE **The Conventional Batboy's Story**

The batboy's story presented in the following pages is an invented first-person narrative. It is made up entirely of familiar, conventional, formulaic elements taken from repeated instances in the interviews and reports. Batboys (at least until the present project) have been interviewed in depth only rarely; in fact, they have largely been sheltered from direct exposure to the media. And yet they seem to have developed a sense of interview techniques and contexts. Indeed, their stories seem at least in part to be the product of their understanding of what their roles, performances, and responses ought to be.[25] If parts of this story sound familiar, they should, or as Yogi Berra is supposed to have said, it's déjà vu all over again.

I always loved baseball, as far back as I can remember. They say that as soon as I could stand I started fielding ground balls, even before I could walk. As a boy I would get out to the ballpark a lot, and I got there so early and stayed so late that pretty soon everyone knew me. I guess it helped that my dad had gone to school with the equipment manager, and when I was fourteen I got hired on as one of the kids who chased down balls in batting practice, you know, long fouls or home runs in the seats. We had a lot of fun racing fans to the balls, and we got to see the games free.

I did that for a couple of years and then, at the beginning of the following season, one day our bullpen catcher asked me to run an errand for him back into the clubhouse. It was just my good luck that that was the day one of the batboys announced that he was going into the service. It was the first time I'd ever gone into the dugout and through the tunnel up into the clubhouse, and I was really in awe. But I went up to the equipment manager and told him what the catcher had asked me for, and he said, "Aren't you the kid who always brings back the most BP balls?" I just grinned and said "Yeah," and then he goes, "How'd you like to be a batboy?" That was it. Nothing about my dad or anything, but I found out later that he knew who I was all along.

They gave me a uniform that was way too big and a locker in the back corner, but I was thrilled to be there. We had a utility infielder whose locker was next to mine, and he sort of took me under his wing, showing me how to get the uniform on right and all. It didn't take long for the feeling of awe to wear off, because I found out pretty soon that baseball players were just like everyone else, regular people, except for this great talent they had for the game.

Nobody told me exactly what I was expected to do, but I grasped the idea right away that I was there to do whatever anyone asked me to do, and there was a sign on the wall that reminded me that I was to do it without opening my mouth to anyone about what happened in the clubhouse. So after about three days, when Lefty asked me to run out to the bullpen for a bucket of knuckleballs, I ran. They kept me running, too, from the bullpen to the visiting clubhouse, and even into the trainer's room, where Doc finally told me it was a joke. Everyone was laughing when I walked back into the clubhouse, and I felt real foolish. But then I knew that they were just letting me know that I belonged, because they only pulled those jokes on new members of the club.

I can't tell you how it felt that first time I ran up the runway and out onto the field dressed in the uniform of the club. It felt good and scary at the same time. I thought everyone was looking at me, maybe watching to see if I tripped on the steps coming out of the dugout or something, but I thought there's a lot of people in the stands who would give anything to be where I was. I know that's the way I felt when I was younger and looking down onto the field.

People think that what you do on the field is all there is to it to be a batboy, but that's just the easiest part of the job. It's not all *that* easy, because you have to be alert all the time, to get the equipment where it needs to be in time and out of the way in time, to make sure you don't attract the attention of players or coaches or umpires—because you only get their attention when you do something wrong. The worst thing is to attract the attention of the fans, because everybody really gets on you for that. Usually, though, if you make a mistake (like the time I handed Big Bill back a bat he'd just cracked hitting a ball that barely curved foul) it's only the dugout that knows. You hear about it from them, but that's OK because everyone on the club gets ragged about inside stuff like that.

For me the hardest part of being on the field during a game was when it was the first game of a home stand, after I'd been up most of the night unpacking the team from a road trip. Usually I'd sleep over in the clubhouse after that to get a fresh start on the day's duties—shining the shoes, laying out all the clean laundry, running errands, and getting a dozen boxes of balls signed—so that by the time I had finished shagging flies during BP I was already exhausted. That was when I found it hard to be alert during the game, and I almost got hit by foul balls a couple of times. By the time we did the laundry and cleaned up the postgame spread on a night like that, I'd be a zombie.

You learn a lot about the players when you unpack their stuff after a road trip. At first I was kind of surprised at what would turn up. And at first I was shocked at other things, like the amount of swearing in the way they talked, the number of them who smoked (some chewed tobacco but not as many as I heard it used to be), and how much beer some of them would put away after a game. But I was also surprised at how hard they worked to get in shape and stay in shape. Taking care of their bodies is a serious part of their jobs. My dad always said I really grew up fast in the clubhouse. But I don't think he meant just the language and smoking and stuff; I think he meant the lessons I learned about working hard to do what you were supposed to do and at the same time enjoying what you were doing. That was all part of learning what it was to be a man.

Toward the end of my first season I got to take my first road trip. Every batboy is entitled to one road trip a year, and I got to go to the

West Coast in August of that year, just before I had to start back to school. It was perfect. I got to see San Francisco and Disneyland. I got to stay with the team in their hotels, fly with them on their charters, and ride to the ballparks on the team bus. Different players took me out to dinner at world-class restaurants almost every day, and I never once had to pay for a thing. You can't imagine what it feels like to go on rides at Disney with a major leaguer on both sides of you.

Like I said, the ballplayers turned out to be just like regular people. Most of them were great to me, whether they were long relievers in the bullpen or all-star sluggers. What really brought home the reality of the game was when someone you'd gotten close to was traded, or released, or sent down. But once in a while there was the thrill of going into a visiting clubhouse and having a former member of your club greet you by name.

Fans sometimes get a wrong idea about a player. On our club they were always getting on Pete for not getting the big hit or coming up with the big catch. They'd boo him for the way he'd react to getting called out and the angry gestures he'd make on his way to the dugout. And they didn't like him because he never gave interviews in the media, and writers and broadcasters would bad-mouth him for being uncooperative and all. But he was the best guy in the clubhouse, always joking with us and keeping everybody loose while also reminding everyone that it was a serious matter to keep winning and that it required hard work and dedication. He behaved the way he did because he cared about the game and the people in it, but he couldn't care less about what outsiders said.

And then there was Marty, everybody's all-American favorite. The press loved this guy and the fans ate up the way he played and the stuff he said in interviews and his "class" on and off the field. But let me tell you, he was a different guy in the clubhouse, aloof, businesslike, all for himself. He'd arrive in his three-piece suit, carrying his briefcase, and he was very polite when he asked you to do something for him, but at the end of the season you'd get a warm handshake and a hearty hope-to-see-you-next-year, but nothing like an envelope with a tip. It was Pete who'd take up the collection for your expenses on your road trip, but Marty who'd have his picture taken at a children's hospital. Don't get me wrong. Marty's a great player, and he deserves to get in the Hall of Fame on the first ballot. But if it was the clubbies who voted, Pete would be first on the list. And the fans, they just get the wrong impressions about who's a great guy and who isn't.

Sometimes, though, they get it right. We had another guy on our club with Hall-of-Fame type figures and a good reputation, and he deserved every bit of it. His public image and his private self were the same. He was the same classy guy on camera and in the clubhouse, at home or on the road. He was never a rah-rah type of leader but led by example. He wouldn't pat you on the back to make himself look good, but if he saw you were down about something he'd have a quiet talk with you. He was the one who really taught me the work ethic and to count your blessings.

Skipper was someone I never figured out. I never had much contact with him, he kept to himself pretty much and out of the way of the crowd in the clubhouse. You just didn't approach him like one of the guys and you kept quiet and out of the way when he was around. But during the times I worked on the visiting side I got to know a lot of the other managers around the league. Richie, of course, was a crazy guy, as big a joker as any player, and Archie had such a temper that you had to watch your head for flying items when he was pissed off. Butch was different: he'd be like a wild man on the field, and the media played up that image, but in the clubhouse he was good-natured and calm and cared about people. He appreciated what you did to take care of him, and he'd stay around the clubhouse and talk for hours after a game. Best of all was Blackie. He'd always have a good word for you, he'd remember your name from one visit to the next, and he'd go out of his way to tell your boss what a good job you were doing. I think that's the key to his success and why he stayed around so long—he never forgot the little guys.

The real unsung heroes in baseball for me were the equipment manager and the trainer. Mac and Doc taught me what it was all about. Doc had more stories than tape. He knew everyone back to the Dark Ages, and he'd taken care of most of them. He didn't just make players feel better physically, he'd entertain them and make them feel like part of a tradition that stretched back forever. Being in his room was an escape from any problem that followed you from the field or outside on into the clubhouse, but being in his hands was to get your whole spirit massaged. He was like your favorite old uncle.

As for Mac, he was like a parent to all of us kids. He was tough on us, demanding, but he was always looking out for us and reminding us to think about the future. He insisted we keep our grades up in school or we wouldn't work for him for long, and he made us think about the value of education in the long run. He wrote one of my letters of recommendation for college, and I'm proud of that. He was always there for us or any player, no matter how late the hour was, and he never wanted any credit for just doing his job as he saw it. A couple of times I remember that he was asked for interviews by media people, and he'd just say something like, "People want to hear from clean-up hitters, not clean-up men."

People think that rubbing shoulders with great players is the best part of the job, or slapping five with a home run hitter after he crosses the plate. But really the best part is being part of the club, playing your role in the clubhouse and being accepted, even taken for granted as if you belong. It was a special time and place in my life. They told jokes about women and body parts and made fun of anything they noticed about you, but it was always good-natured. The kind of stuff that makes trouble between people—politics, religion, sex—just didn't get in the way. A couple of times the senator or the governor or a touring rock band came into the clubhouse, and they acted just like kids thrilled to be there with the players. I had to laugh to think that I was where these bigwigs and stars wanted to be.

All through my last two years I was trying to figure out if there was a way I could stay in the game. I was very anxious to find a place for myself, especially after I got to go to spring training for the first time. I had always heard people talk about spring training, and I couldn't wait to go. It was everything it was supposed to be. It's like the biggest annual reunion of the biggest, happiest family in the world, and everybody gets to be together as an equal part of it. I didn't want to leave, and I didn't want to leave baseball.

The first two years I was out I couldn't stay away. I'd come into the clubhouse whenever I was back home, and as long as people knew my name I felt I still belonged. Mac even let me help unpack a couple of times, but he'd shake his head at me as if he didn't know what I was doing there. I didn't particularly want to be out near the field, just hung out during the games with the clubbies. And then, after a while, I couldn't bring myself to go back at all. Somehow I just didn't belong any more. Watching a ball game from the stands does nothing for me. The fans, even the most knowledgeable ones sitting around me, don't really know what's going on. Sometimes they even believe the stories that sportswriters or so-called analysts of the game make up. Now, I follow the team casually in the papers, but I might go to only three or four games a year, just to be sociable, and I avoid even thinking about what's going on inside.

It was a special time in my life. For four years I lived and breathed baseball. I really believe that whatever I am as a man I owe to what I learned in baseball, in the clubhouse: my work ethic, how I treat people, how I play my role and do what I'm expected to do even when others are letting us down, and to trust my own experience instead of what everybody else thinks and says. I think I've been pretty independent and successful because of that philosophy, and just because I don't go back any more doesn't mean I've turned away from it all. In fact, forget about salary and seniority and all I've accomplished since, if I was offered a chance to get back into the game I'd be there in a heartbeat.

By calling their narratives substantially conventional, I do not mean to suggest that former batboys invent experiences they did not have, acknowledge feelings that are foreign to them, assess personalities without the benefit of personal contact, or subscribe to beliefs that are not their own. What I am asserting is that the nature of the subculture itself dictates and shapes the framework, the structure, and the values of the stories they tell about themselves and others.

Batboys enter the clubhouse primed, prepared, and predetermined to be indoctrinated into a subculture they have dimly perceived but projectively or imaginatively grasped. Their duties are routinized but given value by their contexts. Picking up a bucket of balls and fetching them back to a supervisor is drudgery, but when they are balls hit during a major league batting practice and they are being gathered so that major leaguers can hit them again and the chore is being performed while wearing a major league uniform, it is all endowed with a power of privilege that extends self-importance to the functionary.

The game itself is played in a ritualized context, so that what becomes central to the batboy's experience is the ritual itself rather than the individual occurrences. Extraordinary instances stand out because they are aberrations, rather than because the special event or achievement is the goal. Kneeling in the on-deck circle with each successive batter, carrying off the warm-up jacket of each entering reliever, replacing a cracked bat with a fresh one of the same model, slapping the hand of each home run hitter—that is the treasured, recalled experience, not the competitive performance, because the routine is what pertains to the privileged role and the regular duty is what makes the performer a part of the club.

In the clubhouse itself the batboy learns a code of behavior, an appreciation of hierarchy and membership in the club, an orthodoxy that ridicules and excludes deviants, and most important a self-perpetuating mythology that incorporates a constant set of values. Stability is honored and protects custom; intrusions are abhorred, intruders are shunned, and intrusiveness prompts repudiation or punishment. You watch whom you talk to and you know what you can say.

A sign on the wall of every clubhouse proclaims the rule of separateness and privilege. It implies that if you want to be a part of this world—and who doesn't?—then you agree to keep its secrets. And in return you are made to feel that you belong. You are initiated by being the butt of practical jokes, the victim of more or less innocent, puerile pranks. Suiting up in the uniform of the club is a kind of ritual investiture, and its significance is accentuated by the fact that one of your central duties is to tend the uniforms of the whole club, the trappings of the elect.

Batboys come to feel that they belong by taking part in the intimacies that obtain in a clubhouse environment, intimacies of dressing, showering, eating, and casually rubbing shoulders with the members. They also take part in celebrations, conventional conversations and humor, and ceremonies such as kangaroo court sessions. Their specific roles, of course, place them in special relationship with some of the sacred accoutrements, the equipment they tend— not just bats and uniforms, but the shoes they shine assiduously, the helmets, the weighted bats and donuts, the pine tar, and the rosin bag. The hands-on nature of this relationship is another sign of the batboys' intimacy with the game.

What may be equally significant is what they avoid discussing. Matters of current interest, social and political issues, are not the stuff of baseball clubhouse pertinence. Personal family matters are rarely mentioned. Even religion is avoided, though there is a spirit of religious tolerance that prevails. Those clubs that sanction some form of Sunday morning Christian service, for example, acknowledge it as acceptable but somehow a little off-center (whereas prayer is often encouraged or even formalized, not to say sanctified, in

CLUB HOUSE
PLAYERS ONLY

Separateness and privilege: batboy Stan Strull leaves the players-only door of the Brooklyn Dodgers clubhouse at Vero Beach in the spring of 1951. (photo by Keystone Pictures, Inc., courtesy of Stan Strull)

football locker rooms). The occasional practice of Islam by members is accepted without cavil; and when a secular Jew like Hank Greenberg refuses to play on Yom Kippur, that's all right, too, even when everyone in the clubhouse knows that he frequently has batboys fetch him ham sandwiches. Even the rare practice of voodoo is tolerated in the baseball clubhouse, but the point is that any such matter is not an approved topic of dialogue. The most celebrated line in Penny Marshall's *A League of Their Own* is, "There's no crying in baseball." Well, there's no proselytizing in baseball, either. When members of the baseball brotherhood sit around the clubhouse to talk, there is only one validated topic: baseball.

Nowadays, though, acceptable subjects are extended to include televised and videotaped entertainment, but only since the advent of popular culture media into the clubhouse area itself in the well-stocked entertainment centers of major league clubhouses. That makes it opportune for batboys to share tastes in wrestling, sitcoms, music, video games, and the like with the players with whom they share space in lounge areas. Interestingly enough, when luminaries from the worlds of entertainment and politics are allowed into the clubhouse, they approach the resident deities with the same kind of awe with which the batboys originally arrived. But no matter how much the clubbies (like the players) may admire the visitors, the clubbies are now bonded to the group that the non-baseball stars have come to pay tribute to.

Stories of the road, of spring training, of other clubhouses and training rooms and ballparks and major league cities make up the folkloric material absorbed by batboys from their first entrance into the charmed inner circle, soaked up at the knees of big brothers or Dutch uncles or avuncular, paternal, grandpaternal eminences, as it were. Then, when they are lucky enough to make pilgrimages of their own to the hallowed and storied places, the trips themselves serve to identify them more firmly with the group at large and the club in particular, while intimate sharing of living experiences on the road (planes, buses, hotels, restaurants, movies, amusement parks) with individual players reinforces their membership in the brotherhood.

Finally, what is taken in and fixed at the deepest level of allegiance and belonging is a set of attitudes and values. And these are what is reflected in the stories batboys tell about themselves. Those stories, then, may be seen as the story of the group, and their telling of it rehearses the process by which they came to be part of it, to partake of it, to experience it in such a way as to say they "lived" it.

If batboys have seldom been approached for interviews, it is at least in part because they have not made themselves accessible. This avoidance is not a matter of their having nothing of value to communicate, but a sign that they have embraced the clubhouse ethos of viewing their world as separate from and invaded by the media. The reporters who gather daily in the clubhouse, grouping and bonding in their own little separate circle, deciding among themselves what the story of the day is (or after a game what the appropriate lead has to be), are admitted into the sacred world but are not of it. Players are needed by the media, the media by the players and management, but the batboys adopt the view that the relationship is less symbiotic than parasitic.

Nothing gives a batboy more pleasure than to know the truth of the clubhouse world when the world at large knows only what the media have misled, misguided, or mischiefed them to believe. In that sense, the "truth" is the essential myth. The batboy's story, then, is an expression of what is, I suppose, the defining myth of any subculture—that only if you belong inside that sacred circle, having been adopted into it and having embraced it, can you appreciate the meaning of it.

Baseball has gone to great lengths to hold itself separate and apart, and the batboy's story, if it is to have any value or validity whatsoever in his own eyes, must be supportive of that tenet and creed. His story is derivative, conventional, conformative, complimentary, and complementary, but surely it is his own as well. After all, his story as part of the mythology should reflect the role he played as attendant functionary or acolyte, a role that attaches to, pays tribute to, and gives testimony to the enduring value of the subculture's sacred world.

APPENDIX: FIRSTHAND

SOURCES

The following key indicates the nature of the source:

P = telephone interview/conversation

C = follow-up correspondence

T = reminiscence taped by source, partially in response to open-ended questionnaire

L = live interview/conversation (location by city, so specified if in ballpark)

B = autobiographical book

-s = more than one occurrence

* = interview conducted by Burt Dietch and Phil and Marilyn Isaacs

Mario Alioto   San Francisco Giants (1973–79)   P
Bobby Alldis   San Diego Padres (1981–85)   P
Steve Altman   Washington Senators (1951)   P-s
Mark Andersen   Philadelphia Phillies (1976–80)   L (Veterans Stadium, Philadelphia)
Tony Antonio   Detroit Tigers (1985–89)   L (Detroit)
Tony Atlas   California Angels (1976–80)   P-s, C-s
Buddy Bates   St. Louis Cardinals (1969–71)   P, L (Busch Stadium, St. Louis)
Eddie Baxter   Washington Senators (1967–71)   P, L (Olney, Maryland)
Fred Baxter   Washington Senators (1931–32)   P, L (Bethesda, Maryland)
John Baxter   Washington Senators (1964–67)   P
Craig Beatty   Seattle Mariners (1988–90)   P
Chad Blossfield   Milwaukee Braves (1954–57)   P-s, C-s
Johnny Boggs   Washington Senators (1969), Los Angeles Dodgers (Postseason 1977–78 and 1981)   P-s

Sid Bordman   Kansas City Blues (1940–41)   L (Baseball City Stadium, Baseball City, Florida)

Bill Bush   California Angels (1965–67)   P

Kenny Bush   Philadelphia Phillies (1949–66)   L (Veterans Stadium, Philadelphia)

Tim Buzbee   California Angels (1975–79)   P-s, C

Billy Cahill   St. Louis Browns (1937–39)   P-s

Joe Carrieri   New York Yankees (1953–54)   B

Dennis Cashen   Baltimore Orioles (1980–82)   P-s

Kevin Cashen   Baltimore Orioles (1977–79)   P-s, C, L (Baltimore)

Michael Cashen   Baltimore Orioles (1972–76)   P-s, C, L (Baltimore)

Neil Cashen   Baltimore Orioles (1969–72)   P-s, C, L (Baltimore)

George Catloth   Washington Senators (1932–38)   P-s, L-s (Hyattsville, Maryland)

Charlie (The Greek) Chronopoulos   Boston Braves (1940–49)   P-s, C

Ken Clancy   Milwaukee Braves (1964–65)   P

Phil Cline   Chicago Cubs (1965–66)   P

David (Jigger) Cohen   Washington Senators (1925)   P

Frank Coppenbarger   Decatur Commodores (1967–74)   P-s, L (Veterans Stadium, Philadelphia)

Fred Costello   San Francisco Giants (1985)   L (Osceola County Stadium, Kissimmee, Florida)

Billy Coward   Homestead Grays (1946–47)   P-s

David Cowart   Detroit Tigers (1980–84)   P-s, C

Ivan Crayton   Baltimore Orioles (1990–94)   P-s, L (Memorial Stadium, Baltimore)

Ray Crump   Washington Senators (1949–57)   P

Don Deason   St. Louis Cardinals (1967–70)   P

John Donovan   Boston Red Sox (1948–51)   P-s

Mike Doyle   Milwaukee Braves (1963–65)   P-s

Joe Dunn   Philadelphia Phillies (1989–90)   L (Veterans Stadium, Philadelphia)

John Dykowski   Detroit Tigers (1989–90)   P, L (Tiger Stadium, Detroit)

Rich Eberle   Chicago Cubs (1965–66)   P-s

Jay Edmiston   Houston Astros (1986–89)   P, L (Osceola County Stadium, Kissimmee, Florida)

Bob Elder   California Angels (1965–67)   P-s

Jim (Doc) Ewell   Norfolk (1934)   L (Osceola County Stadium, Kissimmee, Florida)

Bob Farmer   Washington Senators (1957–58)   P-s, L (Rockville, Maryland)

Bob Fenech   San Francisco Giants (1966–68)   P-s, T

Luke Fera   Milwaukee Brewers (1987–89)   P

Tommie Ferguson   Boston Red Sox (1945), Boston Braves (1946–52)   P-s, C

Roy Firestone   Baltimore Orioles (1971–72 spring)   P-s

Don Fitzpatrick   Boston Red Sox (1944–50)   P-s, L-s (Royals Stadium, Kansas City; Tiger Stadium, Detroit)

Eddie Forester   Detroit Tigers (1919–22)   L (Detroit)

Steve Friend   Montreal Expos (1986–88)   P, T

Leonard Garcia   California Angels (1965–67)   P, L (Memorial Stadium, Baltimore)

Garth Garreau   New York Giants (1946–47)   B

Steve Garvey   Dodgers, Yankees, Tigers (spring, 1956–62)   P

Paul Gibson   St. Louis Cardinals (1966–68)   B

Paul Gonoud   New York Yankees (1981–82)   P-s

Paul Greco   New York Mets (1984–87)   P-s, C, L* (New York City)

Ben Grieve   Texas Rangers (1989–91)   P, T

Brad Grimes   Toronto Blue Jays (1988)   P

Greg Grimes   Toronto Blue Jays (1985–88)   P

Ozzie Guillen   Venezuela (1968–69)   P

Jim Hackett   St. Louis Browns (1944)   P-s

Roger Hailey   California Angels (1965–69)   P-s, C

Jeff Hochberg   Baltimore Orioles (and others, exhibition games in Washington, 1986–90)   P

Sid Holland   Houston Astros (1982–86)   P

Jack Hughes   Washington Senators (1956)   P-s, L-s (Columbia, Maryland)

John Milne Kurtz   Washington Senators (1957–58)   P-s

Steve Labatt   Minnesota Twins (1982–86)   P-s

Rene Lachemann   Los Angeles Dodgers (1960–62)   L (Memorial Stadium, Baltimore)

Rick LaCivita   Washington Senators (1970)   P

Hank Le Bost   Brooklyn Dodgers (1915–16)   P-s, C-s, L (Brooklyn)

Gilly Lefebvre   Los Angeles Dodgers (1959–61)   P-s

Jimmy Lefebvre   Los Angeles Dodgers (1961)   L (Memorial Stadium, Baltimore)

Chris Lehr   San Diego Padres (1988–90)   P

Dennis Liborio   Boston Red Sox (1969–73)   P-s, L-s (Veterans Stadium, Philadelphia; Osceola County Stadium, Kissimmee, Florida)

Tracy (Red) Luppe   Pittsburgh Pirates (1985–90)   P, L (Three Rivers Stadium, Pittsburgh)

Scotty MacDougal   Washington Senators (1958–59)   P-s, L (Frederick, Maryland)

Tom MacDougal   Washington Senators (1957–59)   P-s, C, T-s

Mike Macko   Texas Rangers (1983–87)   P-s, C

Rocky Maunakea   Oakland A's (1969)   P

Steve Maunakea   Oakland A's (1977)   P

Jay Mazzone   Baltimore Orioles (1966–73)   P-s, C, L (Hampstead, Maryland)

Pat McBride   Milwaukee Brewers (1970–74)   P-s, C-s

Socko McCarey   Pittsburgh Pirates (1919–21)   P-s

Art McKennan   Pittsburgh Pirates (1920–22)   P-s

Mark McKenzie   Minnesota Twins (1968–70)   P-s, C-s

Roy (Red) McKertcher   San Francisco Giants (1958–61)   P-s, C

Frank McNulty   Boston Braves (1945–50)   P-s

Jim Merritt   Los Angeles Dodgers (1961)   P

Rick Merschbach   Cincinnati Reds (1976–79)   P-s

Chad Meyer   Pittsburgh Pirates (1989–90)   L (Three Rivers Stadium, Pittsburgh)

Bob Mical   Detroit Tigers (1980–84)   P-s

Tony Migliaccio   Milwaukee Brewers (1978–84)   P, L (Memorial Stadium, Baltimore)

John Mitchell   Washington Senators (1941–42)   P, L (Rockville, Maryland)

John Mitchell   Washington Senators (1970–71)   P-s, C

Mickey Morabito   New York Yankees (1970–73)   P, L (Memorial Stadium, Baltimore)

Payton Morris   Atlanta Braves (1989–91)   P, C

Fred Mueller   California Angels (1965–67)   P

Mike Mullane   San Francisco Giants (1983–86)   P, T, L (Three Rivers Stadium, Pittsburgh)

Thad Mumford   New York Yankees (1968–69)   P-s, L (Colesville, Maryland)

Tim Murnin   St. Louis Cardinals (1988–91)   P, C, T, L (Busch Stadium, St. Louis)

Mike Murphy   San Francisco Giants (1958–60)   P-s, L (Three Rivers Stadium, Pittsburgh)

Mahendra Naik   Toronto Blue Jays (1977–79)   P

Ron Nedset   Milwaukee Brewers (1983–85)   P, L (Memorial Stadium, Baltimore)

John Nelson   Detroit Tigers (1979–82)   P, L-s (Tiger Stadium, Detroit; Marchant Stadium, Lakeland, Florida)

Ron Ogle   Los Angeles Dodgers (informal, summers 1964–69)   P

Dan O'Rourke   Philadelphia Phillies (1985–89)   L (Veterans Stadium, Philadelphia)

Tony Pastore   Philadelphia Phillies (1987–90)   L (Veterans Stadium, Philadelphia), B (Solomon)

Wes Patterson   Kansas City Royals (1984–91)   P-s, C, T, L (Royals Stadium, Kansas City)

Johnny Pesky   Portland Beavers (1932–37)   P-s
Bill Philips   Chicago Cubs (1955–56)   P, C
Mike Pieraldi   Oakland A's (1968–70)   P
Ron Pieraldi   Oakland A's (1970–73)   P-s
John Plein   San Diego Padres (1976–78)   P-s, C
David Povich   Washington Senators (spring 1946–47)   P
Maury Povich   Washington Senators (spring 1946–48)   P
Brian Prilaman   San Diego Padres (1971–72)   P-s, L (Busch Stadium, St. Louis)
Patrick Quinlan   San Francisco Giants (1976–79)   P-s, C-s
Bobby Recker   Pittsburgh Pirates (1959–62)   P-s, C-s, L (Colesville, Maryland)
Ken Reitz   informal, college teams in San Francisco Bay area (1965–66)   P
Merritt Riley   New York Yankees (1982–84)   P-s, L* (New York City), L (Levittown, Long Island)
Jeff Risch   St. Louis Cardinals (1984–85)   L (Busch Stadium, St. Louis)
Jerry Risch   St. Louis Cardinals (1966–69)   P, L (Busch Stadium, St. Louis)
Brooks Robinson   Little Rock semipro teams (Fire Dept., Riverside Nursery, 1947–50)   P, L (Baltimore)
Pete Rose, Jr.   Philadelphia Phillies (informal, 1979–83)   L (Harry Grove Stadium, Frederick, Maryland)
Gerald Rosen   New York Giants (1955)   P, B
Mike Rufino   New York Yankees (1982–83), New York Mets (1984–87)   P-s, L* (New York City)
Jim Ryan   Washington Senators (1956–58)   P-s, C-s, T-s
Thomas (Snuffy) Ryza   Houston Astros (1988–91)   P
Jim Sassetti   Chicago White Sox (1984–88)   P-s, C, T
Mark Sassetti   Chicago White Sox (1985–88)   P-s, C, T
Bob Scherr   Baltimore Orioles (1964–66)   P, L (Glen Burnie, Maryland)
Kurt Schlogo   St. Louis Cardinals (1982)   L (Busch Stadium, St. Louis)
Carl Schneider   Houston Astros (1989–91)   P
Jerry Schroer   St. Louis Cardinals (1955–58)   P-s
Jim Schroer   St. Louis Cardinals (1955–57)   P-s
Tony (The Flea) Simokaitis   St. Louis Cardinals (1985–90)   L (Busch Stadium, St. Louis)
Jeff Sipos   Cleveland Indians (1971–72)   P-s, T
Shannon Smith   Milwaukee Brewers (1989–91)   P
Mark Stowe   Cincinnati Reds (1975–76)   P-s
Stan Strull   Brooklyn Dodgers (1943–44, 1946–51)   P-s, C-s
Ray Tarin   Los Angeles Dodgers (1988–90)   C
Brad Tham   San Francisco Giants (1965–72)   P-s, C, T

Gus Tham   San Francisco Giants (1963–67)   P-s, C

Mark Thomson   San Diego Padres (1988–89)   P

Bill Tofant   Cleveland Indians (1929–31)   P, C

Jimmy Triantas   Baltimore Orioles (1984–88)   P, T

Bill Turner   Washington Senators (1956–59)   P-s, L (Gaithersburg, Maryland)

Fred Tyler   Baltimore Orioles (1973–79)   L-s (Memorial Stadium, Baltimore; Oriole Park at Camden Yards, Baltimore)

Jimmy Tyler   Baltimore Orioles (1965–67)   L (Memorial Stadium, Baltimore)

Tom Villante   New York Yankees (1943–45)   P-s

Mike Wallace   Texas Rangers (1973)   L (Royals Stadium, Kansas City)

Barry Waters   Los Angeles Dodgers (1978–79)   L-s (Veterans Stadium, Philadelphia; Osceola County Stadium, Kissimmee, Florida)

Fred Weisman   Cleveland Indians (1936)   P-s, C-s

Paul Wick   Milwaukee Braves (1955–56)   B

Jim Wiesner   St. Paul Saints (1952–57)   P-s, L (Memorial Stadium, Baltimore)

William (Red) Willis   Detroit Tigers (1947–51)   P, C, L (Tiger Stadium, Detroit)

Clayton Wilson   Minnesota Twins (1987–90)   P

Eric Winebrenner   Kansas City Royals (1980–88)   P-s, L (Kansas City)

Steve (Stretch) Winship   Kansas City Royals (1979–84)   P-s, C, T-s, L (Royals Stadium, Kansas City)

Butch Yatkeman   St. Louis Cardinals (1924–31)   P-s, C-s, L (St. Louis)

David Zeigler   Texas Rangers (1984–87)   P-s

Kim Zeigler   Texas Rangers (1983–86)   P-s

Ted Zeigler   Texas Rangers (1982–84)   P-s

NOTES

1. An egregious example of the problematical nature of participant observation, particularly where the participation may be faked, is Laud Humphreys's *The Tearoom Trade*. When the participants are aware of the observations, however, other distortions or complications may arise, as, variously, in Bill Buford's *Among the Thugs*, Tom Wolfe's *Electric Kool-Aid Acid Test*, and the "interview" films of Shirley Clarke.

2. Baseball's legislative and judicial chronicle, from the first labor-management disputes through Justice Holmes and his opinion for a unanimous court on the antitrust exemption, up to the decisions in the Curt Flood, Andy Messersmith, and Dave McNally cases, is well told in Lowenfish and Lupien. This should now be supplemented by the Brookings Institution's *Diamonds Are Forever: The Business of Baseball*, edited by Paul Sommers. The story of Spalding's "Special Commission" is neatly summarized in Rosenburg's *They Gave Us Baseball* 87–89. For a broader historical perspective on baseball and politics, see Dick Crepeau, esp. chapter 9, "Baseball Diplomacy" 196–217.

3. According to the batboys, there is some gambling in almost every clubhouse. Players enjoy playing a variety of card games, take part in pools on early-season NFL games, the Kentucky Derby, and the Indianapolis 500. Many play the lotteries, not quite as many play the horses, and on road trips to New York and Philadelphia there are usually a few who visit Atlantic City casinos between games. The stakes are small; it's all in fun and well within their means. Dick Wakefield's notoriously foolish ten thousand dollar wager with Ted Williams on their season's batting average is an aberration (as are the apparently gambling-addicted behaviors of such sports figures as Pete Rose, Michael Jordan, Mickey Rivers, Lenny Dykstra, Leonard Tose, Chet Forte, and Art Schlicter.) Serious sports betting is clearly taboo in the clubhouse; the mere suggestion of it produces a high level of anxiety bred, I believe, more in lore and legend than in codes of ethics or law. Where some gambling is part of a way of life, excesses are frightening and abhorrent.

4. In 1993, the NCAA basketball tournament, heavily promoted by sports-deprived CBS, became the focus of enormous betting action nationwide. According to industry spokesmen in Las Vegas, the last two weekends of the tournament ranked second and third for sports betting, behind only the Super Bowl.

5. The latter phrase is Lorenz Hart's from the lyric to "I Wish I Were in Love Again" from *Babes in Arms*. The former is Klinkowitz's, from the "Report." As Michael Roberts says, "Sport has been the source of more shameless propaganda, the subject of more nonsense beliefs, and the instrument of more disreputable purposes than any institution but government and religion. And sport seems to be gaining" (196). Coffin's "cant" suggests that baseball is the worst offender. The offenses, in turn, provide fertile fields for satirical plowing. See, e.g., Tony Kornheiser's column, "A Swing and a Myth," where he ridicules the "elegiac symmetry that resonates with the poetry of mankind's universal quest for self-knowledge," the "emerald chessboard upon which modern warriors choreograph ancient battle," the "rich mythology [of] the rhythms of America," and concludes, "Listen, Keats didn't scratch. Yeats didn't spit. Baseball is poetry like this here column is." Or see the ironic Zen/existential meditations of Bill Griffith's Zippy while waiting for a pitch.

6. See Oriard 306–23 for a comprehensive listing. A juvenile audience has been the designated target of prior books on batboys: Wick, Hollander, Garreau, Gibson, and Solomon.

7. A character in Donald Hays's *The Dixie Association* says (310), "We can't contradict the scorebook. Baseball is a historian's delight. Every pitch is recorded." Delight may lead to immoderation, whether in multivolume exhaustiveness (Seymour, Voigt) with its telescopic perspective and authoritative tone, or in microscopic focus with breathless hyperbole, as in atomizations of single seasons, series, games, innings. Regardless of historiographical methodology, however, all such works are labors of fan-love and may be appreciated by fellow fans. A modest, moderate alternative is Alexander's one-volume *Our Game*, which acknowledges the basic ground of baseball history as fandom.

8. Another apt phrase from Klinkowitz's "Report." He may have had in mind the gushing effusion of Giamatti in the essay that may have earned him the commissionership. Or he may have seen the George Grella essay that equates baseball with the "American Dream" itself. In a larger sense, such rhetoric inflates the whole Michael Novak argument heralding sport as America's secular religion. In all fairness, it is difficult to resist being carried away by the phenomena of American sports-minded attitudes. I recall the passage in Michener's *Sports in America* where he describes landing in his "glamour plane" at a small

Nebraska airport campaigning for Kennedy in the 1960 election. Introduced to a silent crowd of conservative ranchers are such luminaries as Ethel Kennedy, Angie Dickenson, Arthur Schlesinger, and Jeff Chandler. And then, well, listen to the even-handed reporter as he shifts into a different gear altogether: "Then Stan Musial appeared, and before the announcer could name him, a low rumble rose from the crowd, and men pressed forward, dragging their boys with them, and one man shouted, 'It's Stan the Man!' And a great cry rose from the night, and Musial walked into the glare, a tall, straight man in his late thirties, an authentic American folk hero, and the men fell back to let him pass" (240). Breathless with adoration, the writer no less than the congregation, the language itself chants of man and men and the rising sounds.

9. The periodical bibliography is extensive, another thriving ancillary baseball cottage industry. Lowry and Ritter both include ample references. Earlier books include Shannon and Reidenbaugh.

10. Another splendid example of overblown rhetoric. But see Gordon et al., eds., *Diamonds Are Forever: Artists and Writers on Baseball*. A handsome collection of photographs, photographic reproductions of paintings and sculptures, and snippets of poetry and highly charged or emblematic or devotional prose, it is a book "organized by the New York State Museum in association with the Smithsonian Institution Traveling Exhibition Service." It is no mean accomplishment for a sport to educe such an abundance of high-cultural artifacts: the nonliterary objets d'art are only infrequently overblown, but the rhetoric has been explicitly institutionalized.

An example of the blending of rhetoric, art object, mysticism, and iconography occurs with a brilliant reproduction of Jim Markowich and Paul Kuhrman's "The Ace of Bats (from the Tarot of Cooperstown)," acrylic and colored pencil on canvas, 1983, accompanied by the oblique caption, "A Louisville Slugger; a baseball, that perfect object for a man's hand; the smell of varnish and leather; and a well-worn and well-used, older brother's glove."

11. Bouton, *Ball Four* 219: "The same sign hangs . . . I suppose, in the CIA offices in Washington. If I were a CIA man, could I write a book?" The answer is yes, provided it was approved by the CIA's Publication Review Board—though some have found their way into print without official sanction. The irreverent Bouton, hardly a company man, would probably have skirted the approval of "the Company."

12. In the Introduction to his collection *Writing Baseball*, Klinkowitz says, "There is something in the nature of baseball that makes writing the subject . . . [let] one act purely reflexively while still having a universally recognizable object on the table when one's done." And beyond "the way it is played, managed, administered (even

scouted), watched, and remembered," the foremost reason for that "is its affinity with the play of language itself" (1). Bjarkman identifies specific elements of "the way" that nurtures that "affinity": "Baseball is a game of endless mythic potential—a spectacle of breathing legends and heroic deeds. The timely home run blow of unsung Bobby Thomson, the circus catch of Willie Mays, the prodigious home run blasts of Babe Ruth are the stuff of pure nostalgia, much of it summoned with the names and faces of our ball player heroes. Baseball's constant interplay of pregnant pause and frenetic action creates time for reflection and thus for indelible memories. Its field of play is spread openly in full view so that each action and each athlete-turned-actor stands uncomplicated, clearly displayed, before us" (64). The attraction and the accomplishment of a literary baseball of the mind are accounted for in this pair of passages. For another account of the interface between baseball and literature, see Billy Herman's tale of Ernest Hemingway and Hugh Casey during spring training in Havana in 1942 (Honig 152–5). David Remnick once observed that the "purple prose that marks baseball's opening day like a bruise is fast becoming as much a rite of spring as rickety statesmen throwing out the first balls" (C1) but concluded that "the best of baseball literature [provides] something that is without apparent importance and yet full of human effort, feeling and grace" (C4). There is no better example of the grace than Marianne Moore's "Baseball and Writing," though it may serve to modify Remnick's view of the significance of the special worlds of both.

13. My use of the term "jockocracy" in *Jock Culture, U.S.A.*, as a more appropriate and suggestive alternative to Lipsyte's *SportsWorld*, was not original—but I cannot identify my source. When the term was subsequently given wide currency (without attribution) by Howard Cosell, it was after he had taken it from a copy of *Jock Culture* I presented to him as a gesture of respectful deference.

14. Even the Hall of Fame Game has produced a batboy anecdote. Chad Blossfield remembers the 1951 game, when his little brother Paul, wearing his Hartford Chiefs batboy uniform with number 1,000 on it, was supposed to appear for the benefit of the Jimmy Fund (a New England charity, named for a young cancer victim, long associated with baseball). But it was the Red Sox versus the Giants, and when Charlie Blossfield, Chiefs general manager, asked manager Durocher to interrupt the exhibition game for the little routine, Leo just said no. No matter—Birdie Tebbetts, the Boston manager, said, "Sure, Charlie," and next inning little Paul pinch-hit for big Walt Dropo to face an underhand toss from big Jim Hearn.

15. When Orlando was himself a clubby, according to Halberstam in *Summer of '49* (162), it was his chore to drive Ted Williams to the bus

station the last time he was sent to the minors. Above and beyond the call of duty, he lent Williams five bucks for the trip to Daytona. Orlando knew he would get it back but not the generous dividends anyone who tended Ted would receive. Williams's more famous departure from the Red Sox is famously recorded in Updike's playful but reverent rhetoric.

16. Like a good trouper, Firestone rehearsed this material for the present project (and no doubt elsewhere) before refining and developing it for the first chapter of his book ("Batboy" in *Up Close* 1–10). The versions presented here, however, are not modified from our original conversations.

17. Salvon's present participle is by far the most common expletive in the clubhouse, occurring between words and even between parts of words. Jane Leavy skewers this practice throughout her novel *Squeeze Play*, both capturing and mocking baseball dialect.

18. A study of the clubhouse would provide an abundance of material in support of the social learning theories of Parsons and Bales, Bandura, and especially Goffman.

19. A legend in his own time, Kawano is pictured by Brosnan as "rushing from the Cub [sic] clubhouse on one of his mysterious and urgent errands" and credited as one who "could usually figure out most of my ballplayer's problems" (163). Maury Allen devotes a chapter to him, "Clubhouse Confidential" (34–48), suggesting that Kawano has replaced Pete Sheehy as the archetypal clubhouse man. On Sheehy, see Sullivan's chapter "Clubhouse Attendants" (106–9).

20. A full-blown treatment of what the batboy called "foul" is presented in Donald Hall's *Dock Ellis in the Country of Baseball*. Hall's definition says, "Baseball is a country all to itself. It is an old country . . . . Seasons and teams shift, blur into each other, change radically or appear to change, and restore themselves to old ways again" (*Fathers* 67). Ellis's iconoclasm, his civil disobedience against the country, is presented against the backdrop of substance abuse. But when the original 1976 edition was expanded for 1989 publication, the substances themselves had been radically changed. It is instructive to read Hall's account of why the earlier version participated in a kind of official mythologizing in which even foulness played an acceptable role.

21. Writer, teacher, critic, editor, and former co-owner of the Waterloo (Iowa) Indians, Klinkowitz has become a baseball hero in his own self. Refusing to be the Walter O'Malley of Waterloo, he resigned as executive director of the club rather than go along with his fellow owners' plan to sell the franchise and have it moved to Springfield, Illinois, and he sold back his share for the designated nominal amount. That splendid gesture left him obligated to pay a substantial "gift tax" on the six-figure value of his share (less the fifty bucks he took for it).

22. Conrad's 1931 hit song "You Call It Madness (But I Call It Love)" was the long-time theme song of Russ Columbo.

23. The subject of scouting is thoroughly examined by Kerrane 1984. Like every other aspect of the game, it too has been mythologized, whether in fiction (e.g., Malamud) or in analysis (e.g., Maury Allen's tribute to exemplary performers of such baseball functions as scouting, equipment-managing, and groundskeeping). But for the essential *sporting* nature of scouting, see my friend and colleague Jack Russell's illuminating, engaging portrait of (and tribute to) his father, *Honey Russell: Between Games, Between Halves*, esp. 168–76.

24. Irwin Shaw's "Eighty-Yard Run" and Tennessee Williams's *Cat on a Hot Tin Roof*, both dealing with ex-football stars, are perhaps the best-known treatments of this theme. But the theme frequently appears in a baseball context as well. Kahn's *Boys of Summer* has it as a persistent undertone. Its prevalent strain in the fiction is in anticipation: the refusal of the aging star to hang 'em up, the pathetic insistence on one more comeback. That there is life after baseball is but a dim dream, a slim hope, or a comic justification—as in Ron Shelton's *Bull Durham*, loosely based on the persistent minor-league odyssey of the historical Lawrence (Crash) Davis, whose major league career was over at age twenty-three after 148 games over three seasons (1940–42) as a reserve infielder for the Philadelphia Athletics, the worst team of that era. In Mark Harris's *Bang the Drum Slowly*, and even more clearly in John Hancock's movie version, a literal dying is a metaphor for the baseball "dying" of playing out a last season.

25. This chapter owes a substantial debt to my friend and colleague Barry Pearson, whose study of bluesmen is a model of appreciation for what may aptly be called the performance context of oral history.

WORKS CITED

Abbott, George, and Stanley Donen, dirs. *Damn Yankees*. Warner Bros., 1958.

Aldrich, Adell, dir. *The Kid from Left Field*. Dena Silver-Kramer, 1979.

Alexander, Charles C. *Our Game: An American Baseball History*. New York: Holt, 1991.

Allen, Maury. *Baseball: The Lives Behind the Seams*. New York: Macmillan, 1990.

Angell, Roger. *Five Seasons: A Baseball Companion*. New York: Simon, 1977.

——. *Late Innings: A Baseball Companion*. New York: Simon, 1982.

——. *Season Ticket*. Boston: Houghton, 1986.

——. *The Summer Game*. New York: Viking, 1972.

Asinof, Eliot. *Eight Men Out: The Black Sox and the 1919 World Series*. New York: Holt, 1987.

Bacon, Lloyd, dir. *It Happens Every Spring*. Twentieth Century Fox, 1949.

Baker, William J., and John M. Carroll, eds. *Sports in Modern America*. St. Louis: River City, 1981.

Bandura, A. *Social Learning Theory*. Englewood Cliffs, NJ: Prentice, 1977.

Bjarkman, Peter C. *The Brooklyn Dodgers*. Secaucus, NJ: Chartwell, 1992.

Blake, Mike. *The Incomplete Book of Baseball Superstitions, Rituals, and Oddities*. New York: Wynwood, 1991.

Borges, Jorge Luis. "An Examination of the Work of Herbert Quain." *Ficciones* 73–78. New York: Grove, 1962.

Boswell, Thomas. *Game Day*. New York: Doubleday, 1990.

——. *The Heart of the Order*. New York: Doubleday, 1989.

——. *How Life Imitates the World Series*. New York: Doubleday, 1982.

——. *Why Time Begins on Opening Day*. New York: Doubleday, 1984.

Bouton, Jim. *Ball Four*. New York: World, 1970.

Boyd, Brendan. *Blue Ruin: A Novel of the 1919 World Series.* New York: Norton, 1992.

Brashler, William. *The Bingo Long Traveling All-Stars and Motor Kings.* New York: Harper, 1973.

Brosnan, Jim. *The Long Season.* New York: Harper, 1960.

Brown, Clarence, dir. *Angels in the Outfield.* MGM, 1951.

Buford, Bill. *Among the Thugs.* New York: Norton, 1992.

Carkeet, David. *The Greatest Slump of All Time.* New York: Harper, 1984

Carroll, John M. "The Rise of Organized Sports." Baker and Carroll 3–15.

Charyn, Jerome. *The Seventh Babe.* New York: Arbor, 1979.

Coffin, Tristram Peter. *The Illustrated Book of Baseball Folklore.* New York: Seabury, 1975.

Cohen, Philip. "Sub-Cultural Conflict and Working Class Community." *Working Papers in Cultural Studies* 2 (1972).

Cohen, Sidney. *Dodgers! The First Hundred Years.* New York: Birch Lane, 1990.

Conrad, Con. "You Call It Madness (But I Call It Love)." ASCAP, 1931.

Coover, Robert. *The Universal Baseball Association, Inc., J. Henry Waugh, Prop.* New York: Random, 1968.

Creamer, Robert W. *Babe: The Legend Comes to Life.* New York: Simon, 1974.

———. *Stengel: His Life and Times.* New York: Simon, 1984.

Crepeau, Richard C. *Baseball: America's Diamond Mind 1919–1941.* Orlando: U Presses of Florida, 1980.

DeLillo, Don. "Pafko at the Wall." *Harper's Magazine* 287 (October 1992): 35–70.

Dillard, R. H. W. *The First Man on the Sun.* Baton Rouge: Louisiana State UP, 1983.

DiMaggio, Dom, with Bill Gilbert. *Real Grass, Real Heroes.* New York: Zebra, 1990.

Donovan (Donovan Leitch). "Atlantis." BMI, 1968.

Durocher, Leo, with Ed Linn. *Nice Guys Finish Last.* New York: Simon, 1975.

Empson, William. "Another Version of Pastoral." Kerrane and Grossinger 54.

———. *Seven Types of Ambiguity.* New York: New Directions, 1947.

———. *Some Versions of Pastoral.* New York: New Directions, 1960.

Falkner, David. *The Short Season.* New York: Times, 1986.

Fiffer, Steve. *How to Watch Baseball.* New York: Facts on File, 1987.

Firestone, Roy, with Scott Ostler. *Up Close and In Your Face with the*

Greats, Near-Greats, and Ingrates of Sports. New York: Hyperion, 1993.

Ford, Whitey, Mickey Mantle, and Joseph Durso. *Whitey and Mickey*. New York: Viking, 1977.

Forman, Milos, dir. *One Flew Over the Cuckoo's Nest*. United Artists, 1975.

Fraser, James George. *The Golden Bough: A Study of Magic and Religion*. New York: Macmillan, 1963.

Garreau, Garth, with Joe King. *Bat Boy of the Giants*. New York: Westminster, 1948.

Gerlach, Larry. *The Men in Blue: Conversations with Umpires*. New York: Viking, 1980.

Giamatti, A. Bartlett. "The Green Fields of the Mind." *Yale Alumni Magazine and Journal* 41, 2 (November 1977): 9. Rpt. Kerrane and Grossinger 295–97.

———. "The Story of Baseball: You Can Go Home Again." *New York Times*, April 2, 1989.

Gibson, Jerry, with Ed Wilks. *Big League Batboy*. New York: Random, 1970.

Goffman, Erving. *The Presentation of Self in Everyday Life*. New York: Doubleday, 1959.

Golenbock, Peter. *Bums: An Oral History of the Brooklyn Dodgers*. New York: Putnam, 1984.

Gordon, Peter H., ed., with Sydney Waller and Paul Weinman. *Diamonds Are Forever: Artists and Writers on Baseball*. San Francisco: Chronicle, 1987.

Greenberg, Eric Rolfe. *The Celebrant*. New York: Everest, 1983.

Greenberg, Hank, with Ira Berkow. *The Story of My Life*. New York: Times, 1989.

Grella, George. "Baseball and the American Dream." *The Massachusetts Review* 16, 3 (Summer 1975): 550–67. Rpt. Vanderwerken and Wertz 267–79.

Griffith, Bill. "Zippy." King Features Syndicate, June 2–9, 1989.

Halberstam, David. *The Summer of '49*. New York: Morrow, 1989.

Hall, Donald. "The Country of Baseball" (first chapter of *Dock Ellis*). Rpt. *Fathers* 67–110, Kerrane and Grossinger 191–96.

———. *Fathers Playing Catch with Sons*. San Francisco: North Point, 1985.

Hall, Donald, with Dock Ellis. *Dock Ellis in the Country of Baseball*. New York: Simon, 1989 (expanded from 1976).

Hancock, John, dir. *Bang the Drum Slowly*. United Artists, 1973.

Harper, James. "Baseball: America's First National Pastime." Baker and Carroll 53–62.

Harris, Mark. *Bang the Drum Slowly*. New York: Knopf, 1956.

————. *It Looked Like Forever*. New York: McGraw, 1979.

————. *The Southpaw*. Indianapolis: Bobbs-Merrill, 1953.

————. *A Ticket for a Seamstitch*. New York: Knopf, 1957.

Hart, Lorenz, and Richard Rodgers. "I Wish I Were in Love Again." *Babes in Arms*. ASCAP, 1937.

Hays, Donald. *The Dixie Association*. New York: Simon, 1984.

Hebdige, Dick. *Subculture: The Meaning of Style*. London: Methuen, 1979.

Heiman, Lee, David Weiner, and Bill Gutman. *When the Cheering Stops . . . : Former Major Leaguers Talk about Their Game and Their Lives*. New York: Macmillan, 1990.

Hemingway, Ernest. *The Old Man and the Sea*. New York: Scribner's, 1953.

Hemphill, Paul. *Long Gone*. New York: Viking, 1979.

Herrin, Lamar. *The Rio Loja Ringmaster*. New York: Viking, 1977.

Higgs, Robert J. *Laurel and Thorn*. Lexington: UP of Kentucky, 1981.

————. "The Unheroic Hero: A Study of the Athlete in Twentieth Century American Literature." Ph.D. diss., University of Tennessee, 1967.

Higgs, Robert J., and Neil D. Isaacs. *The Sporting Spirit: Athletes in Literature and Life*. San Diego: Harcourt, 1977.

Hollander, Zander. *Yankee Batboy*. New York: Prentice, 1955.

Honig, Donald. *Baseball When the Grass Was Real: Baseball from the Twenties to the Forties Told by the Men Who Played It*. New York: Coward, McCann & Geoghegan, 1975.

Howe, Steve, and Jim Greenfield. *Between the Lines*. Grand Rapids, MI: Masters, 1989.

Humphreys, Laud. *The Tearoom Trade: Impersonal Sex in Public Places*. Chicago: Aldine, 1975.

Isaacs, Neil D. "The Importance of Being Batboy." *Witness* 6 (1992): 162–69.

————. *Innocence and Wonder: Baseball through the Eyes of Batboys*. Indianapolis: Masters, 1994.

————. *Jock Culture, U.S.A.* New York: Norton, 1978.

Jones, Harmon, dir. *The Kid from Left Field*. Twentieth Century Fox, 1953.

Kahn, James M. *The Umpire Story*. New York: Putnam, 1953.

Kahn, Roger. *The Boys of Summer*. New York: Harper, 1972.

————. *Good Enough to Dream*. New York: Doubleday, 1985.

————. *The Seventh Game*. New York: New American Library, 1982.

Kerrane, Kevin. *Dollar Sign on the Muscle*. New York: Beaufort, 1984.

Kerrane, Kevin, and Richard Grossinger, eds. *Baseball Diamonds: Tales*,

Traces, Visions, and Voodoo from a North American Rite. Garden City, NY: Anchor, 1980.

Kesey, Ken. *One Flew Over the Cuckoo's Nest.* New York: Viking, 1962.

Kinsella, W. P. *The Iowa Baseball Confederacy.* Boston: Houghton, 1986.

———. *Shoeless Joe.* Boston: Houghton, 1982.

———. *The Thrill of the Grass.* New York: Penguin, 1984.

Klinkowitz, Jerry. "Report" to UP of Mississippi on batboy ms. 1993.

———. *Short Season and Other Baseball Stories.* New York: Collier, 1989.

———, ed. *Writing Baseball.* Urbana: U of Illinois P, 1991.

Kornheiser, Tony. "A Swing and a Myth." *Washington Post,* October 17, 1993: F 1, 5.

Kuklich, Bruce. *To Every Thing a Season: Shibe Park and Urban Philadelphia 1909–1976.* Princeton, NJ: Princeton UP, 1991.

Landis, John, dir. *National Lampoon's Animal House.* Universal City, 1978.

Lardner, Ring. "Lose with a Smile." *Saturday Evening Post,* 1932.

———. *You Know Me Al.* New York: Scribner's, 1916.

Leavy, Jane. *Squeeze Play.* New York: Doubleday, 1990.

Lehmann-Haupt, Christopher. *Me and DiMaggio: A Baseball Fan Goes in Search of His Gods.* New York: Simon, 1986.

Levine, Peter. *A. G. Spalding and the Rise of Baseball.* New York: Oxford UP, 1985.

Levinson, Barry, dir. *The Natural.* Tri-Star, 1984.

Lipsyte, Robert. *SportsWorld.* New York: Quadrangle, 1975.

Lowenfish, Lee, and Tony Lupien. *The Imperfect Diamond.* New York: Stein and Day, 1980.

Lowry, Philip J. *Green Cathedrals: The Ultimate Celebration of All 271 Major League and Negro League Ballparks Past and Present.* Reading, MA: Addison, 1992.

Malamud, Bernard. *The Natural.* New York: Farrar, 1952.

Marshall, Penny, dir. *A League of Their Own.* Columbia, 1993.

McCarthy, Colman. "My Son in Yankee Stadium." *Washington Post,* August 3, 1991: A3.

Michener, James A. *Sports in America.* New York: Random, 1976.

Millar, Jeff, and Bill Hinds. "Tank McNamara." Universal Press Syndicate, July 13, 1990.

Miller, Walter B. "Lower Class Culture as a Generating Milieu of Gang Delinquency." *Journal of Social Issues* 14 (1958): 5–19.

Moore, Marianne. "Writing and Baseball." In *The Complete Poems of Marianne Moore,* 221–23. New York: Macmillan, 1967. Rpt. Higgs and Isaacs 169–72

Nettles, Graig, and Peter Golenbock. *Balls.* New York: Putnam, 1984.

Novak, Michael. *The Joy of Sports.* New York: Basic, 1976.

Okrent, Daniel. *Nine Innings.* New York: Ticknor & Fields, 1985.

Oleksak, Michael M., and Mary Adams Oleksak. *Beisbol: Latin Americans and the Grand Old Game.* Grand Rapids, MI: Masters, 1991.

Oriard, Michael V. *Dreaming of Heroes: American Sports Fiction, 1868–1980.* Chicago: Nelson-Hall, 1982.

Parsons, Talcott, and R.F. Bales, eds. *Family Socialization and Interaction Process.* New York: Free, 1955.

Pearce, Donn. *Cool Hand Luke.* New York: Scribner's, 1965.

Pearson, Barry Lee. *"Sounds So Good to Me."* Philadelphia: U of Pennsylvania P, 1984.

Phillips, Louis. "The Day the Walrus Hit .400." *Aethlon* 6 (1988): 53–71.

Reidenbaugh, Lowell. *The Sporting News Take Me Out to the Ball Park.* St. Louis: Sporting News, 1987.

Remnick, David. "Forget the Bores of Summer; Take Me Out to the Library." *Washington Post,* April 6, 1986, C1, 4.

Ritter, Lawrence. *The Glory of Their Times.* New York: Macmillan, 1966.

———. *Lost Ballparks: A Celebration of Baseball's Legendary Fields.* New York: Viking, 1992.

Roberts, Michael. *Fans!* Washington, DC: New Republic, 1976.

Robinson, Phil Alden, dir. *Field of Dreams.* Universal City, 1989.

Rose, Pete, and Roger Kahn. *Pete Rose: My Story.* New York: Macmillan, 1989.

Rosen, Gerald. "Dreams of a Jewish Batboy." Klinkowitz, *Writing Baseball* 50–57.

———. *Growing Up Bronx.* Berkeley: North Atlantic, 1984.

Rosenberg, Stuart, dir. *Cool Hand Luke.* Warner Bros.-7 Arts, 1967.

Rosenburg, John M. *They Gave Us Baseball.* Harrisburg, PA: Stackpole, 1989.

Roth, Philip. *The Great American Novel.* New York: Holt, 1973.

Russell, John. *Honey Russell: Between Games, Between Halves.* Washington: Dryad, 1986.

Sayles, John. *The Pride of the Bimbos.* Boston: Little, 1975.

———, dir. *Eight Men Out.* Orion, 1988.

Seymour, Harold. *Baseball: The Early Years.* New York: Oxford UP, 1960.

———. *Baseball: The Golden Age.* New York: Oxford UP, 1961.

———. *Baseball: The People's Game.* New York: Oxford UP, 1990.

———. "Big-League Batboy." *Sports Heritage* Spring 1988: 13–17. Rpt. *Drew Magazine* 15 (May 1988):8–13.

Shannon, Bill, and George Kalinsky. *The Ballparks*. New York: Hawthorn, 1975.

Shaw, Irwin. "The Eighty-Yard Run." *Selected Short Stories of Irwin Shaw*. New York: Random, 1940.

———. *Voices of a Summer Day*. New York: Delacorte, 1965.

Shelton, Ron, dir. *Bull Durham*. Orion, 1988.

Smith, H. Allen. *Rhubarb*. New York: Doubleday, 1946.

Solomon, Chuck. *Major-League Batboy*. New York: Crown, 1991.

Sommers, Paul M., ed. *Diamonds Are Forever: The Business of Baseball*. Washington, DC: Brookings Institution, 1992.

Spalding, Albert G. *Base Ball: America's National Game 1839–1915*. San Francisco: Halo, 1991.

Stern, Daniel, dir. *Rookie of the Year*. Twentieth Century Fox, 1993.

Sullivan, George. *Baseball Backstage*. New York: Holt, 1986.

Talley, Rick. *The Cubs of '69*. Chicago: Contemporary, 1989.

———. *Out of the Blue*. Chicago: Contemporary, 1985.

Tullius, John. *I'd Rather Be a Yankee*. New York: Macmillan, 1986.

Updike, John. "Hub Fans Bid Kid Adieu." In *Assorted Prose*, 127–47. New York: Knopf, 1965. Rpt. Kerrane and Grossinger 237–50.

Vanderwerken, David L., and Spencer K. Wertz, eds. *Sport Inside Out*. Fort Worth: Texas Christian UP, 1985.

Veeck, Bill, with Ed Linn. *Veeck—As in Wreck*. New York: Putnam, 1962.

Voigt, David Quentin. *American Baseball: From Gentleman's Sport to the Commissioner System*. University Park: Pennsylvania State UP, 1983.

———. *American Baseball: From the Commissioners to Continental Expansion*. University Park: Pennsylvania State UP, 1983.

———. *American Baseball: From Postwar Expansion to the Electronic Age*. University Park: Pennsylvania State UP, 1983.

Ward, David S., dir. *Major League*. Morgan Creek-Mirage, 1989.

Warren, Robert Penn. "The Love and the Separateness in Miss Welty." *Kenyon Review* 6 (1944): 246–59.

Welty, Eudora. "A Still Moment." *The Wide Net and Other Stories*. New York: Harcourt, 1943.

Wick, Paul, as told to Bob Wolf. *Batboy of the Braves*. New York: Greenberg, 1957.

Will, George. *Men at Work: The Craft of Baseball*. New York: Macmillan, 1990.

Williams, Raymond. *The Long Revolution*. Westport, CT: Greenwood, 1975.

Williams, Tennessee. *Cat on a Hot Tin Roof*. New York: New Directions, 1955.

Wolfe, Tom. *The Electric Kool-Aid Acid Test.* New York: Farrar, 1968.

Wood, Sam, dir. *The Pride of the Yankees.* RKO, 1942.

Young, Dick. "He Walked with the Stars." *Coronet* 46, 3 (July 1959): 25–28.

INDEX